NEEDLE FELTING
Masks and Finger Puppets

Terese Cato

Copyright © 2016 by Terese Cato
All rights reserved.
ISBN-10: 1530996309
ISBN-13: 978-1530996308

Cover Designer: Adriana Mendoza
Copy Editor/Proof Reader: Gia Benevento
Illustrator: Terese Cato
Photographer: Terese Cato

All rights reserved. No part of this work may be used in any form or reproduced by any means- graphic, electronic, or mechanical, including photocopying, recording, taping, or information storage and retrieval systems- without written permission from Terese Cato. These designs may be used to make items only for personal use or donation to nonprofit groups for sale or display only at events, provided the following credit is included on a conspicuous label: Designs copyright © 2016 by Terese Cato from the book **NEEDLE FELTING Masks And Finger Puppets**. Permission for all other purposes must be requested in writing from Terese Cato.

Attention Copy Shops: Please note the following exception- author gives permission to photocopy pages 144 -154 for personal use only.

A Special Thank You To

Linda Williams
Adriana Mendoza

And To The Mask And Puppet Models:
Sheila DeSimone
Gia Benevento
Vanesa Mendoza
Tyler Verheyen
Crosby Verheyen

Thank you to my sweet husband for his unending patience and support.

*For
Caeden, Emma, and Annalise*

Contents

Preface 7
Introduction 9
Tools And Supplies 10
Felting Needles 10
Needle Tools 10
Folded Cardboard 11
Needle Felting Pads 12
More Helpful Tools 13
Wool 14
Techniques 15
Choose The Right Needle For The Job 16
Take Care Of Your Needles 16
Is It Felted Yet? 16
Use Core Wool For A Base 18
Felt Fabric 18
Using Templates To Make Ears 18
Making Ears With A Felt Fabric Base 18
Making Ears Without A Felt Fabric Base 20
Blending Colors 22
Blending Colors As You Felt 22
Felting A Firm Ball 23
Creating Edges 24
Felt An Edge On The Sculpture 24
Felt An Edge On The Foam Work Surface 25
Felting Ropes 26
Shaping The Sculpture 28
Attach An Elastic Strap To A Mask 29
Making Masks 31
Cat Mask 33
Colorful Cat Mask 42
Dog Mask 46
Mouse Muzzle 48

Owl Mask 49
Rat Mask 49
Wild Hare Mask 51
King Of The Jungle Lion Mask 59
Ram Mask 71
Giraffe Mask 80
Displaying Masks 83
Making Animal Finger Puppets 85
Making A Base For Finger Puppets 86
Red Fox 88
Raccoon 94
Lion 98
Elephant 102
Horse 106
Zebra 111
Farm Animal Finger Puppets 112
Pig 112
Sheep 113
Goat 114
Cow 114
Rooster And Hen 115
Making People Finger Puppets 117
Making A Base For People Finger Puppets 118
Making Arms And Hands 119
Mitten Girl 122
Pirate 128
Sheriff 132
Forest Elf 136
Make Your Own Finger Puppets 140
Make A Stand For Displaying Puppets 141
Puppet Theatre 142
Templates 144
The Old Man 156
Resources 155
About The Author 158

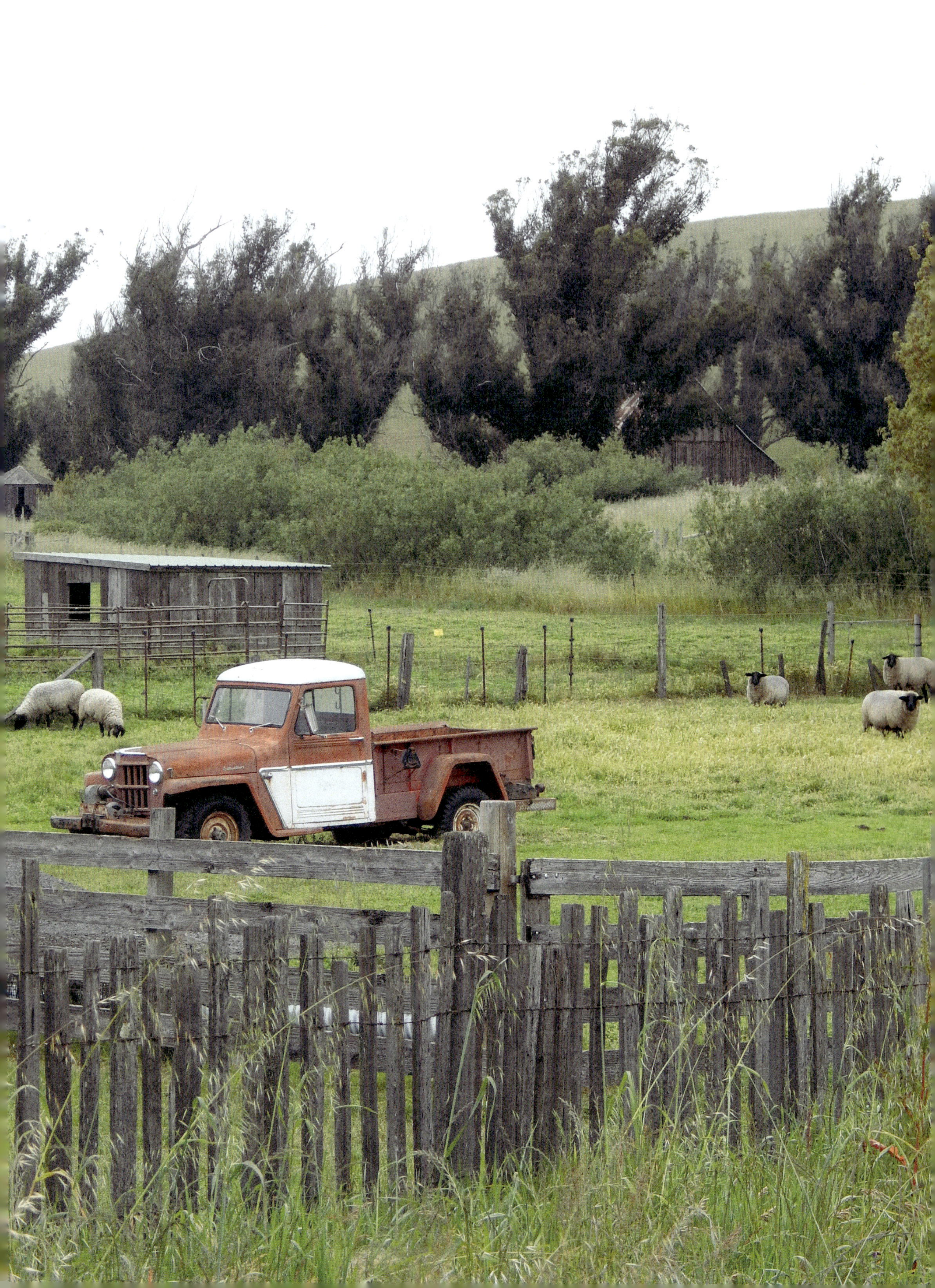

Preface

When I decided to write this book I thought I knew exactly what I would write about. I wanted to share how to create three-dimensional needle felted sculptures and use animals as my subjects. I began making the projects and, while I was happy with my work, my thoughts started going off in a different direction. I was thinking that it would be fun to create projects that were usable in some way. I wanted to create functional art. Art with a purpose beyond being something beautiful to look at. Once you have needle sculpted **anything** with wool fibers you know that it is a piece of art. Needle felting is so amazing in the way that you can make something very simple to something with incredible detail using the same techniques.

I had never needle felted a mask before. I pushed everything on my worktable to one side and just started. I always get excited to try something new. The *idea* is knowing where you want to go. The *challenge* is figuring out how to get there. There are times when things just do not work out. That should never discourage you. These are most likely the times that we learn the most. The first mask I made was a cougar. I can't even say why I chose a cougar. I was amazed at how easily it came together. I believe once you learn the techniques and understand how to manipulate the wool, you can get it to do whatever you want. I was so pleased with the outcome that I couldn't start the next mask fast enough. Somewhere along this journey I started thinking about puppets. I had very elaborate puppets dancing around in my head. I decided to start simply with finger puppets. One day while making puppets I just dropped everything to go see what wood I had in my bin. I knew I had to make a puppet theatre.

I thoroughly enjoyed creating every project in this book. I finally had to make myself stop felting and start writing. The ideas for more masks and puppets just keep coming. I hope that these projects will inspire you and give you lots of your own ideas.

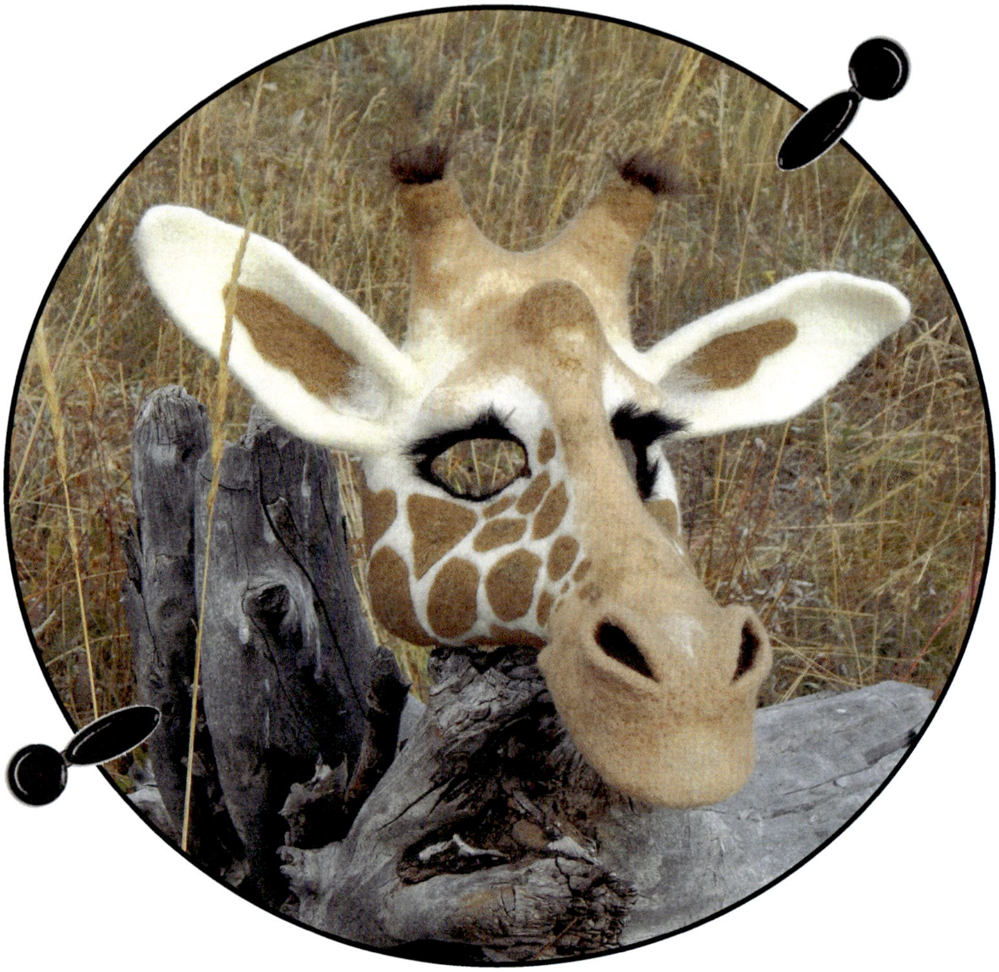

Introduction

As you read through the project instructions you will notice that I often refer you to the chapter on **Techniques** beginning on *page 15*. The projects in this book all use the same techniques and I have compiled many of them together for you to use as a reference.

Once you have tried a couple of finger puppets or masks you will notice that the instructions are quite repetitive. Both the animal and people finger puppets begin with **Making A Base For Finger Puppets** on *page 86*. The basics will always be the same and it will be the size, shape, and detail that will change. Once you have made a few projects and understand the basics you will be able to explore some of your own ideas. I have also included some projects that are not accompanied by detailed instructions. However, once you have made a few of the projects you will notice that they are very similar to each other.

There are some words in the text that should be mentioned. The word "**poke**" has a dual meaning. Poking is an action but it also means to **felt**. When the instructions are telling you to poke, it is telling you to felt the piece. I often instruct you to "**felt on the foam work surface**". Take notice that some items are completely felted on the foam work surface and then attached to the sculpture. Other items may be felted directly on the sculpture. I will often say to leave the wool "**fluffy**". For example, felting the animal's ear but leaving the bottom edge fluffy for attaching to the sculpture. If the wool is *fluffy* it is not felted. It is easier to blend a fluffy edge into a sculpture than a felted edge. The fluffy fibers will disappear into the sculpture without leaving a line or edge.

On the **Resources** page at the back of the book I have named my source for the plastic eyes I used on some projects. You can also choose to use black beads or make the eyes completely from felt. You may have some tiny buttons that can also be used for eyes.

The elastic that is used for the strap on the back of the masks come from the sewing department of the store. Elastic cording is used for the small masks. Flat elastic in 1/8" and 1/4" widths is used for the larger masks. The elastic is easy to find in black or white. Simply choose the color that works best with your mask.

The most important thing is to simply have fun with it. If you are needle felting for the first time start by focusing on the techniques. Once you get a feel for the wool and learn how to manipulate it you can just relax and enjoy the process.

Tools and Supplies

Felting Needles

Felting needles are made from carbon steel and are extremely sharp. They will last a long time if you don't bend or break them. If you are breaking or bending needles frequently then you need to examine your poking technique. Only use the needle while your project is on a foam mat. Never twist or turn the needle while it is in the wool. A quick poke with the needle following the same path on the way into the wool and out of the wool is the proper poking technique. Never use the felting needle to pick or pull at the wool.

Notches are cut in the edge of the felting needle blade. The barbs grab the fibers each time the needle is poked into the wool tangling and condensing it. There are many variations in the number of barbs, their placement, and spacing. The blade of the felting needle will be a triangle shape or a star shape. A star shaped blade has more edges for barbs than a triangle blade.

The most common size felting needles you will find available are gauge 32, 36, 38, 40, 42, and 46. The lower numbers (32, 36, 38) are a thick, coarse needle and the higher numbers (40, 42, 46) are a thin, fine needle. If you are felting something large and want to felt it quickly you would use a coarse needle. If you are felting small items or felting the final surface layer of wool you would use a fine needle. As you gain experience using the needles you will know which gauge is best for a specific job.

There are also twisted needles with the blade in a spiral shape. This needle will push and twist the fibers at the same time as you poke. You may also come across a reverse felting needle. A reverse needle will pull the wool fibers out instead of pushing them in. These needles are great for blending colors or creating a furry look on an animal sculpture.

If you are trying needle felting for the first time you do not need a needle in every size to get started. I would suggest that you purchase a variety pack of needles that will give you several sizes to try. The gauge I used the most on the projects in this book were a triangle 40 and 42 and a star 38.

Companies that sell felting needles color code them to identify the size and others do not. Unfortunately, there is not a universal color coding system. You may want to create your own color coding system so you can identify the sizes easily. A dot of paint or nail polish can be used. Mark the needles just below the area where you hold it so it does not rub off with repeated use.

Felting needles are made for industrial use and not the comfort of the artisan. You may find that holding onto the crank at the top of the needle is not comfortable for extended periods of time. You can find needles that have been dipped into a rubber coating or have clay or beads attached to the crank for a more comfortable grip.

Needle Tools

There are needle felting tools that will hold one or multiple needles. The tools are made to hold the same industrial needles with the crank at the top. If you are felting often and find that you enjoy it, you may decide to explore some of the tools available. If you are new to felting all you really need to start are needles. You do not need tools to complete a project. I used a single needle to make the puppets in this book.

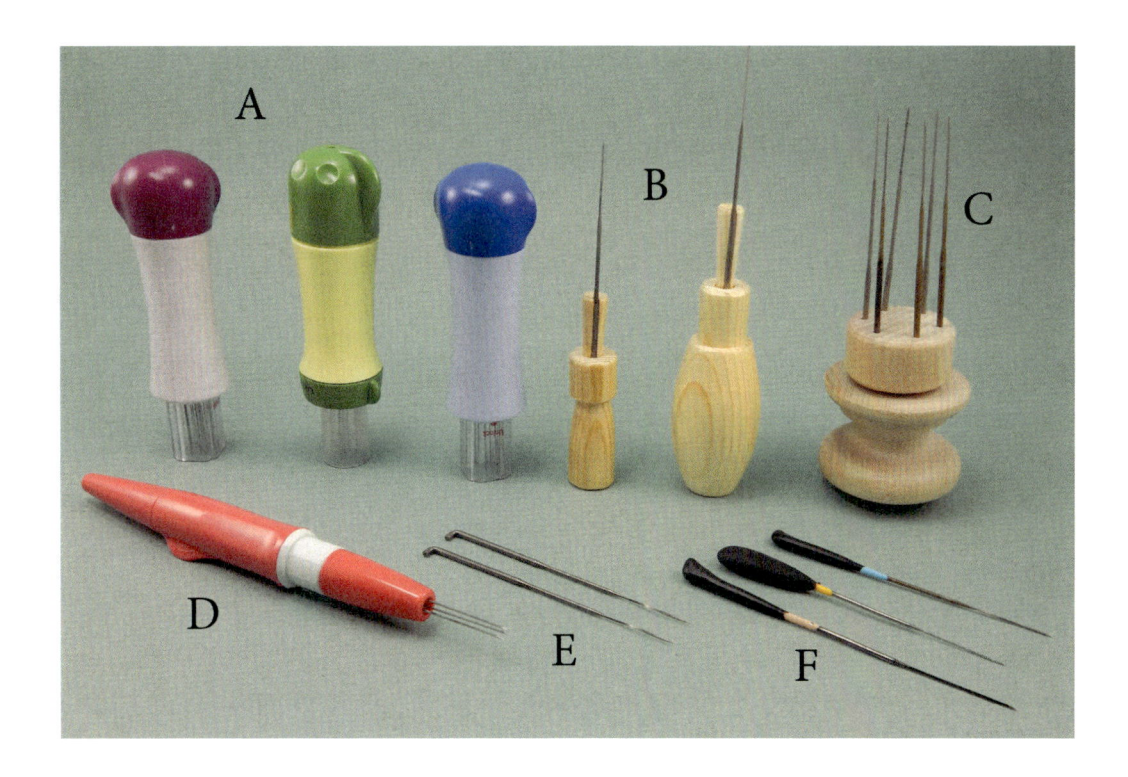

Shown in the photo above are:

A These holders fit comfortably in the palm of your hand and hold 5 to 7 needles that are spaced close together. Among other things, they are great when making animal ears.

B Single needle holders give you more to hold onto for comfort. They can be made of wood, plastic, or metal.

C There are many larger tools like this one that hold multiple needles that are widely spaced apart. They are better suited for large projects.

D The pen tool holds 1 to 3 needles that are spaced close together. It is one of my favorite needle holders.

E Single felting needles. Working with multiple needles together will make the felting process go quicker. However, small items and detail work is best done with a single needle.

F Felting needles that have been dipped in rubber coating are comfortable to hold.

Folded Cardboard

One of the most useful tools is perhaps one of the simplest. A piece of cardboard folded in half will hold small items while you felt. It will keep your fingers away from the needle and is often easier than working on the foam. It can be used for tiny hands, the edge of an eyelid or ear, tiny balls, and many other small items as seen on *pages 20, 26, 121*.

Needle Felting Pads

You should always use an appropriate work surface while needle felting. If you work on the tabletop you will run the risk of the needle hitting the table and breaking. Do not get into the habit of holding your work in the palm of your hand as you will eventually poke yourself with the sharp needle.

Choose a foam mat that is at least 2" thick to keep your needle a safe distance from the tabletop. The width and length of the foam is a personal preference. You may be surprised to know that while making the projects in this book I used a 2" thick foam that was only 6" x 9". The part of your project that you are working on is the only part that needs to be on the foam.

Any foam will work, however, a dense foam will last longer against the repeated poking of the sharp needles. A high density foam is very firm, while a low density foam is softer with more air filled pores. If you purchase foam that is sold as a *needle felting pad* you can expect it to be high density. If you purchase a chair pad or upholstery foam it is available in regular density, high density, and extra high density. Foam can be very expensive so choose the highest density you can find so it will last longer.

You may have some foam around the house and wonder if you can use it. If the foam is thick enough to prevent your needles from hitting the tabletop then you can use it as a pad. However, if the foam is low density it will be soft and easy to condense when you push on it. It will not offer much resistance when you apply pressure while working. The foam will quickly begin to fall apart and small pieces will fall off leaving holes in the foam. The tiny pieces of foam will start to embed themselves in the wool. The answer is yes, you can use a lower density foam you may already have on hand but with the understanding that it will not last long. On *page 86* I explain **Making A Base For Finger Puppets**. I cut a piece of foam to use for making the finger tube for the puppets. I used a lower density foam that just happened to be around the house. I knew that the foam would fall apart quickly. As soon as it started to fall apart I threw it away and cut another piece. Using what I had on hand meant that I did not have to cut up my needle felting pad.

The lifespan of your foam pad depends on how much you use it. If you get into the habit of always working in one spot on the foam, it will begin to show wear quickly. Use all areas of the foam, including both sides so it will wear more evenly. You can also help extend the life of your pad by covering it with acrylic craft felt. It is readily available at most craft supply stores in 9" x 12" sheets. I like to use the white sheets so that the colored wool is visible on it. The sheet can be cleaned with a lint brush and replaced when it gets too dirty.

Your project will pick up fibers from the foam. This may be a problem if red fibers are showing up on your white sculpture. When you are finished working use your fingers to remove the largest part of the fibers on the foam. Then use a lint roller to remove the rest. I do a lot of felting so I find it helpful to have a pad for dark colors and a pad for light colors.

It may be your preference to use a brush style mat instead of foam. The large brushes are 4" x 6" and I find them just a bit small for myself. While I prefer foam, use what you are comfortable with and works best for you.

More Helpful Tools

The felting needles and your work surface are the two items that are a must have for needle felting. There are a few more tools that are helpful to have on hand while felting. Most of them you may already have.

A **large sewing needle** may be used to push, pull, and stretch the wool. Some people prefer to use an **awl**. I like to use a **3" or 5" doll needle**. They are thick and strong enough for pulling and poking. If you use your felting needle it will surely break so have one of these items on hand while felting.

You will also need an assortment of **sticks and dowels** on hand. *Lollipop sticks* come in several sizes and are smooth. They can be found in the baking department of the grocery or craft store. *Wood dowels* come in a larger selection of sizes. You need to choose them carefully to make sure they are smooth, if not sand them with fine sandpaper. If they are not smooth, the rough surface will catch and grab the wool. Sticks and dowels are great for pushing and pulling the wool and also making shapes. Felt can be wrapped around a dowel to make a log or rope shape that may be used for fingers, arms, legs, lips, and more. Refer to **Felting Ropes** on *page 26*. I used this technique to make thin ropes to outline the eyes on some of the masks (*page 27*). Wool that has been wrapped around a stick or dowel will give you a clean, even edge to attach to your sculpture. You can also rub the wool against the side of a dowel to stretch the fibers. They can also be used as a guide to poke a straight line while you **Felt An Edge On The Foam Work Surface** on *page 25*. The photo at the bottom of *page 113* shows a stick being used to hold onto the wool while making a tiny ball for the sheep's fleece. This helps to keep your fingers away from the sharp felting needle as you are poking.

Tweezers are another helpful tool to have on hand. When you are building the base of a sculpture that will be covered with more layers of wool, a stray black fiber on the light core wool is not important. However, when you are felting a pink nose on a bunny, a stray black hair can be very visible and need to be removed. It can be difficult to grab one tangled fiber with your fingers. Tweezers will easily grab the fiber to remove it.

Core wool, batting, and curly locks may have vegetable matter tangled in the fibers. Vegetable matter is grass, hay, or weeds that get matted into the wool while the sheep are in the fields. The process of washing and carding (combing) the wool will remove most of this debris but it is still common to find some in the wool. Curly locks has not been carded so it may have the most vegetable matter present. Batting has been carded and will have less vegetable matter than curly locks. Roving is carded more than batting and will have little debris or none at all. When you are purchasing wool there may be a reference to how much VM is in it. VM is referring to *vegetable matter*. Picking debris from the wool is easier with a pair of tweezers.

Straight pins may be used to hold a template in place on the foam work surface while you poke around it (top of *page 21*). Straight pins will also hold a puppet's arm or an animal's ear in place while you are deciding where to attach it. They are also an extra set of hands to hold a rope in place as you attach it to the sculpture.

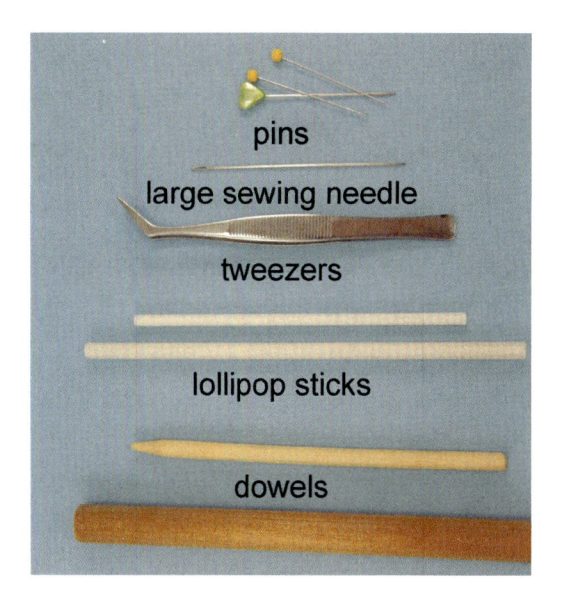

Wool

The projects in this book are made of wool batting. You may also see it referred to as *batt*. Batting has been carded (combed) to break up all the locks and clumps of fiber. The carding process stops before all the fibers are completely parallel. This means that the fiber will felt without much effort.

Core wool is undyed batting. It is used as a base or filler for a project and then covered with a more expensive dyed batting. Core wool is usually not a bright white. It is left in its natural color which ranges from white to beige. If it is the color you need, it may also be used as the outer layer of wool on a project. Core wool was used for the **white ram** and the **eagle masks**. It may also be used on the muzzle of animals. When you are purchasing wool you may consider a collection or variety pack that includes a group of colors. This will give you a larger color palette to work with as you are felting.

Curly locks and wool roving are used for hair on the finger puppets, the lion and horse's mane, and other details like hair in the ears or on the chin. Curly locks are the natural curls just as they were sheared off the sheep. Wool roving has been carded (combed) until the fibers have been well aligned and straightened. It does not felt up as easily as batting. For this reason it is best used for the details (like hair) rather than the sculpture.

On the **Resources** *page* (*155*) I have listed the sources for the wool that was used to make all the projects in this book.

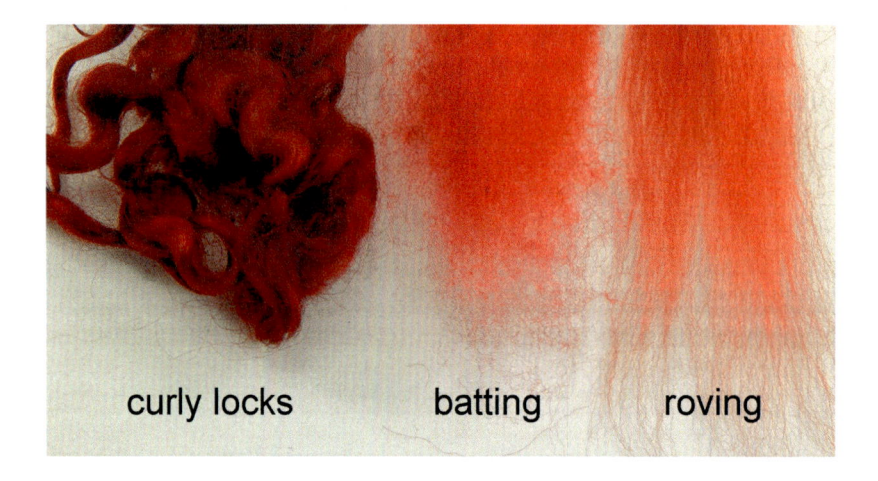

curly locks   batting   roving

Notice the different textures of the wool. The curly locks has not been combed or carded. The batting has been carded to break up the locks, but the fibers are not completely parallel. The roving has been carded until all the fibers become parallel.

Techniques

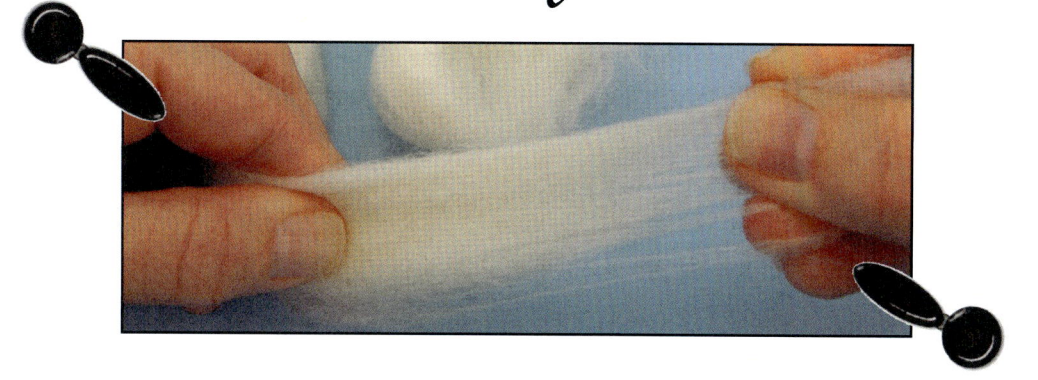

This is perhaps the most important chapter in this book. All needle felted projects use the same techniques. As you are following the directions for a project it will refer you back to this chapter for a detailed explanation. Some of the techniques are general needle felting information. For this reason you should familiarize yourself with this chapter and refer back to it as needed.

The directions use the word "*poke*". In the context of the directions the words "*poke*" and "*felt*" have the same meaning. When the directions instruct you to "*poke the entire area*" it is telling you to "*felt the entire area*".

So many crafts require that you be precise in every aspect of the process to result in a successful outcome. However, this is not the case with needle felting. You **can** get the measurement wrong. If you add the wrong amount of wool you **can** remove some or add some more. Needle felting is very forgiving. You will learn something with each new project. Gain some experience working with wool and you will learn how to manipulate it to result in your desired outcome.

If I were to break it down as simply as possible, I would give each project three main steps. **First** is building the basic form or shape of the sculpture. **Second** is adding the detail and getting the shape just right. **Third** is covering the form with color. All of the core wool is covered with a layer of color.

You should finish all your needle felting projects with a final surface felting. This will create a consistently smooth surface to the sculpture. Shallow poking with a fine needle, while holding the needle at a 45 degree angle to the surface, will felt the top layer without changing the shape. It will bury all the hairy ends and firm up the surface. After a sculpture gets older and has been handled a lot, you may want to touch it up with some surface felting to take care of any stray fibers.

Choose The Right Felting Needle For The Job

Purchase felting needles in variety packs so you will have several sizes to work with. Experiment with them and you can feel and see the difference between fine and coarse needles.

When you are building a core shape use a coarse needle (#36 and #38 triangle or star needles). A core or base shape needs to be dense and firm so you can add detail on top of it. A coarse needle will create a dense felt quickly. It can also be used to firm up an area that is too fluffy or attach two shapes together. Poke close together in a line and it will make strong deep lines in the wool.

A fine needle can do the same job as a coarse needle but will require more pokes to get the same result. A fine needle (#40, #42, #46) is used to work the surface of the wool and for detail. The smallest detail requires the finest needle. It may also be used to tack pieces in place for positioning and will easily pull off to reposition the piece. When a project is complete, a final shallow surface felting with a fine needle will create a smooth finished surface.

Take Care Of Your Needles

Take care of your needles and they will last a long time. Felting needles are made from carbon steel and are extremely sharp. Chances are you will break or bend a needle before it becomes dull. If you are breaking or bending needles frequently, then you need to stop and examine your poking technique. It is always easier to develop proper techniques than to try and break bad habits later.

Always work on a foam surface to protect the needle from hitting the tabletop. Never twist or turn the needle while it is in the wool. A quick poke with the needle following the same path on the way into the wool and on the way out of the wool is the proper poking technique. Never use the felting needle to pick or pull at the wool. Keep a large, thick sewing needle handy for picking, pulling, and pushing the wool. Use tweezers to pull out vegetable matter and other debris from the wool.

Is It Felted Yet?

It is easy to show examples of felted wool when you can hand someone a completed project that they can feel for themselves. Once you feel a felted piece you can understand how firm it needs to be. Explaining it in writing will leave my words open to your individual interpretation. If you have never handled a needle felted sculpture and you are working on your first project, you may need to read this again when your project is complete. Once you have experienced working with the wool you may be able to grasp the meaning of my words with a deeper comprehension.

You begin a project by poking (felting) a core or base shape. You continue to add layers of wool as you sculpt. The sculpture will become firmer as you poke each layer of wool. **Felt** is a nonwoven material or fabric. When your sculpture is felted it becomes one piece of nonwoven material. When you press your finger into felted wool it will depress slightly but feel firm.

Felted wool is tangled and compressed so there is no room to push your finger deep into the wool. Wool that is *not* felted is fluffy and full of air and will allow you to push your finger into it. If you are able to push your finger deep into the wool then it is not completely felted as shown in the photo below.

When you begin to construct a mask it is very flimsy. If you lay it down it will relax until it is flat. As you continue to add wool and poke (felt) you can feel the wool continually getting firmer until it will hold its shape. The fibers are compressed into the sculpted shape.

Pinch the surface of felted wool with your thumb and index finger. Do the fibers pull away?

If you can easily pull the fibers from the surface then it is not felted. The final layer of wool is adding color over the base sculpture. Before you add the color, the base should be felted in the shape of the final project. The color is not meant to change the shape in any drastic way. Once the final layer of color is added a final surface felting will create a consistently smooth exterior to the sculpture. Use a fine felting needle (#42) and poke at a 45 degree angle. Shallow poking while holding the needle at a 45 degree angle to the surface will felt the top layer without changing the shape. It will bury all the hairy ends and firm up the surface. Poke the entire surface in one direction and then repeat in the opposite direction. Turn the sculpture again and repeat the process until you have poked in all four directions. Work in rows poking back and forth. If your pokes are close together the wool will felt quickly leaving a smooth even surface.

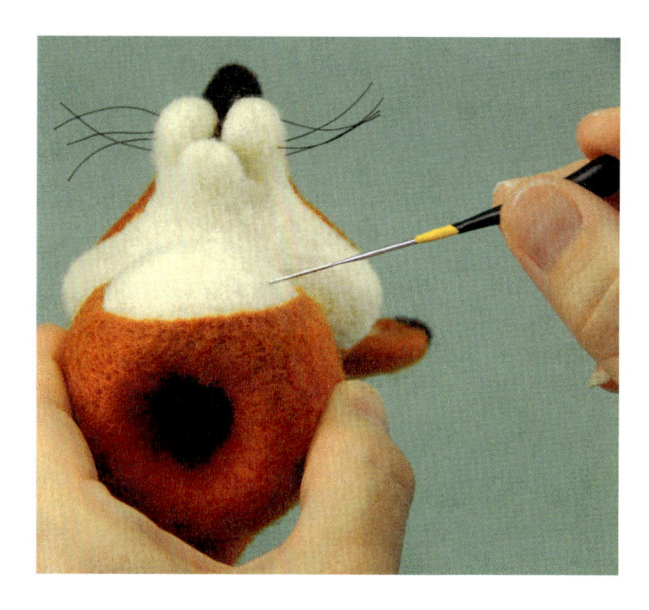

It is best to perform the final surface felting in several passes rather than trying to do it in one. Trying to do it all at once will push and bunch the wool. Changing the direction of your pokes with each pass will help to tangle and grab all the loose fibers. As you are working, add more color to any area that seems too thin or where the core wool is visible through the color.

Use Core Wool For A Base

Curly locks wool (*has the natural curl of the sheep*) and roving (*has been combed straight*) are used for some of the details in the sculptures. The majority of each project is made from wool batting. Core wool is undyed batting. It is less expensive than dyed wool batting so it makes more sense to use it as a base for needle felting. You can purchase core wool by the pound and save the dyed wool for the final layer of your sculpture. Core wool may be used on the final layer anytime you need an off-white color. The **Ram project** (*on page 71*) uses core wool for the entire project except for bits of shading and a final layer of brown on the horns.

Felt Fabric

Most fabric stores have bolts of **felt fabric** that can be purchased by the yard. Read the label carefully and you will see that it comes in acrylic, wool blend, and 100% wool. A wool blend is usually 80% acrylic and 20% wool. I have noticed that often the wool blend is simply called "*wool*" making you assume that it is 100% wool. A careful look at the label on the end of the bolt will reveal the fiber contents of the fabric. The cost of these fabrics will also alert you to their differences. 100% wool fabric may cost up to 4 to 5 times the cost of the acrylic fabric.

Most of us are familiar with **craft felt sheets** that are readily available at craft supply stores and online. They are acrylic sheets cut into 9" x 12" pieces and are very inexpensive.

Prefelt is batting that has been partially felted into thin sheets. It is not strong enough to be used as a fabric without further felting. It can be torn easily with the hands creating a soft feathered edge along the tear. It can be used as a base for wet felting or needle felting. The loose fibers of the prefelt allow you to easily blend other colors into it.

I prefer using 100% wool fabric on many of my projects. I feel like it gives me a head start and I can cut it in the exact shape I need. This doesn't mean that you can not make the projects in this book without wool fabric. You can use wool fabric or you can felt the shape yourself. Refer to **Making Ears Without A Felt Fabric Base** on *page 20* for an example of this.

Using Templates To Make Ears

I have included templates at the back of this book for some of the projects. Make a copy of the templates and cut them out.

All of the animal ears in this book are different sizes and shapes but they are all constructed the same way. I will demonstrate how to make ears *with* a felt fabric base and *without* a felt fabric base.

Making Ears With A Felt Fabric Base

1. Pin the ear template to 100% wool felt fabric. Cut out the ear around the template.

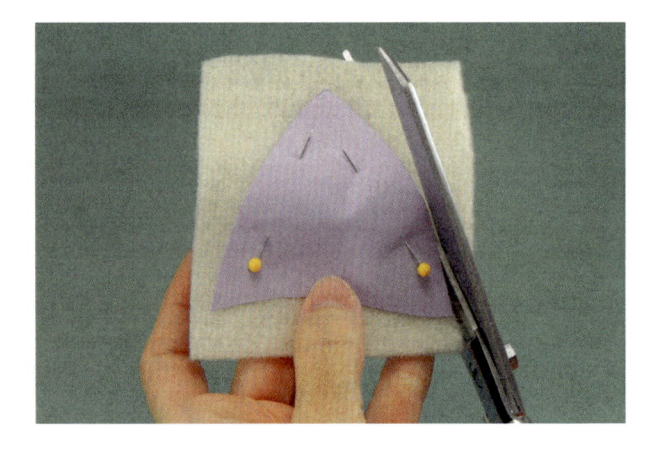

2. Lay the ears on the foam work surface and cover them with a layer of wool. The wool should extend past the edges of the cut felt fabric. Poke the entire ear up to the edges of the fabric cutout. It will not be completely felted at this point, but the wool should be attached to the ear cutout.

3. Pick up the ear and turn it over. Fold the fluffy wool over the edges of the fabric cutout and poke to hold it in place. Do not fold over the edge that will be attached to the head.

When you are working on a piece and poking into the foam you should lift the piece frequently as you work. The needle will push the fibers into the foam. If you don't pull the piece off the foam it will begin to attach to the foam. If your piece is embedded into the foam, the shape may become distorted as you pull it off the foam.

4. Cover the second side of the ear with a layer of wool that extends past the edges of the ear. Poke the entire ear up to the edges of the fabric cutout.

5. Pick up the ear and turn it over. Fold the fluffy wool over the edges of the fabric cutout and poke to hold it in place. Do not fold over the edge that will be attached to the head.

6. The entire ear is covered in wool and ready to be felted. Add additional colors or designs now if the pattern calls for it, and then felt the ear on both sides. The ears are felted before they are attached to the head. Always leave the bottom edge of the ear fluffy so it can be attached to the head. Work on both ears at the same time. It is easier to keep them the same shape if you work on them together. Ears are never completely flat. You must felt the curves and bends into the ears

so they will hold that shape permanently. Some ears have a definite front and back. Lay both ears on the foam with the front facing up so you don't end up with two left ears. With the ear on the foam work surface bend the ear. Poke the ear along the bend on the inside and outside of the ear. Keep working back and forth between the ears so they match.

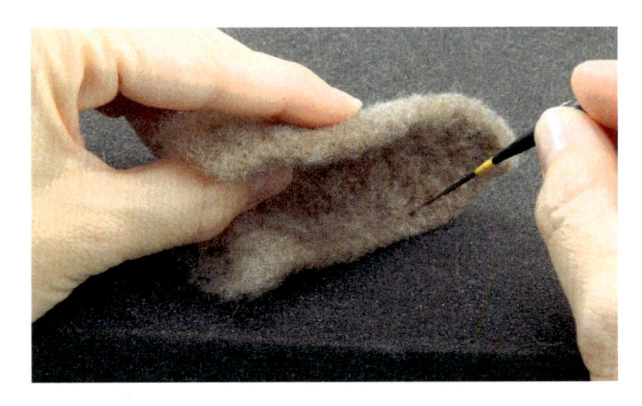

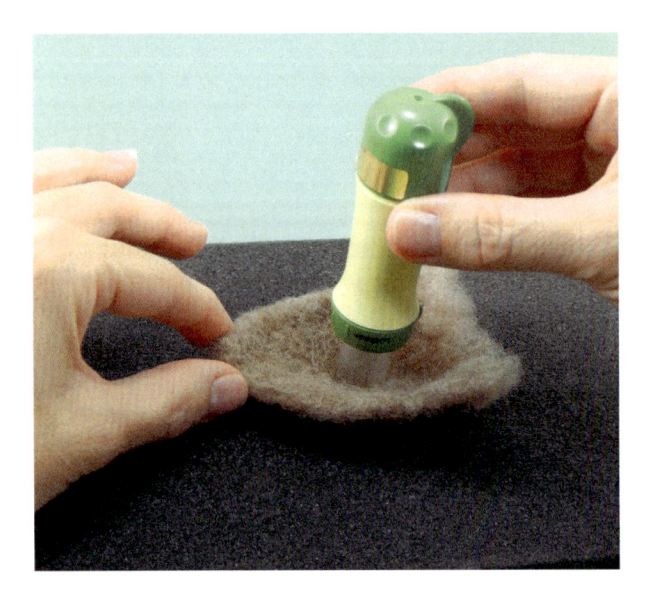

Make sure that as you felt both sides of the ear you are also felting the edges of the ear. Holding the ear in a piece of folded cardboard allows you to felt the edge with your fingers out of the way.

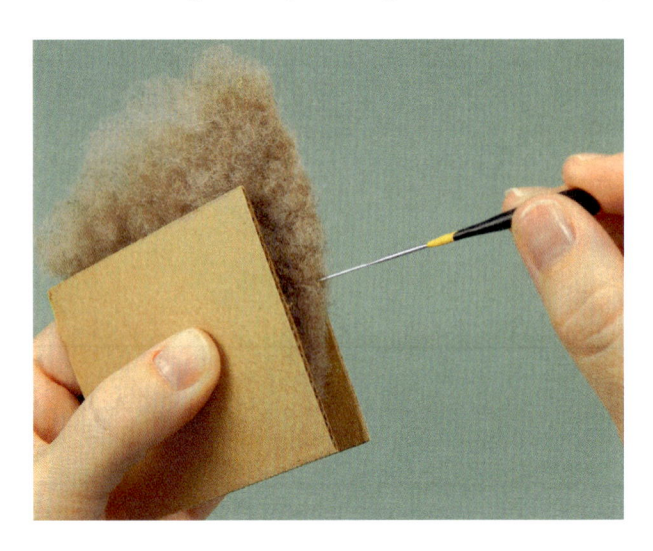

Making Ears Without A Felt Fabric Base

1. Lay wool on the foam work surface that is wider and taller than the ear template. The wool should be thick enough so you can not see the foam through it. Once you have made an ear you will have a better understanding of how much wool is needed. If you discover that the ear is too thin once you begin felting it, you can add more wool.

2. Place the ear template in the center of the wool. Stick straight pins through the template and into the foam. This will keep the template in place.

3. With a slow and controlled action, poke around the outline of the ear template. The pokes should be close together so this may require poking around the template 2 or 3 times. Do not poke across the bottom edge of the template on the side of the ear that will be attached to the head. The bottom edge of the ear will remain fluffy.

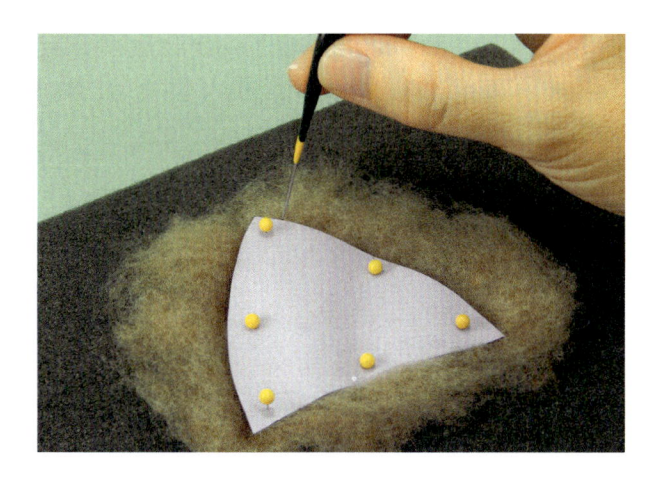

4. Remove the straight pins and the template. Inspect the poked line for any areas that may not have enough pokes. It should be a solid line without gaps. Poke along the line in any areas that have gaps.

5. Poking the outline of the ear has lightly attached it to the foam. It is not secure and will easily pull off the foam so be gentle with it. Use your finger to gently fold over the wool along the ear outline. Poke to hold it in place.

6. Poke the entire ear. If you completely felted the ear at this point you would have some trouble pulling it off the wool. Poke it just enough so it is holding its shape and can be lifted off the foam. With each poke you are pushing fibers into the foam. Keep your pokes shallow and the fibers will not embed deep into the foam.

Notice the bottom edge of the ear. You did not poke a line along the bottom edge of the ear. As you are poking the surface of the ear do not poke beyond the ear template. This will leave a fluffy edge along the bottom of the ear so it can be attached to the head.

7. Slowly and gently pull the ear off the foam so you do not distort the shape of the ear. Turn the ear over and poke on the other side. Pick the ear up frequently so it does not get embedded into the foam. Now that the felting process has begun you can see where the ear may be too thin. You can also hold it up to the light and see thin areas. Add wool where needed so the ear has a consistent thickness. Check the folded edges of the ears for consistent thickness also. Wrap additional wool around edges that are too thin.

Add additional colors or designs now if the pattern calls for it, and then felt the ear on both sides. Work on both ears at the same time. It is easier to keep them the same shape if you work on them together. You must felt the curves and bends into the ears so they will hold that shape permanently. Some ears have a definite front and back. Lay both ears on the foam with the front facing up so you don't end up with two left ears. With the ear on the foam work surface bend the ear. Poke the ear along the bend on the inside and outside of the ear. Keep working back and forth between the ears so they match.

TECHNIQUES

Blending Colors

Wool that contains two or more colors can add interest to a sculpture. Creating animals offer many opportunities for using blended colors. You can purchase wool that contains a mixture of colors or you can create your own. Purchasing blended wool will give you a consistent color when you are using it for a large area.

If you decide to mix your own colors make sure you prepare enough wool to cover the area you are working on. If you are a handspinner then you are familiar with hand carding and may have the tools. Hand carding is a traditional method of preparing fleece and fibers for spinning yarns. Hand carders are a pair of wooden paddles with wire faces. Do not buy these tools if you don't already have them. Purchase the wool already blended or mix your own if you only need a small amount.

Decide what colors you would like to blend. In the example below there are three colors.

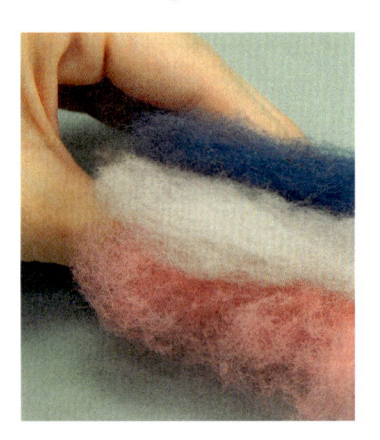

Pull off equal amounts of each color and stack them on top of each other.

This sample used bright colors so the layers are easily seen.

Pull the stack in half.

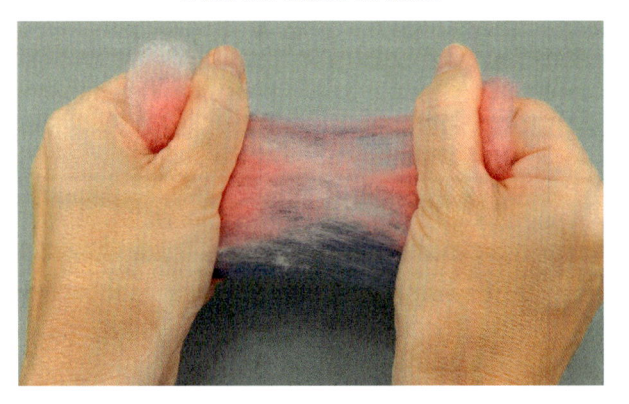

Put one stack on top of the other and pull it in half again. Keep repeating this process until you are happy with the mix of colors.

Blending Colors As You Felt

Colors may also be blended on the sculpture as you are felting. The **wild hare mask** is an example of this. The mask was first covered in light brown. The brown was poked just enough to attach it but not completely felt it. Small amounts of medium brown, dark brown, and off-white were added on top of the base color. Add the colors in thin layers so the base color will show through. The light brown is still fluffy so the other colors will mix with it as you felt.

22

Sometimes it looks better or more realistic if there is not a hard edge where two colors meet. The inside of the hare's ears and the muzzle are off-white with brown around it. The off-white is the core wool that was used to make the base of the mask. The edge of the brown is very thin and wispy so it creates an irregular line. This makes a gradual transition from one color to the next that has a softer look.

Tip: Wool is graded according to its characteristics. There are variations in wool fibers from different sheep breeds. There are also variations in fibers within the same fleece depending on which part of the body they come from. Many things are looked at when grading the wool. The fiber diameter may be fine or coarse. The crimp or waviness in the fiber and the length of the fiber are a few examples. Wool is graded to determine market value and how the wool will be used. A carpet manufacturer would not use the same wool that is used for a fine sweater.

When you search for wool for needle felting projects the description of the wool usually will not mention the specific grade of the wool. It will usually describe the wool as "great for needle felting". As you start to collect wool from various sources you will notice slight differences in the wool and this is fine. As you gain experience working with the wool you will discover that some wool will work better for different parts of the sculpture. The felted surface of one wool may appear smoother than that of another wool. As you start to compare wool you can see and feel their differences and know how to best use them in your projects.

If you are working with a coarse wool you may find it difficult to felt very small items with a lot of detail. On the other hand, a coarse wool may be the perfect choice for the coat of an animal. If you are blending colors choose wool that has a similar texture and they will tend to mix evenly. If you blend several colors and one is more coarse than the others, it may be more prominent in the mix. Learn to use the differences to your advantage.

Felting A Firm Ball

If you want a round shape it is often easier to make a ball and then felt it onto the sculpture. They can be made in any size and be used for eyes, noses, chins and other body parts. I often use balls for eyes on the finger puppets. It will give you a round protruding eye rather than a flat eye. You can add the iris, pupil, eyelids, and eyelashes on the foam work surface to complete the eyes before attaching them to your puppet. This allows you to hide the thread knots from the eyelashes behind the eyes.

1. Pull off a piece of wool and lay it on the foam work surface. Start to roll one edge of the wool. Poke the wool as you are rolling it.

2. Fold in both sides of the wool toward the center and continue poking.

3. Roll up the remaining felt. Poke all around the ball. Roll the ball between the palms of your hands as if you are rolling a clay ball. This will help to create a more rounded shape. You may add wool if you need to increase the size of the ball. Continue poking the ball and rolling it in your hands until it is round and firm.

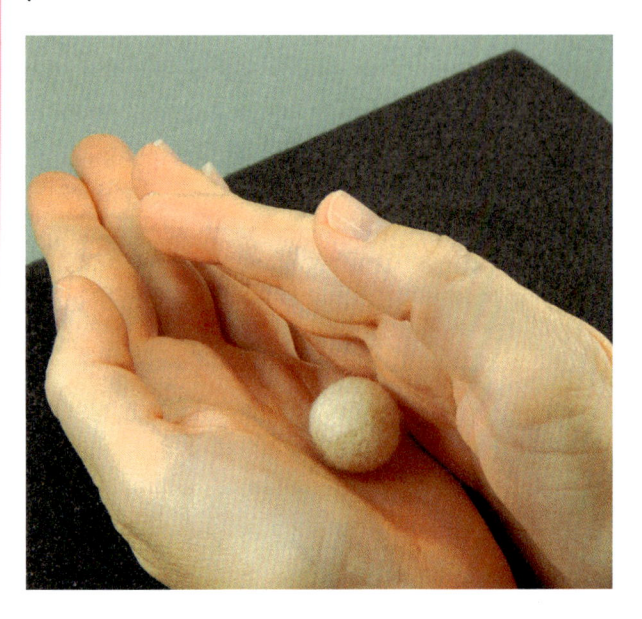

Creating Edges

There are times when you want two pieces or two different colors to gradually fade into one another. Then there are times when you want to create a straight, clean line. The yellow beak against the white face of a bald eagle, the spots on a giraffe, or perhaps your white rabbit is in need of a jacket. There are a couple of variations to creating edges depending on how you intend to use them.

Felt An Edge On The Sculpture

Creating a clean line directly on the sculpture can be used to make stripes, dots, and designs in an animal's coat.

1. Lay wool in the area where you want to add a shape. Poke the outline of the desired shape through the wool and directly into the sculpture. Use a slow controlled poking action. Once you have the shape marked out you can go back and poke over the line again. The first time you can concentrate on making the shape you want. The second time you can concentrate on poking a strong line without gaps.

2. The photo above shows the spots on a giraffe. Poke inside the shape to begin to attach the wool. Use your finger to gently fold over the fluff along the poked line. Push the fluff inside the outline and poke to felt the shape to the sculpture. Short, shallow pokes around the shape will clean up any stray fibers. The photo below shows the stripes on a cat mask. They are made the same as the giraffe's spots.

24

The photo below shows the tiny feet of a rabbit finger puppet. The feet are 1 1/4" long and 3/4" wide. The pink foot pads, though small, are made the same as the giraffe's spots.

Felt An Edge
On The Foam Work Surface

When you create edges directly on the sculpture (as shown previously on the giraffe, cat, and rabbit) you can felt the shape so it is even with the surrounding color. You can also add more wool so the shape is raised above the surrounding color. Now we will felt a thick edge on the foam work surface and attach it to the sculpture.

1. Decide how long the edge needs to be. A soft tape measure from your sewing kit works great for measuring around curves. Lay wool on your foam work surface wide enough to accommodate your measurement. Lay a stick or dowel in the center of the wool to use as a guide to poke a straight line.

Poke in a slow and controlled action. Hitting the stick may bend or break your needle. Once you have the line marked out you can go back and poke over the line again. The first time you can concentrate on making the straight line. The second time you can concentrate on poking a strong line without gaps.

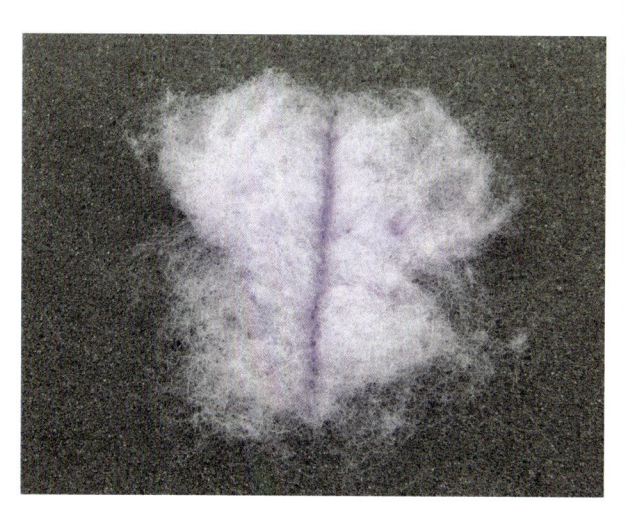

2. Use your finger to fold over the wool along the poked line. Poke along the edge so the wool will stay folded. Use the stick to hold down the wool as you felt.

3. Poke the edge of the wool until the fold is stable enough to hold together. Gently pull the wool off the foam. Turn the wool over and poke the edge on the other side. Felt the edge of the wool completely.

25

TECHNIQUES

4. When you are felting an edge you may need to poke directly into the edge. A thin piece of cardboard folded in half will hold the wool and keep your fingers safe from pokes. You can use the cardboard whenever you need to felt edges or small items.

All the edges for *Alex's* blue jacket were made on the foam work surface. The edges were attached to the rabbit's body in the outline of the jacket. Once all of the edges were attached, the blue wool was felted to the body within the outline of the jacket. Letting some of the edges, like the collar, hang off the jacket give the illusion that the entire jacket is a separate piece.

Felting Ropes

Outlining a nose or filling in the seam of a mouth with a dark color will help add detail. Pull off a very thin strip of wool.

Roll the strip of wool between the palms of your hands to gather all the loose fibers.

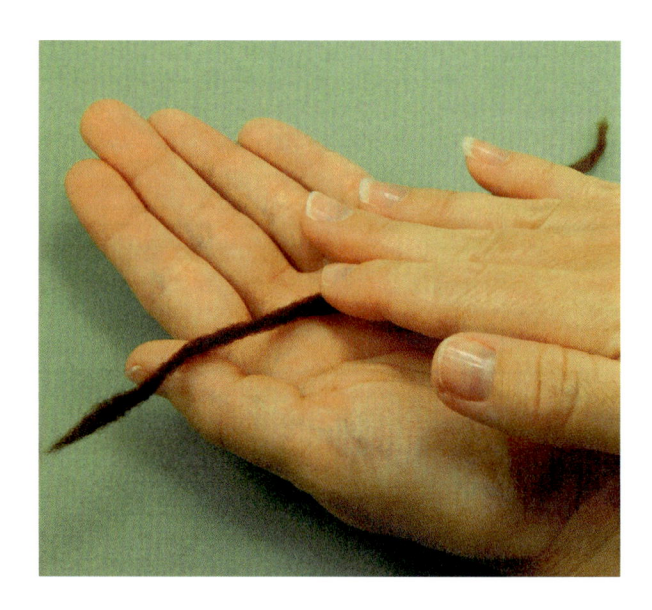

26

There are times when you may need a thicker string or rope of wool. You could use it for the mane of a lion or fleece on a sheep. I often use ropes to outline the eye openings on my masks. Wool that has been wrapped around a stick or dowel will give you a clean, even edge to attach to your sculpture.

1. Gather an assortment of sticks and dowels. The sizes you will use the most will have a diameter less than 1/2". In the wood section of your craft store you will find a package of dowels with varying diameters. The cake and candy decorating section has small and large *lollipop sticks* and *candy apple sticks*. You can even use an unsharpened pencil.

2. Pull off thin strips of wool and wrap them around a dowel. It is better to wrap several thin layers of wool than to wrap one thick layer.

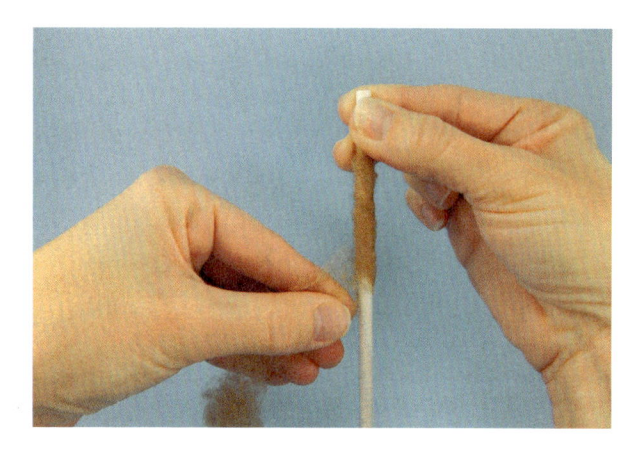

After wrapping each layer, twist the dowel in the palm of your partially closed hand. You will feel the wool tighten around the dowel.

3. Once you have all the wool, continue to twist it in your hand. Twisting in your hand starts the felting process. wool off the dowel. You will notice that the will stretch out a bit longer once removed from the dowel. The rope is ready to use. A brown rope was used to make the stripe under the eyes on the *owl mask* (*shown below*).

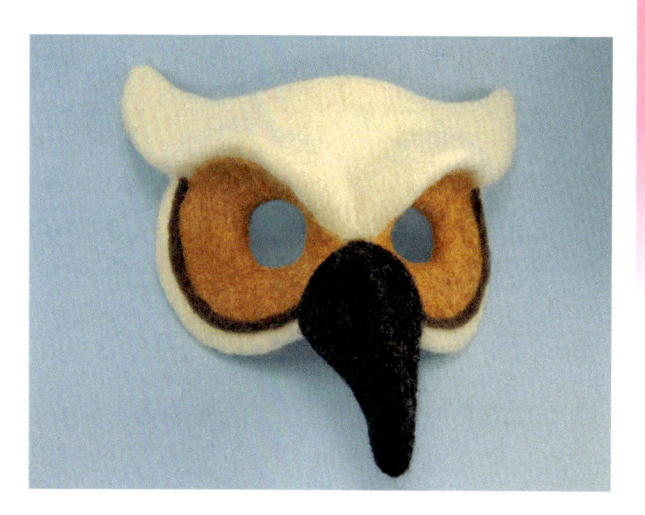

A black rope was used to outline the cat's eyes. The black wool has a bit of white mixed in to soften the look of it.

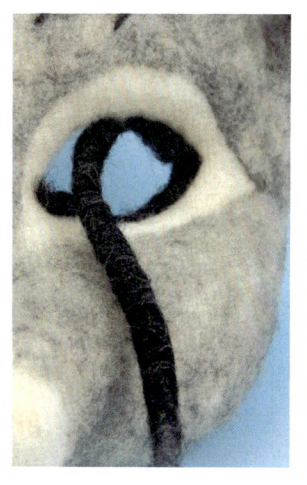

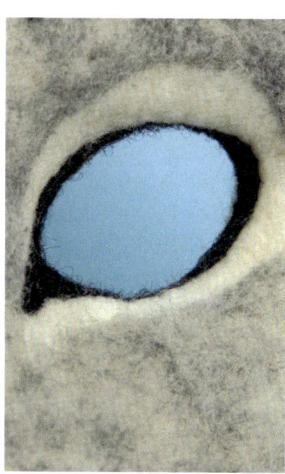

If the rope is too long, simply pull off the excess. Two pieces of rope may be joined together as you are felting them to the sculpture. Slightly overlap the ends of the rope and felt. You may also blend two or more colors together as you are wrapping the wool on the dowel.

27

ture

...ing or model-
...ng is removing
...modeling is add-
... Many materials
...m including stone,
...d wool. Before you
...n your sculpture you
must first ... rm of your subject. If
you are carving wood ... stone you would rough
out a basic shape by removing material from
a block of wood or stone. If you are modeling
in clay or wool you build up the basic shape by
adding material.

As you are building a wool form you are continually poking (felting) the shape. Each layer that is added is felted to the previous layer of wool. The wool sculpture will become firmer as each layer of wool is felted. Once you have achieved the form, you add thin layers of wool to cover up and fill in seams and lines for a smooth surface.

As you are building up an area it may require a log or ball shape of wool to fill it in. It goes without saying that the size and amount of wool you add is determined by the size of your sculpture.

Roll a ball shape and leave a fluffy tail. Lay a piece of wool on your foam work surface and start rolling one edge poking as you roll. Tuck in the sides as you roll. Roll the ball up completely or leave a fluffy tail.

This is a great shape for filling in cheeks, a snout, or making a chin. The shape is felted to the base form and then more wool may be added to refine the shape.

If you want to round an area like a cheek or the top of the head, **make a circle** that has the same thickness all the way across. While holding the wool in your hands, fold under all the fluffy edges (shown below).

Lay the piece on your sculpture and poke around the perimeter of the circle. Once the edge is attached you can poke the entire piece.

Some shapes are difficult to name. Building up a long snout is a **triangle with a tail** on it. The tail is attached between the eyes up toward the forehead. Continue to build on this and refine the shape.

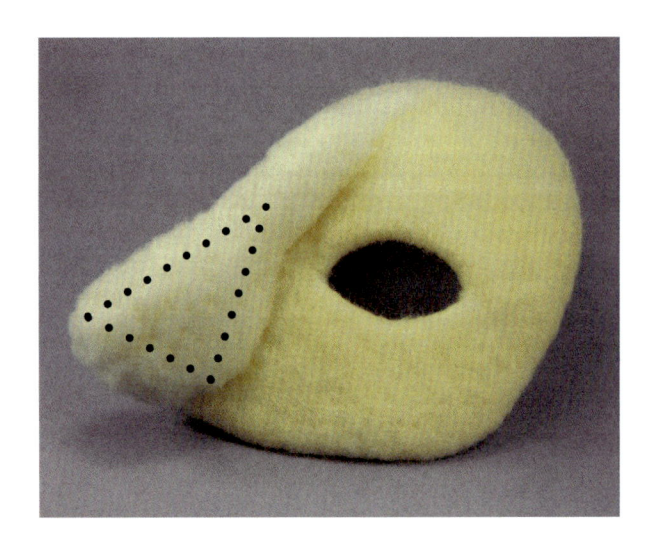

28

To fill in a long area **make a log**. Lay a piece of wool on the foam work surface in the size you need. Roll the wool tightly, poke as you roll. A log (*shown below*) connects the snout to the side of the face.

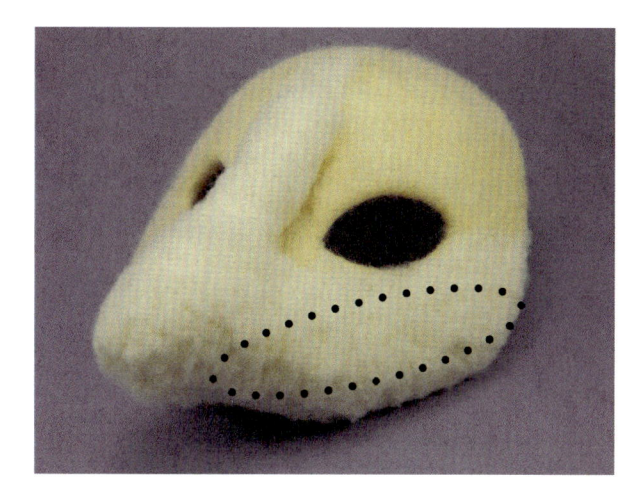

Notice how the area on the side of the snout has been filled with the log shape. (*photo right*)

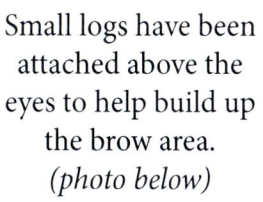

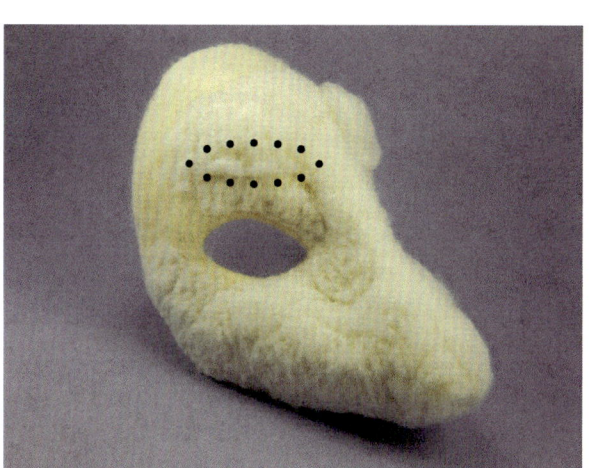

Small logs have been attached above the eyes to help build up the brow area. (*photo below*)

Attach An Elastic Strap To The Back Of The Mask

Elastic may be found where you shop for sewing notions. The 1/8" width comes in a round cord or a flat band. It is available in many colors, but I usually choose black or white. You will also need a sewing needle with an eye large enough to accommodate the elastic.

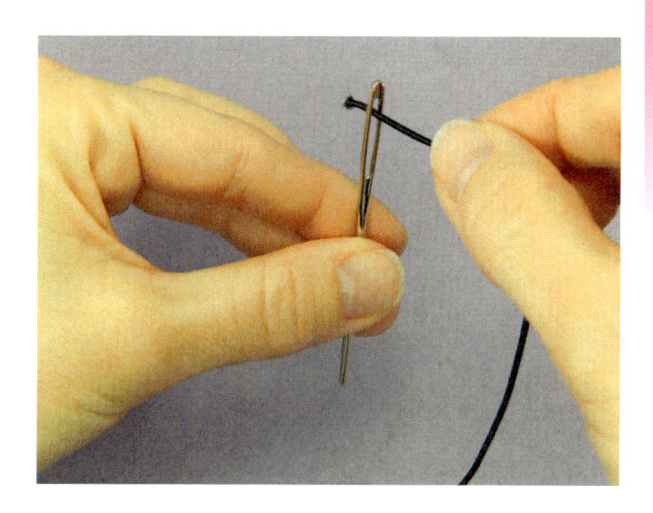

Thread a large sewing needle with the elastic. When you are wearing the mask the elastic should be above your ears. Push the needle through the side of the mask and tie a knot. Try the mask on to get an idea how long the elastic needs to be and then knot the other side. For large or heavier masks use thicker elastic.

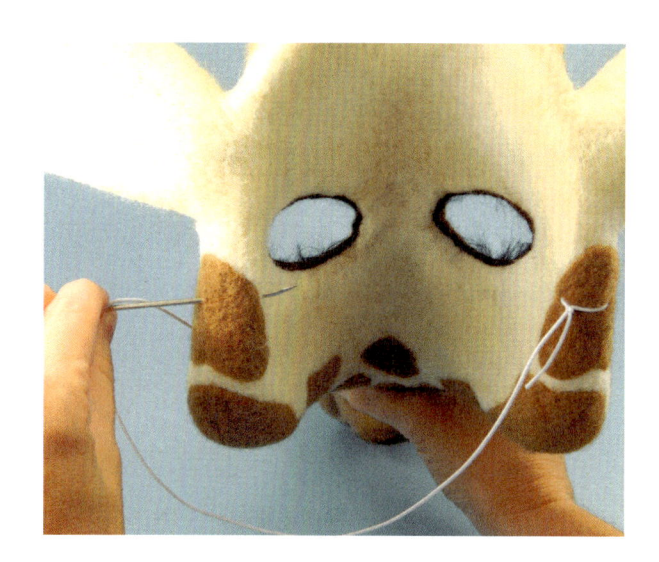

29

30

MAKING *Masks*

Masks are beautiful, wearable art that can be displayed when you are not using them. You can hang them on a wall or make a stand and display them on a shelf.

Wool, whether dyed or left in its natural color, make amazing animal masks. They are incredibly light weight which makes them comfortable to wear. Perhaps the most difficult part about making masks is deciding which animal to make first.

At first I thought I needed to make the masks in several sizes. But then as people started trying them on I noticed that some adults fit into the child size masks and some children fit into the adult size masks. The eye holes on the adult mask are farther apart than those on the child's mask. The size depends on the person wearing the mask. The masks are very flexible so they will adjust to fit the face of the wearer. The same mask may appear different depending on the shape of the face wearing it.

A mask can cover the entire face or it can be a half mask that covers the eyes and nose. Take into consideration who you are making the mask for. A young child may not be comfortable in a full face mask. The masks are made with a void in front of the wearer's nose and mouth. This makes them feel less confining and easy to breathe and talk while wearing them.

The procedure for making different animal masks always begins the same. The base of the mask may cover the wearer's forehead or extend to the top of the head to accommodate an animal's ears or horns. While the size or shape may change, the process remains the same.

I find it very helpful to refer to a photo of the animal I am felting. Some animals have very distinctive features. If you get these attributes correct, you will capture the essence of the animal and the end result will be a pleasing resemblance.

MASKS

Cat Mask

You do not need to be a cat lover to love these masks. They are fun to make, wear, and display. Cats come in a diverse range of coat colorings and patterns. You could make several cat masks and each one could look different, but constructing each mask will always be the same.

There are other animals in the cat species that include the cougar, cheetah, jaguar, leopard, and tiger. The instructions for the cat mask can be used to make any of these animals. You may find it helpful to look at photos of these animals to see the colors or patterns of their coat. Also notice the size and shape of their ears and nose.

Supplies

core wool for the mask base
white wool for the lips, chin, and eyes
light gray wool for the face and ears
dark gray wool to shade the face and ears
medium brown wool to shade the face
black wool for the stripes and to outline the eyes and nose
medium peach wool for the nose

felt fabric for the mask base and the ears
craft or button weight black thread for the whiskers
straight white roving for the hair inside the ears
elastic cord for the strap on the back of the mask

Create A Base For The Mask

Use the **cat template** to cut a mask from felt fabric. *Refer to page 18 for information about using* **Felt Fabric** *or how to create a base without it.*

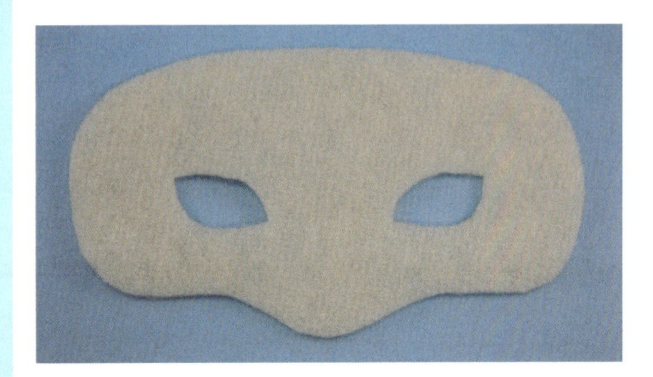

Cover the entire mask on the inside and outside with core wool. Pull off small pieces of wool and poke to attach. A tool that holds several needles will make the felting go quicker. Once both sides of the mask are covered, wrap core wool around the edge of the mask and the edge of the eye openings.

Bend the mask at the center and the nose area will stick out. Hold the mask in this position on your foam work surface and poke on the front and back sides of the mask and on the bend or curved area. As the wool becomes felted, the mask will begin to stiffen. Each layer of wool that is added will continue to stiffen the mask.

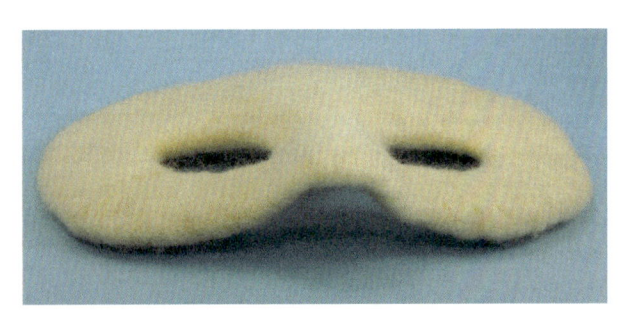

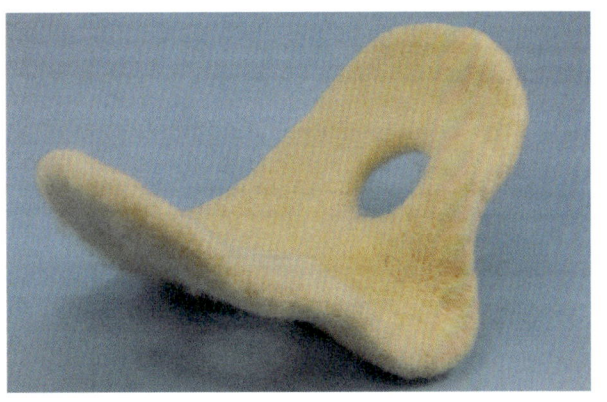

Shaping The Mask

The shape of a cat's face can vary among breeds. There are some breeds that have a very flat face like a Persian cat. This mask is meant to resemble the more common domestic cat. The muzzle of a cat projects out from the head and includes the jaw, mouth, and nose. Do not make a muzzle that is too long or pointed. The measurement on this mask when completed is 2 1/2" from the tear duct of the eye to the tip of the nose. Be mindful of this as you build up the muzzle area.

One of the important things that experience will teach you is how much the wool will shrink and compact after felting. As you get a feel for this, it is easier to understand how much wool is needed to build up an area. Fortunately, wool is so forgiving that you may add or remove wool as you are sculpting.

Make two logs that are 3" long and about 2" wide for the muzzle. Fold over one end and poke it in a rounded shape. Leave the other end fluffy. Put the rounded ends of the log against each other and poke until they hold together.

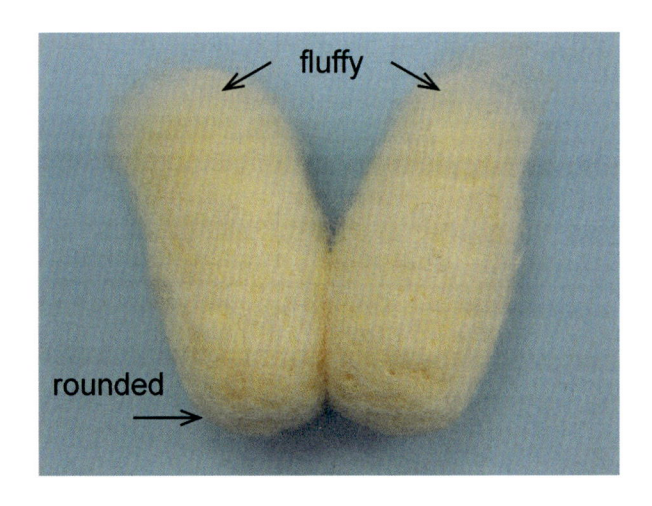

Put the fluffy open end of the muzzle at the bottom of the mask. Previously you poked out the nose area on the mask. Push the nose area between the logs and poke to hold them in place. The mask is not very stiff at this point so be careful that you do not flatten the nose area on the mask.

Roll a ball of wool that is 1 1/2" wide for the chin. Push the ball up between the muzzle and poke to attach. The chin is slightly indented from the muzzle above.

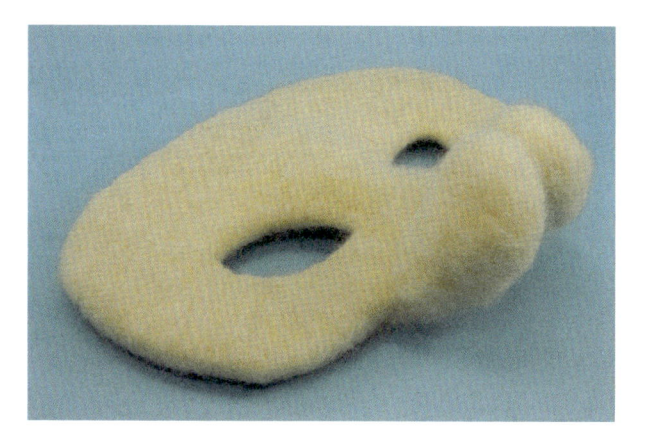

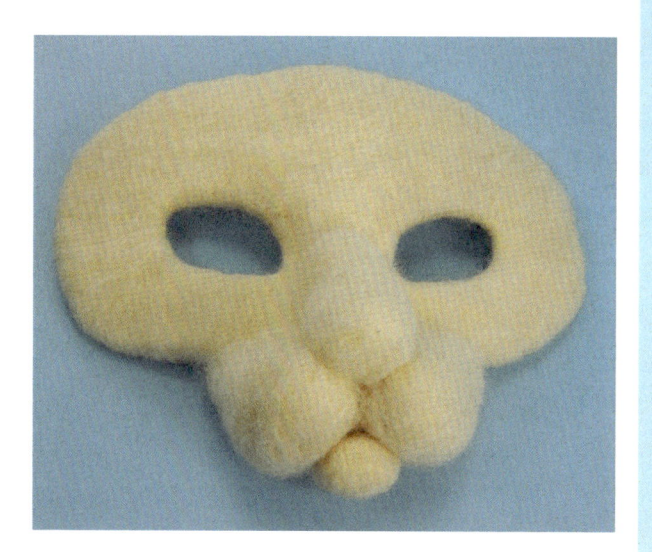

Make a third log that is 3" long and 1" thick for the nose. Fold over one end and poke it in a rounded shape. Leave the other end fluffy. Lay the nose on top of the muzzle with the rounded end extending even with the muzzle. Poke the nose to attach it to the muzzle below it and the mask behind it.

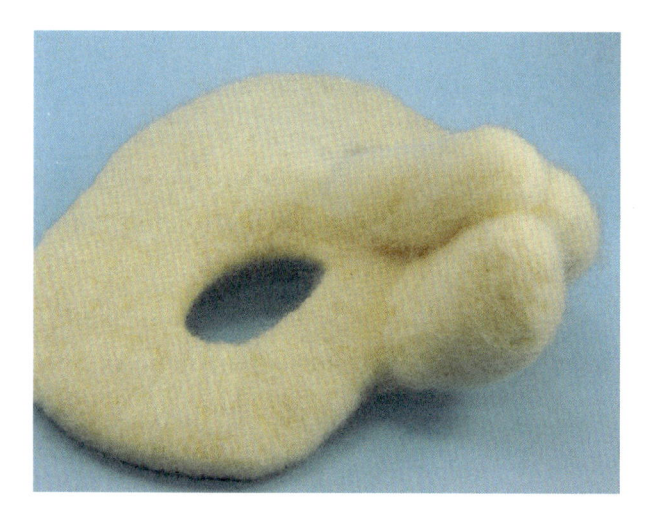

All of the elements of the muzzle are in place and wool is added to smooth the transition from the mask to the muzzle. Add wool on the seam between the nose and muzzle. Then add wool to connect the muzzle to the mask. This will also help shape the curved sides of the mask. Build up the area under the eyes. Poke the wool in place with each layer you add and you will feel the mask becoming stiffer and stronger.

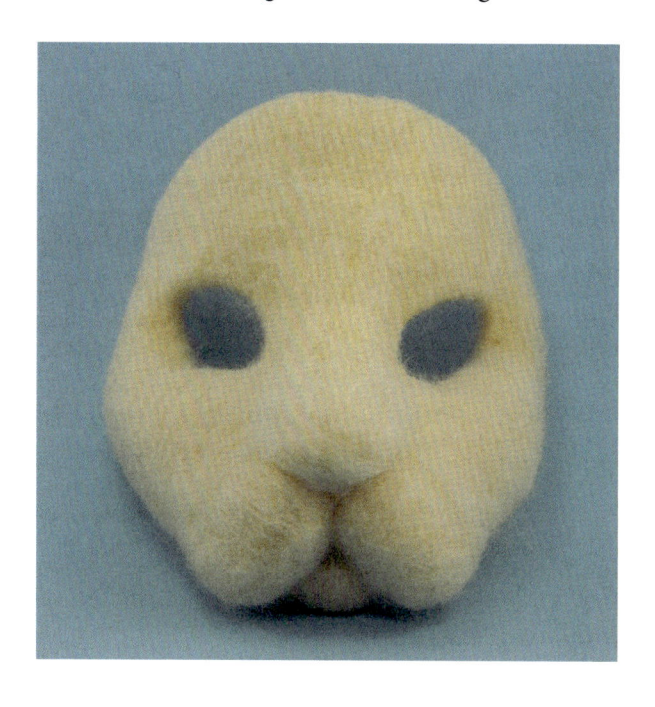

The curve on the sides of the mask may flatten out as you are attaching the muzzle. This happens because the mask is not stiff enough to hold its shape yet.

The basic shape of the cat's face is in place. Now you will refine that shape. As we go on to add detail and color to the mask it will not change the overall shape. Any changes or adjustments need to be made prior to adding color to the mask. The mask should be felted and firm to the touch before you are ready to add detail and color.

The top of the cat's nose should be somewhat flat. Poke back and forth in rows along the top of the nose to flatten it out. The nose should be firm. If you have lost some of the dimension of the nose, add more wool to build it back up.

Roll a 2" log for each brow. Curve the log over the eye and poke in place. You may also add some wool to the center of the forehead. *Refer to page 28 for more information on how to fill in or build up an area.* In the sample project below I added wool to the muzzle to make it more rounded.

Once you are happy with the shape, poke the entire mask on the front and back. At this point the mask should be felted and firm. If an area is too flimsy, it may not be thick enough. Add wool to build up the area and felt it.

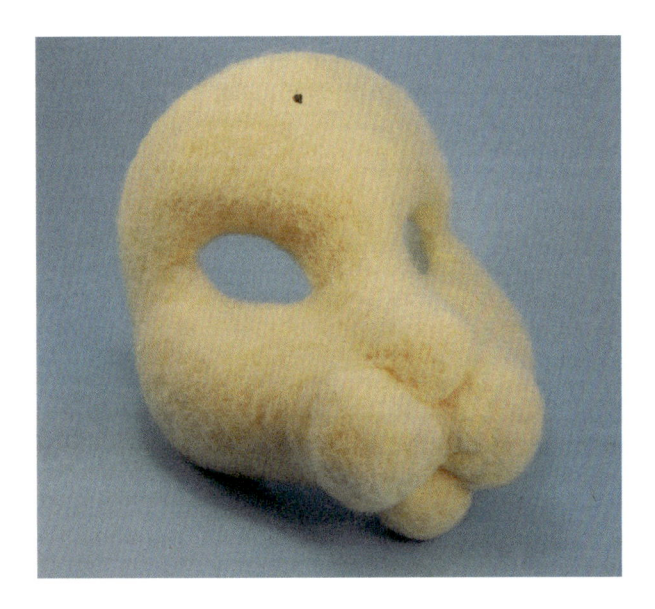

Tip: Sporadic poking will not result in quick felting. A systematic approach with closely spaced pokes will produce more effective results.

Felting The Nose

Use the cat's nose template to shape the nose. Lay a piece of light peach colored wool on the foam work surface that is larger than the nose template. Place the template on top of the wool. Stick a few straight pins through the template and into the foam to hold the template in position. Use a slow and controlled poke to outline the nose template on the wool.

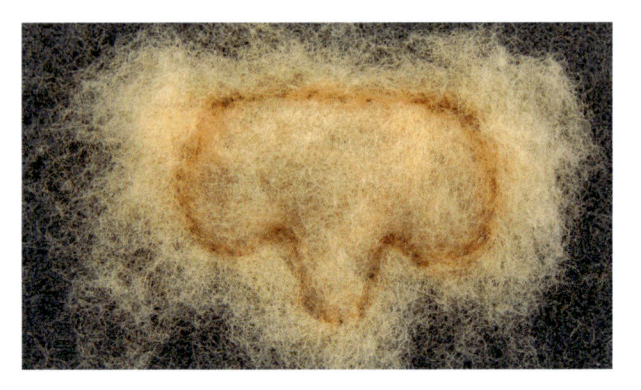

Remove the template. Fold over the fluffy edge along the outline and poke.

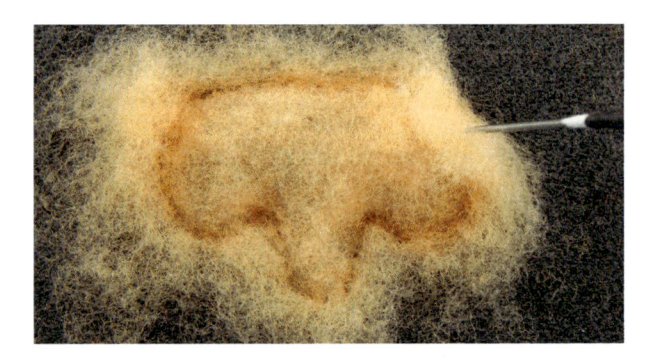

Pull the nose off the foam carefully so the shape is not distorted.

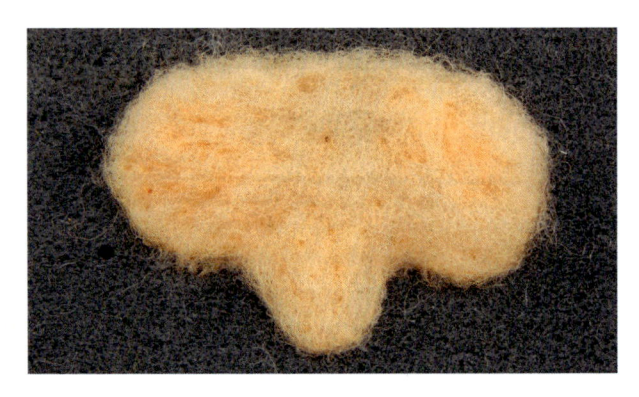

Place the nose on the mask and poke a few times in the center to hold it in place. Poke around the edge of the peach nose to attach.

The excess wool will be pushed toward the center of the nose. The nose resembles the shape of a mushroom. Use a fine #42 needle to felt the nose. This is one instance where you want to felt slowly as you sculpt.

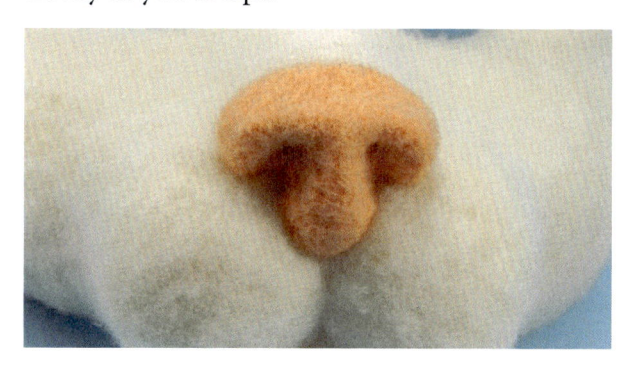

Felt a line about 1/2" long from the bottom of the nose. Twist as you gently push a sharpened dowel into each nostril. Poke inside each nostril with your needle and then with the dowel again. Repeat this until the nose is felted and very firm.

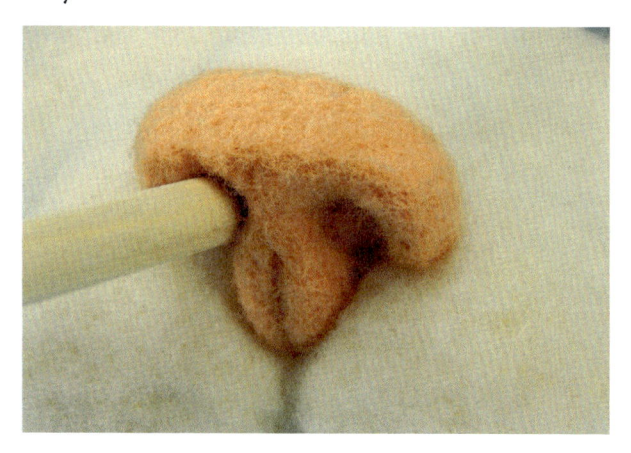

Before outlining the nose you need to put some of the color around the nose. Felt some gray wool with a bit of brown shading around the nose.

I used black wool to outline the nose because this cat has black in its coat. If it were a lighter colored cat that did not have black anywhere else I would have chosen to use a dark brown on the nose.

Pull off a thin strip of black wool and roll it in your hands as you would roll a clay snake. Poke the wool all around the edge of the nose. If the wool disappears, do not pull it out. Add more wool on top of that area.

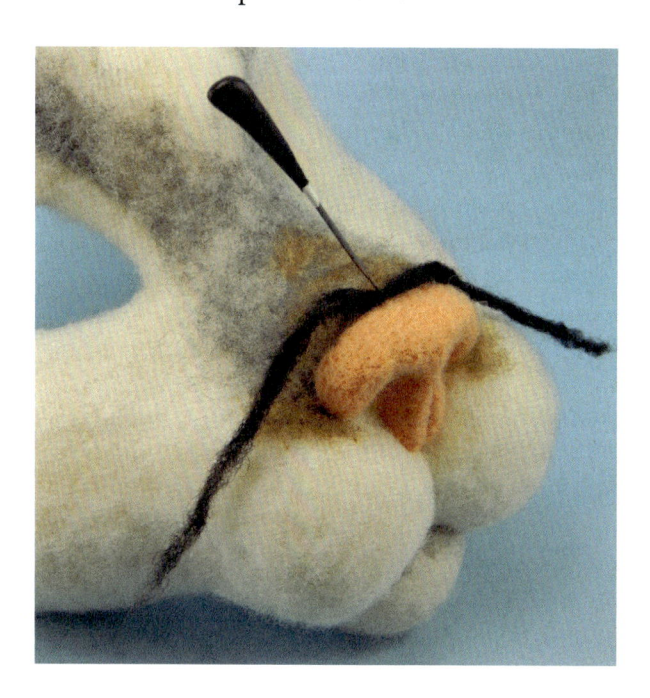

Pull the wool around the sides of the nose and down into the separation between the muzzle.

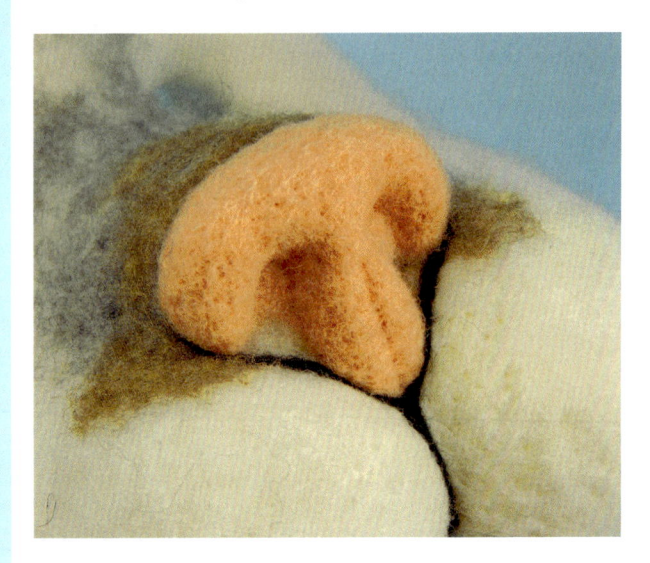

Fill in the nostrils with black. Poke a very fine piece of black in the line at the base of the nose. Add black at the mouth between the upper and lower lips.

Felting The Ears

Use the **cat's ear template** to create the ears. You may use the template to cut two ears from felt fabric and cover them with gray wool or shape your own from wool. (*Refer to page 18 for more information on using templates to help shape the wool.*) Pull off a piece of wool that is larger than the ear template. Lay the wool on your foam work surface. Lay the template on top of the wool. You may use a few straight pins to push through the template and into the foam to hold the template in place. Use a slow, controlled poke to outline the shape of the ear around the template. Poke around the ear template and leave the end of the ear fluffy for attaching to the head. Remove the template and fold over the wool along the poked line to create an edge. Completely felt both sides of the ears before they are attached to the mask. The ears need to be at least 1/4" thick. Add more wool to the ears until they are thick and firm. Bend the ear down the center so that it will curve. Poke the ear in this position.

Spread open the fluff at the base of the ears to attach them to the mask. Position the ears at the edge of the mask. Add additional pieces of gray wool to the ears on the inside and outside until they are securely attached.

Adding Detail

Cover the mask with gray wool. You may cover the core wool completely or let some of it show through the gray. Leave the front of the muzzle, the chin, and around the eyes white. This can be white wool or off-white core wool. Leave an irregular edge of gray around the muzzle. Pull off a thin strip of black wool and roll it in your hands as you would roll a clay snake. Use the strings to make the stripes on the cat.

Wrap black wool around a stick or dowel to make a rope for adding color to the eye openings. *Refer to page 26 for more information on using dowels to make ropes.*

Using the dowel method will allow you to control the thickness of the rope. It will also give you a more defined edge. It is more difficult to produce a rope with consistent thickness when you are rolling it in your hands.

Poke the rope around the eye opening. Simply pull off the excess rope when you get to the end. Add a tear duct shape at the corner of the eye with a small bit of wool. Completely felt the black wool neatly around the eye.

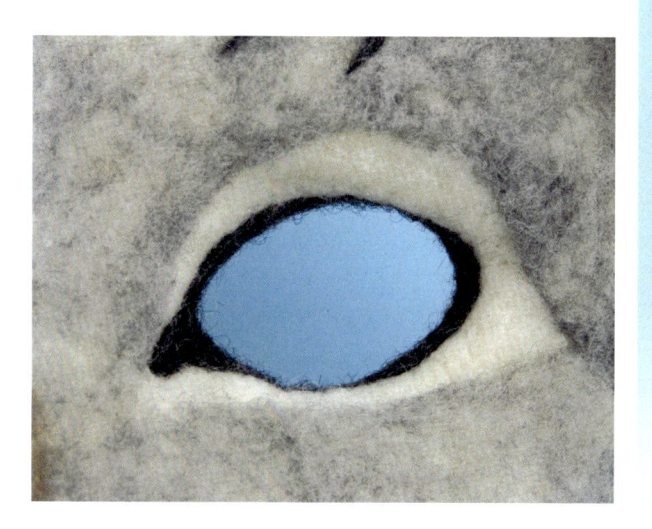

Use brown to shade around the nose, eyes, and ears. You could also use a dark gray or small bits of black to shade the face.

Wool roving makes great hair in the ears. Lay the straight fibers across the ear and poke a line through the center. Brush the fibers with your finger to stand them up and poke a bit more. Use scissors to trim the ear hair. This is one of the rare times I will tell you to cut the wool with scissors.

Whiskers And Elastic Strap

A craft or button weight black thread is used for the cat's whiskers. A 5" or 7" sewing needle will be long enough to reach from one side of the muzzle to the other. Insert the needle on one side of the muzzle and come out in the same area on the opposite side. Put a small dot of white craft glue on the thread and pull the thread until the glue is inside the wool. Once the glue is dry the whiskers will not pull out of the wool. Cut the whiskers about 2 1/2" long. Repeat the process until there are 5 or 6 whiskers on each side of the muzzle. Refer to *page 29* to **Attach An Elastic Strap To The Back Of The Mask**.

Cats In Other Colors

The cat mask below does not use any black wool. Shading with brown suits the colors in this mask better than black.

You may also notice that the nose does not have a line at the base like the gray cat. It is simple and still looks just as good.

Stiff, white bristles cut from a broom are used for the whiskers on this cat. A thick sewing needle is inserted in the muzzle and then wiggled to create a hole in the wool. The end of the broom bristle is dipped in white craft glue and then carefully inserted in the hole left by the needle. The whiskers will be quite secure once the glue dries.

A very small amount of white roving was used to give the cat a little fuzz on his chin. A reverse felting needle pulls fibers out instead of pushing them in. Use the reverse needle as an option for creating some chin fuzz.

The inside of the mask can be left with the core wool showing or you can cover it. I do it both ways. If I am making something with dark colors, like the **black crow**, I would cover the core wool in black. Sometimes it just comes down to whether or not I have enough wool left to cover the back. If you decide not to cover the inside, make sure to bring the color from the front of the mask completely around the edges.

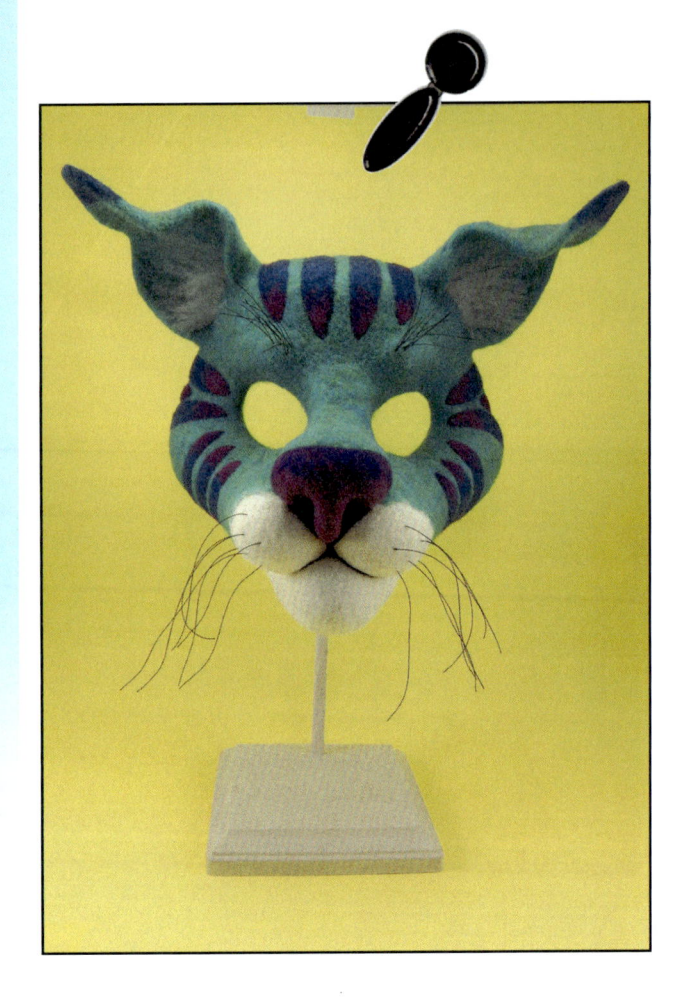

Colorful Cat Mask

The **gray cat** (*on page 32*) and this colorful cat are created using the same steps. The differences are the size and shape of the features and the choice of color. I chose wool dyed in rich jewel tones and used black for the whiskers and also to outline the nose and mouth. I did mix up the steps a bit. The main reason was because I was unsure of the color I wanted to use for the nose. I covered the mask in turquoise wool and then added the two-tone stripes. Once that was done I was able to decide on a nose color. This is an example of how accommodating the wool can be.

The template used for this mask is similar to the one used to make the gray cat. The difference is that the template for this colorful cat has a taller forehead. I wanted to give this cat large ears so it was necessary to increase the size of the forehead. A smaller forehead would have placed the ears too close to the eyes. I also gave him an oversized nose and very round features to resemble a cartoon cat rather than a realistic cat.

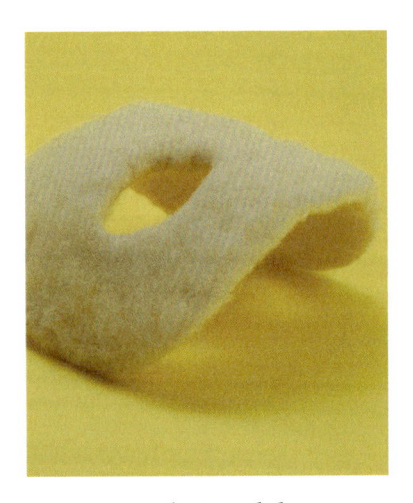

1. Create the mask base.

2. The muzzle is very round and about 2" wide.

3. Make a 5" log for the nose.

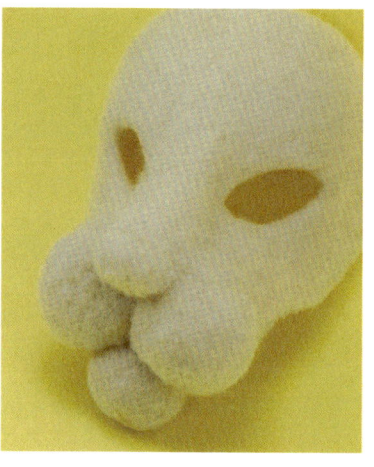

4. The chin is very round like the muzzle.

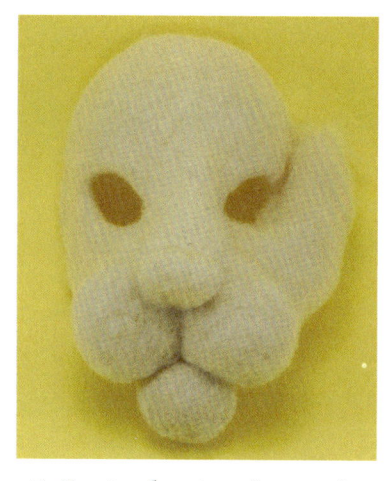

5. Begin shaping the mask.

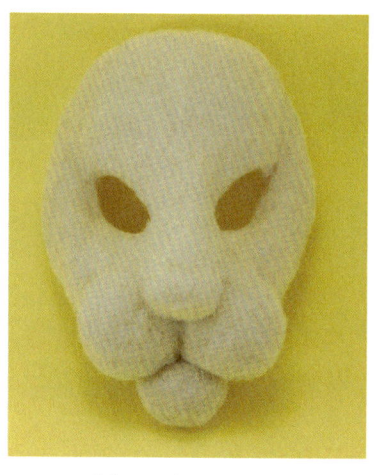

6. Build up the cheeks and blend into the muzzle.

7. Build up the forehead.

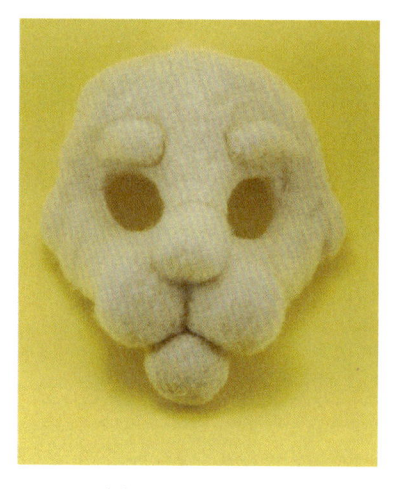

8. Build up the brow area.

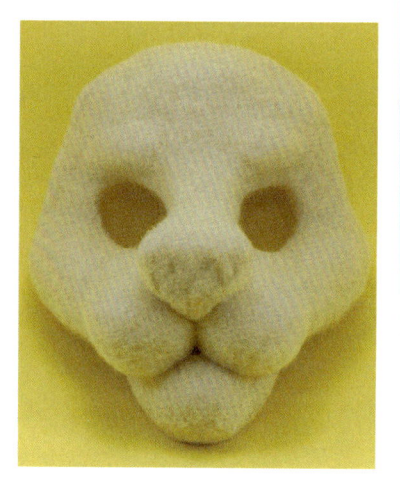

9. Add wool to cover seams and refine the shape.

10. Felt the ears before attaching them to the mask.

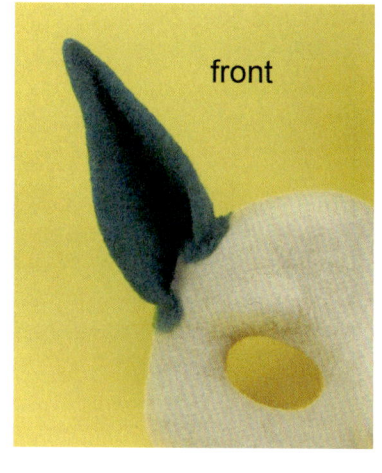

11. Attach the ears with a curve at the base.

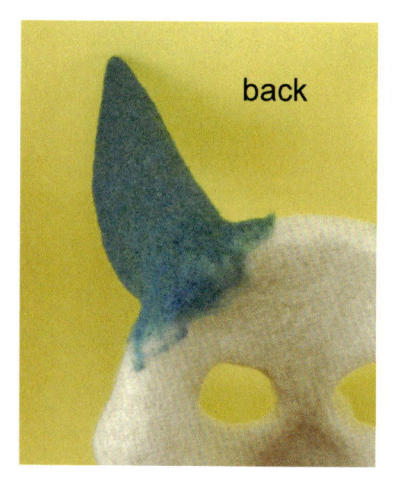

front

12. The back of the ears are at the edge of the mask.

back

MASKS

MASKS

13. Cover the entire mask with color.

14. Shape the ears.

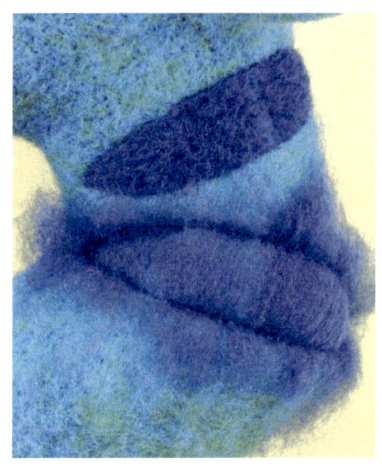

15. Outline the stripes and fill them with color.

16. Add a second color to the tip of each stripe.

17. Add as many stripes as you like.

18. Use the template to shape the nose.

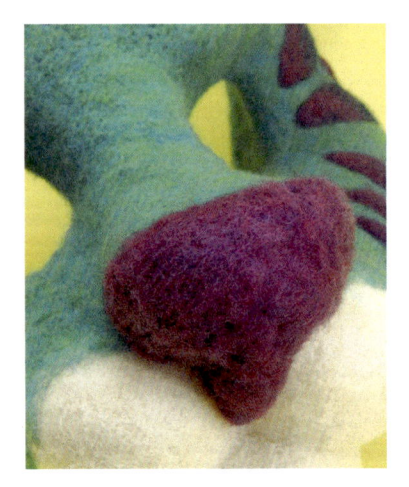

19. Poke along the outer edge of the nose to attach.

20. Shape the nose as you felt with a fine needle.

21. Outline the nose in black wool.

22. Fill in the nostrils and the line of the mouth.

23. Poke a line of white roving in each ear.

24. Trim and mess up the ear hair a bit.

25. Add a bit of color to the tip of each ear.

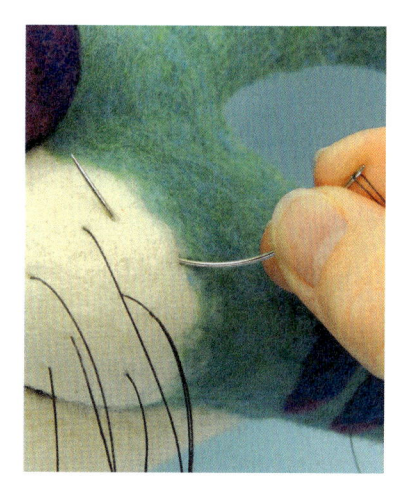

26. Use black heavy weight thread for the whiskers.

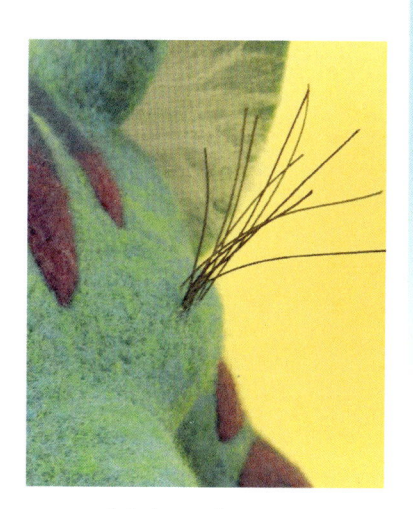

27. Add thread at each brow and trim unevenly.

28. Attach an elastic strap to the mask and it's ready to wear. Refer to the **gray cat** (*page 32*) for more detailed instructions. You can change the shape and proportions of any mask to bring your own ideas to life. Your choice of vivid colors and exaggerated shapes will help create lively characters full of personality.

MASKS

45

MASKS

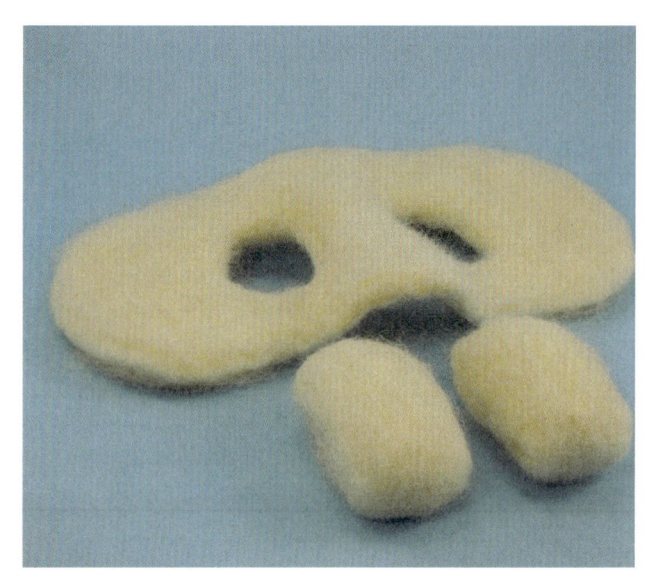

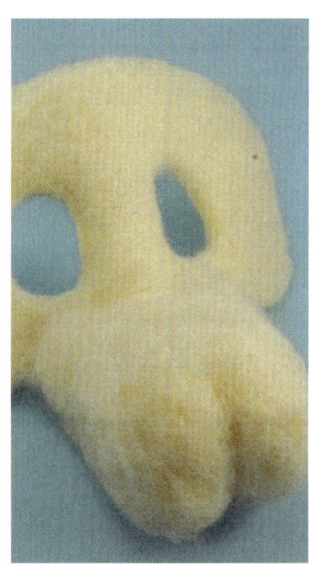

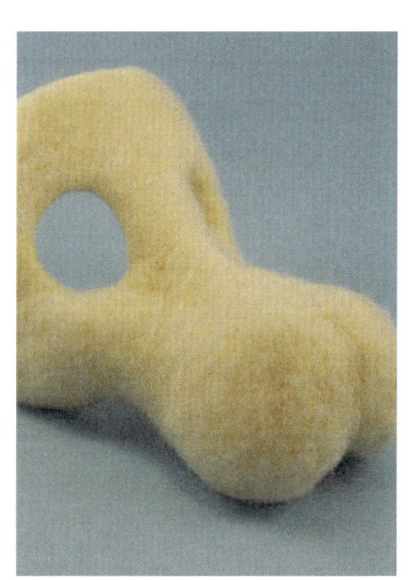

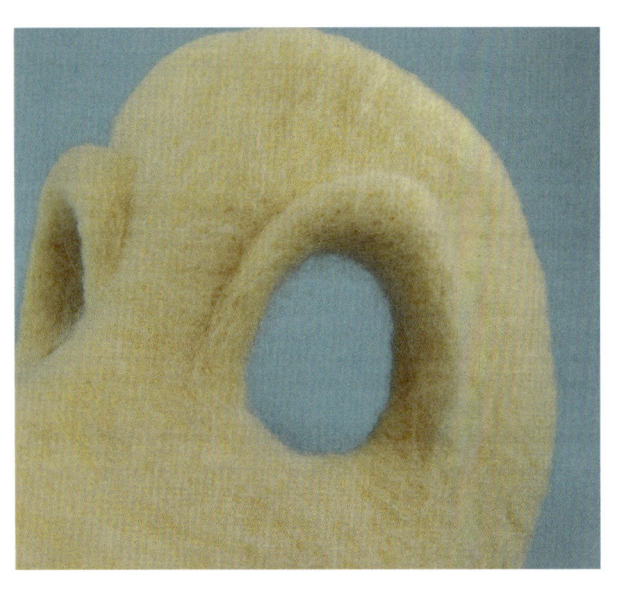

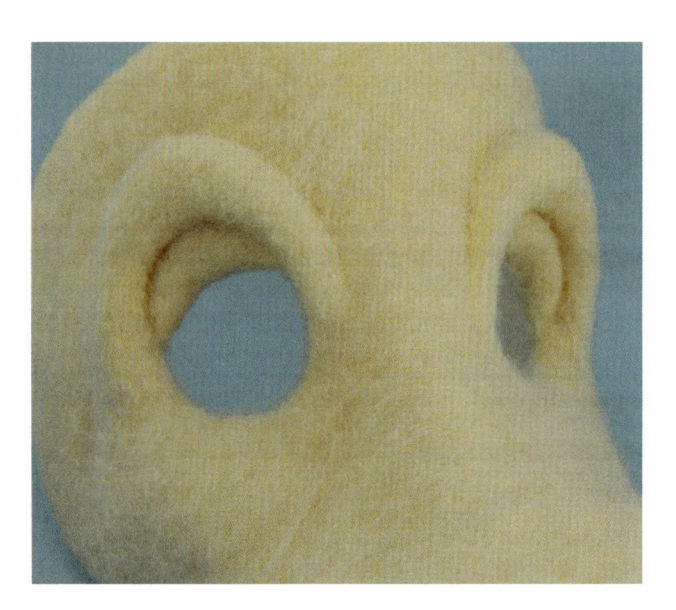

Dog Mask

46

MASKS

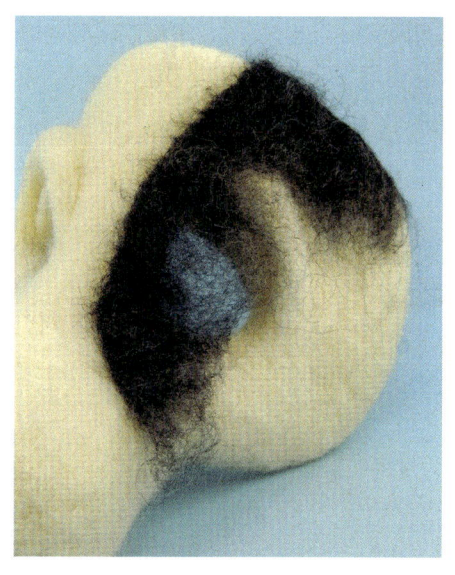

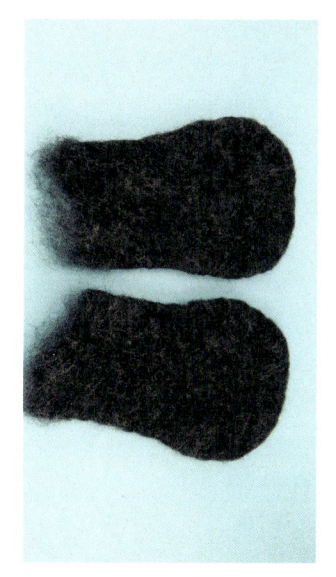

Woof

47

Mouse Muzzle

Instead of making an entire mask, you could make just the muzzle or nose. The size of the base can be 3" wide for a small child or up to 5" wide for an adult. Very young children may be more comfortable wearing a nose rather than a mask.

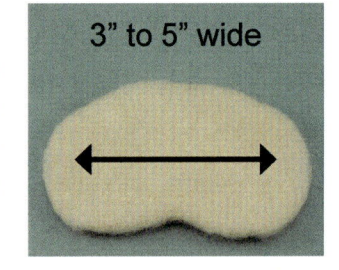

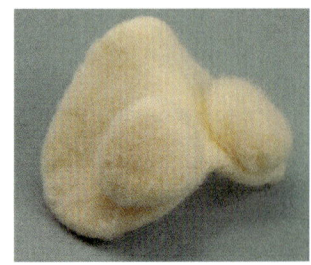

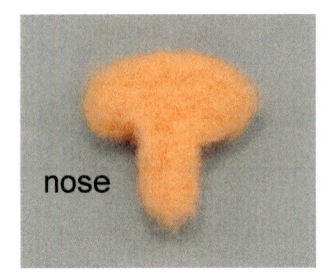

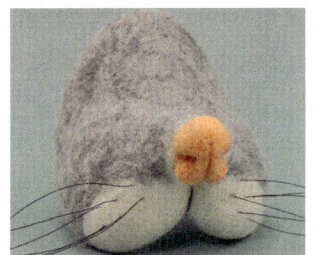

3" to 5" wide

nose

An elastic cord is attached to the muzzle in the same way as the masks. You can also create the ears that go along with the nose. The mouse ears are felted around an elastic headband. If you make large ears that need to stand up, like a rabbit, a hard plastic headband works very well.

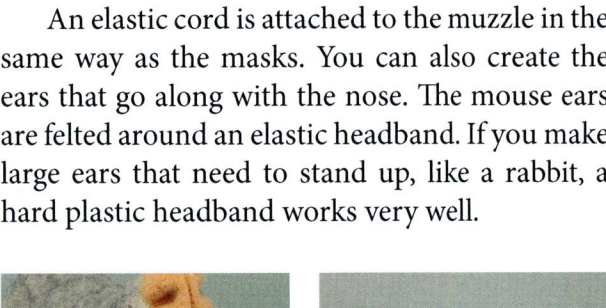

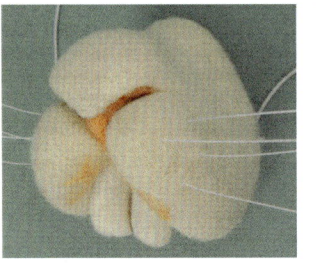

(*photos right*)
plastic headband with rabbit ears, rabbit nose, and dog nose.

48

Owl Mask

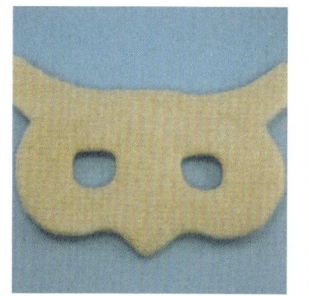

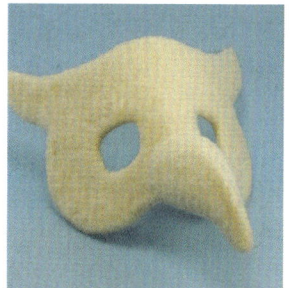

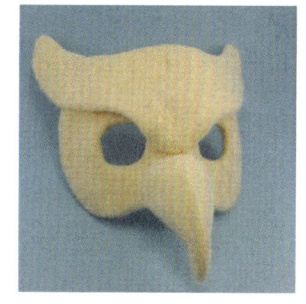

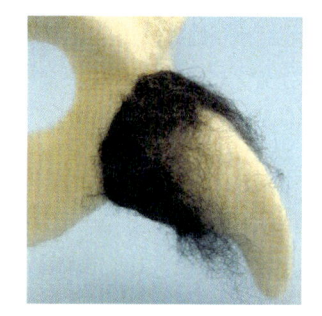

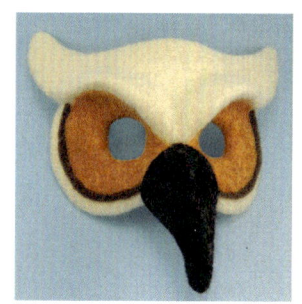

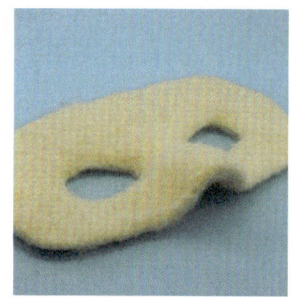

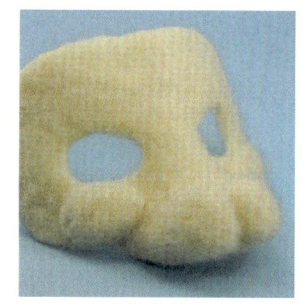

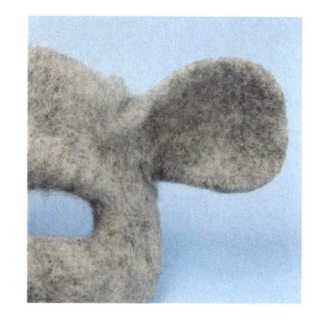

Rat Mask

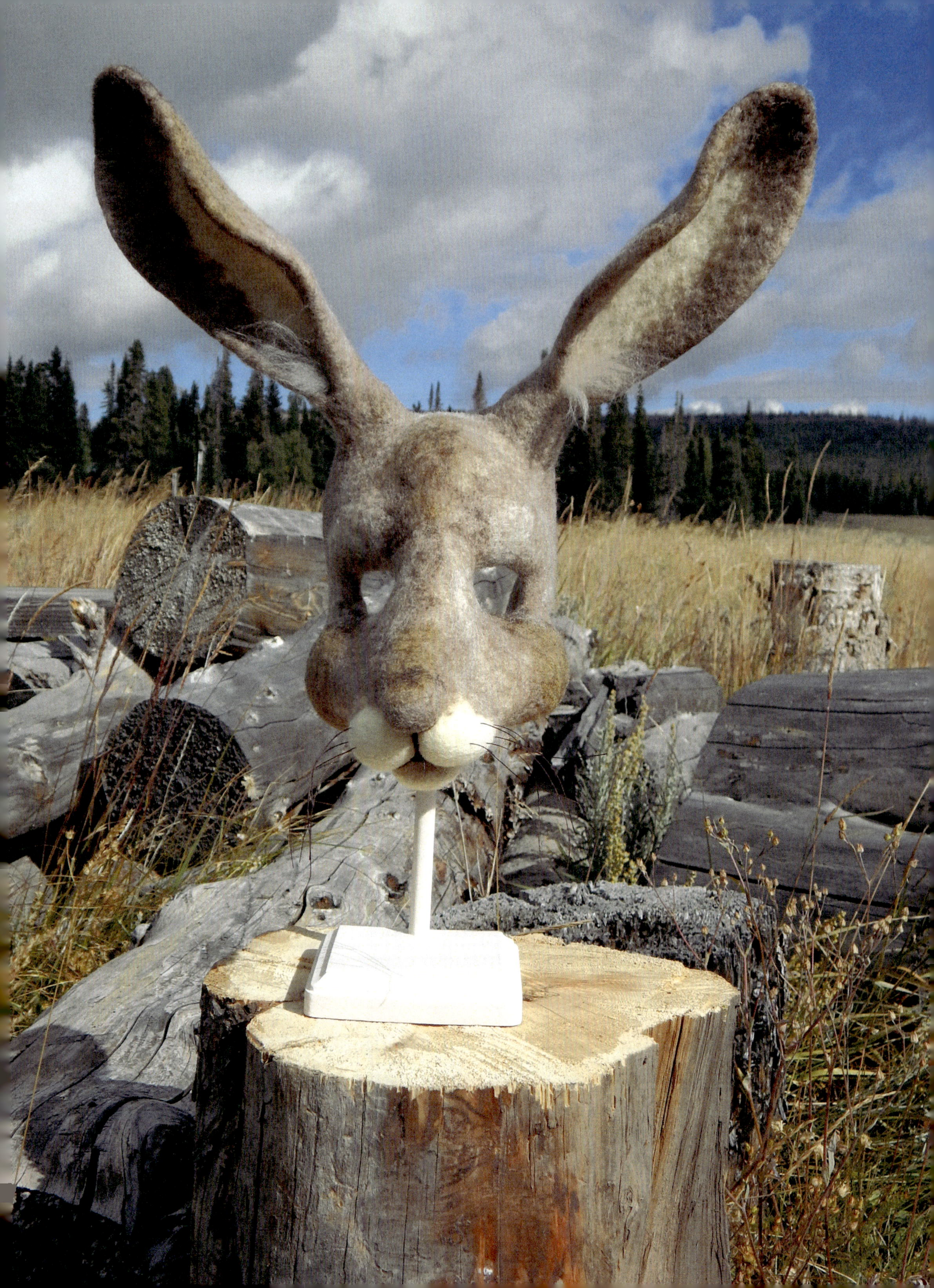

Wild Hare Mask

The wild hare template is a medium size mask. The base for this mask requires a tall forehead. Darts cut into the top of the mask will allow it to curve onto the top of the head of the person wearing the mask. This creates space for the ears to be attached on top of the head.

Even though you may think they look the same, hares and rabbits belong to different species. They actually have more differences than similarities. They differ in the way they are born and their behavior and lifestyle. Hares are usually larger than rabbits and have longer ears and larger feet.

The ears on the wild hare mask are about 3/8" to 1/2" thick. Ears on the other masks in this book are only about 1/4" thick. The hare's ears are very long. They are not meant to flop over like those of a bunny. Making the ears thick and firmly felted will help them to stand up straight on the hare's head.

The majority of the wool used to construct this mask is core wool. White and several shades of brown wool are put over the core wool base in thin layers. Then the thin layers are felted on the mask blending the colors as you felt. Thin layering of the wool allows the colors underneath to show through. This creates subtle areas of dark and light without hard edges where the colors begin and end.

Supplies

core wool for the mask base
white wool for the muzzle and chin and shading the face
light brown wool for the face and ears
medium brown wool to shade the face and ears
dark brown wool to shade the face and outline the mouth, nose

felt fabric for the mask base and the ears
craft or button weight dark brown thread for the whiskers
straight white roving for the hair in the ears
1/4" wide elastic for the strap on the back of the mask

Create A Base For The Mask

Use the **wild hare template** to cut a mask from felt fabric. *Refer to page 18 for information about using **Felt Fabric** or how to create a base without it.* Cut slits in the forehead using the dotted lines on the template as a guide.

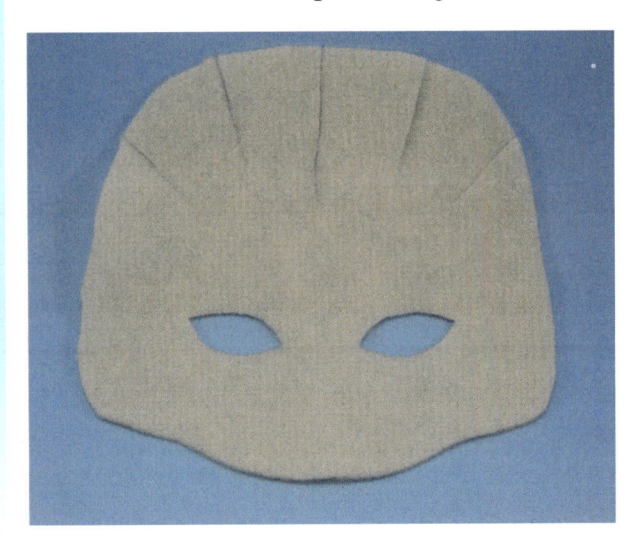

Overlap the cut edges and poke to hold them in place. This will shape the forehead so it will curve over the top of the head. Making a taller forehead creates more room to attach the ears.

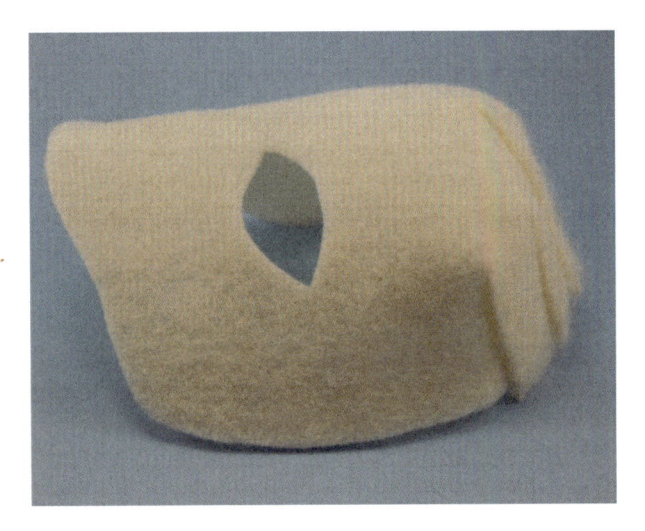

Cover the entire mask on the inside and outside with core wool. A tool that holds several needles will make the felting go quicker. Once both sides of the mask are covered, wrap core wool around the edge of the mask and the edge of the eye openings.

As the wool becomes felted you will notice the mask will begin to stiffen. At this point the mask is very flimsy. Handle it gently. Bend the mask at the center and the nose area will stick out. Hold the mask in this position on your foam work surface and poke on the front and then on the back of the mask. Curve the sides of the mask and poke the area. Keep it in the curved shape as you poke and it will eventually hold the shape on its own.

Shaping The Mask

When I think of a bunny I think of a plump domestic rabbit with a full round face. This mask is a wild hare. If you look at photos you will see the differences. This hare has very long ears and a narrow face. Keep this in mind as you sculpt so you don't give him full round features.

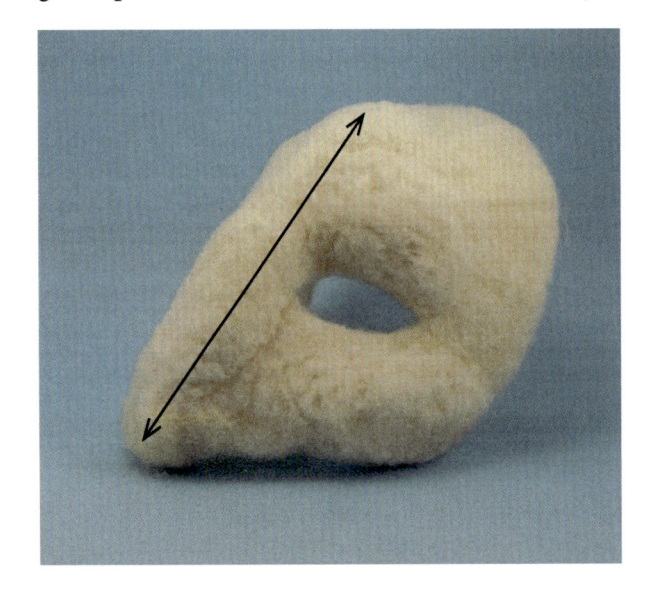

Make a log that is 7" long and about 1 1/2" wide. Fold over one end and poke it in a rounded shape. Leave the other end fluffy. Put the rounded end of the log at the bottom of the mask where the nose is. Let the log hang off the mask base just a bit. The other end of the log goes up the center of the mask, between the eyes and up onto the forehead. Do not let the area between the eyes get so thick that it obstructs your sight when the mask is worn.

Roll two logs that are 4" long to build up the cheek area under the eyes. Poke to attach the logs along the jawline. *Refer to* **Shaping The Sculpture** *on page 28 for more information on building up and filling in your sculpture.*

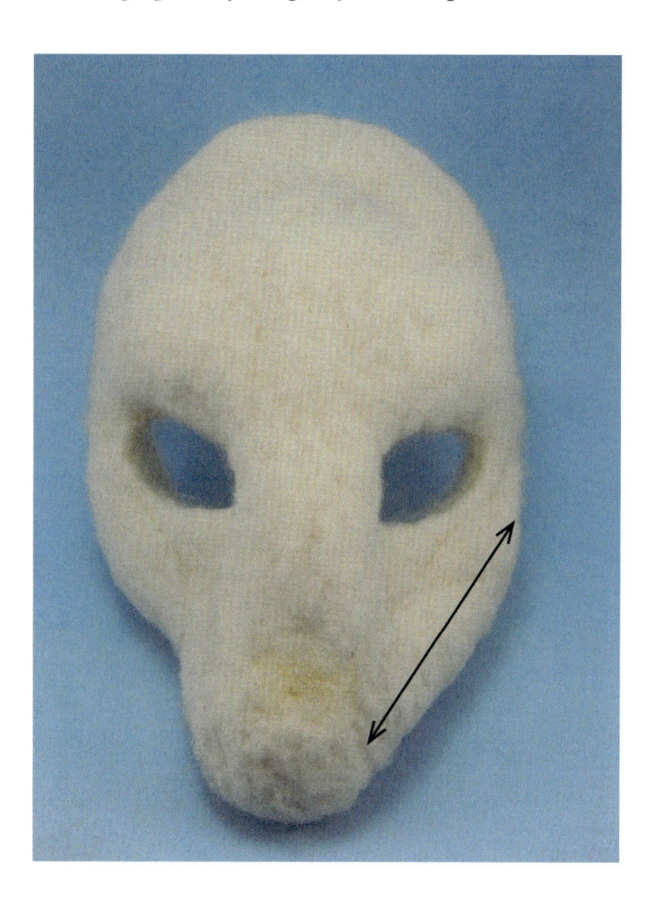

Roll two logs that are 2" long to build up the brow area. Poke to attach the logs above the eye openings. Round the top of the head. Pull off a piece of wool to make a circle that has the same thickness all the way across. While holding it in your hands, fold under all the fluffy edges (*shown on page 28*). Lay the piece in the center of the forehead and poke around the perimeter of the circle. Once the edge is attached you can poke the entire piece. Look at the photo on *page 57* that shows the profile of the hare. Notice the profile line that starts at the forehead and goes to the tip of the nose.

The hare's face shou about it. Create some on the forehead above t the eyes on the sides of t

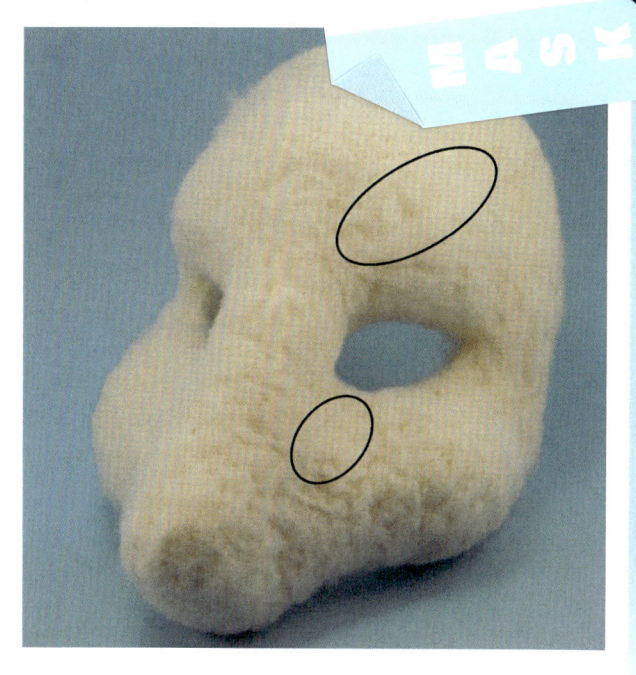

Roll four ball shapes and leave a fluffy tail for the nose, muzzle, and chin. The two balls for the muzzle will be the largest at 1" across. (*refer to page 28*) Lay a piece of wool on your foam work surface and start rolling one edge poking as you roll. Tuck in the sides as you roll. Leave a tail on the ball to blend into the face without leaving a seam. Attach the muzzle first, then the nose, and then the chin. Keep the face lean and do not let the muzzle become too plump

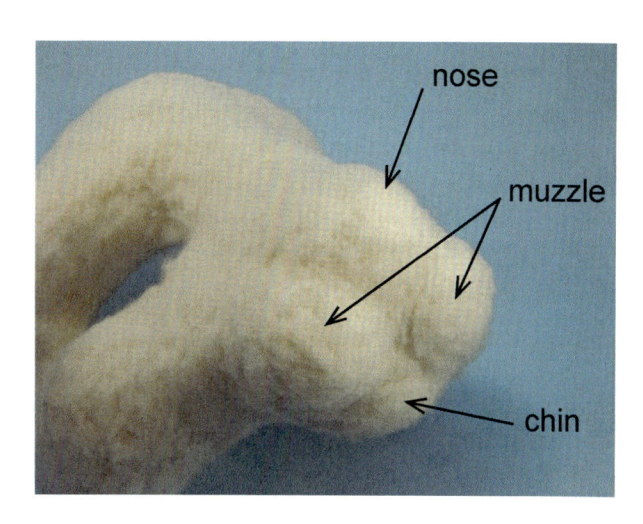

...ext step is to add detail. Before moving ...ur sculpture should possess the shape of ... final form. Remember that adding color will not make any drastic changes to the shape of the sculpture.

Felt the entire mask. Refine the form. Add a thin layer of wool to cover any unwanted seams.

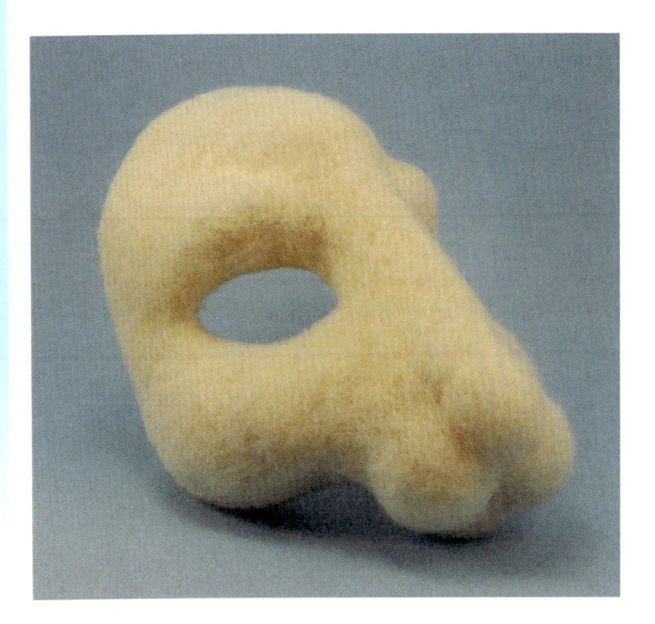

Adding Detail

The wild hare mask is an excellent exercise in learning how to blend colors on the sculpture. (*Refer to* ***Blending Colors as You Felt*** *on page 22*) The hare is brown and does not have any design in his coat. However, look close at a photo of a hare and you will see many shades of brown. If you simply covered the mask with a solid brown wool the final look would be somewhat flat.

For the base color choose a heather brown. Heather colors are typically a mix of multiple shades of the same color. Then choose two more browns that are darker than the base color. One should be a medium brown and the other should be much darker. For the cream color I have used the core wool. There will be no hard lines that separate the brown colors. Subtle blending of all the browns will add dimension to the mask.

Use the **wild hare's ear template** to create the ears. You may use the template to cut two ears from felt fabric or shape your own from wool. (*Refer to page 18 for more information on using templates to help shape the wool.*) While it is certainly acceptable to make the ears without the aid of felt fabric, I do recommend it in this instance. The ears on the hare are quite large and you do not want them to be floppy ears. Start with felt fabric to provide a stable base to build firmly felted ears that will hold their shape. The finished felted thickness is about 3/4".

Make two ears and felt them on the front and back. Leave the bottom edges fluffy for attaching to the head.

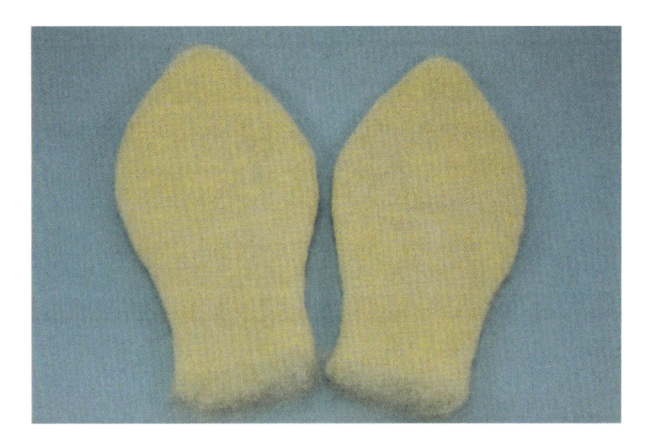

Lay the base color brown on top of the ears so it extends past the edges. This will be the back of the ear. Felt the wool to the ear. Turn the ear over and wrap the wool around the edge to the front of the ear. Leave an irregular edge to outline the center lighter color of the ear front.

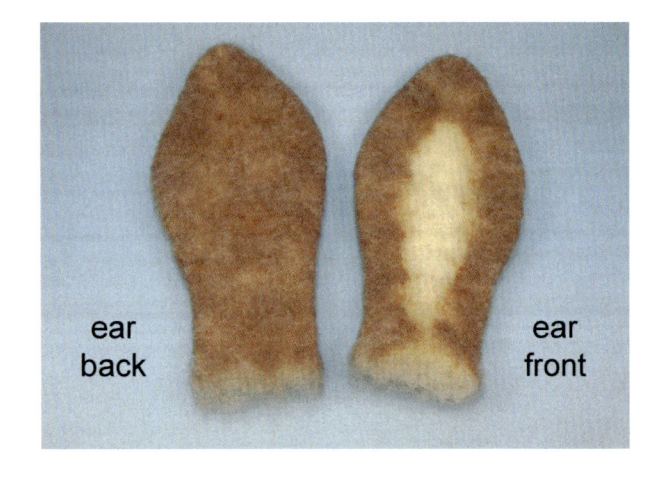

ear back

ear front

Add darker brown to the ears for shading. Do this before the ears are completely felted. Remember that adding fluffy wool to fluffy wool will help them blend together without creating hard lines of color. Hares usually have dark tips on their ears so shade with your darkest color of brown.

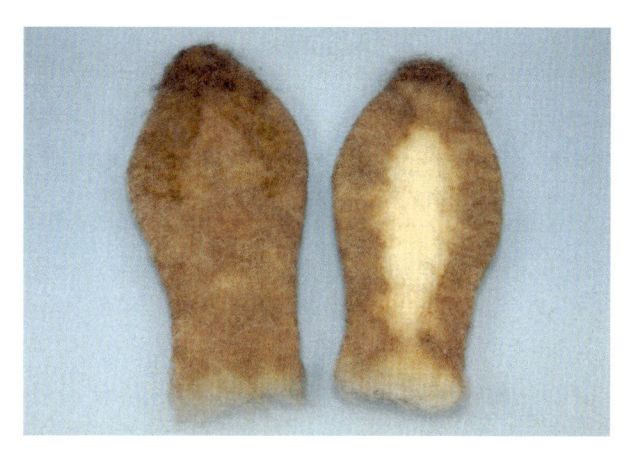

As you are felting and shaping the ears work on them both at the same time. This will help you create a matched set. They do not need to be a mirror image of each other, but they should be the same size and have similar curves. The ears will condense and shrink as they are felted.

Bend the ear. While holding the ear in the bent shape, poke the front and back of the ear around the bend. This will condense the wool along the bend so it will hold the shape permanently. You will poke the ears on the front and back several times to completely felt them.

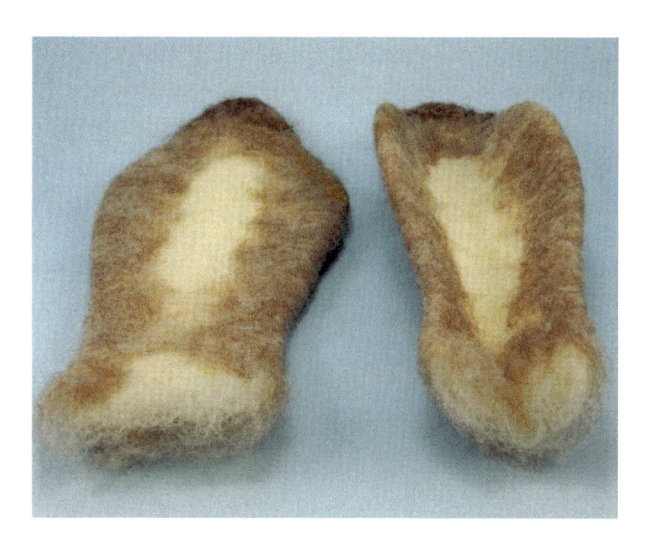

The ears may seem firm while laying on your foam work surface. Hold them up and wiggle them. If they seem floppy they may not be completely felted or they may be too thin. The ears should be a consistent thickness of about 3/8".

Roll the bottom of the ears and connect the edges for about 1". Cover the seam with wool and felt so the seam disappears.

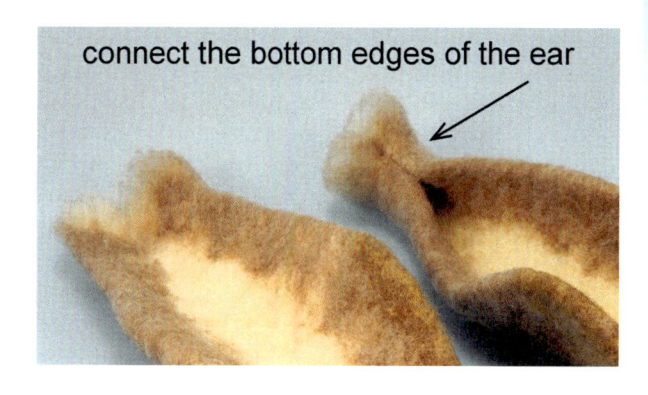

connect the bottom edges of the ear

Spread apart the fluff on the bottom of the ears to prepare them for attaching to the head.

55

Spread the fluff of the ear out on the head. The back of the ear is at the back edge of the mask. Push the ear firmly into the head and poke. Poke slow and deep with a coarse needle (#36 or #38) so you are pushing the ear fibers into the mask. Add more brown wool to secure the attachment if you need to.

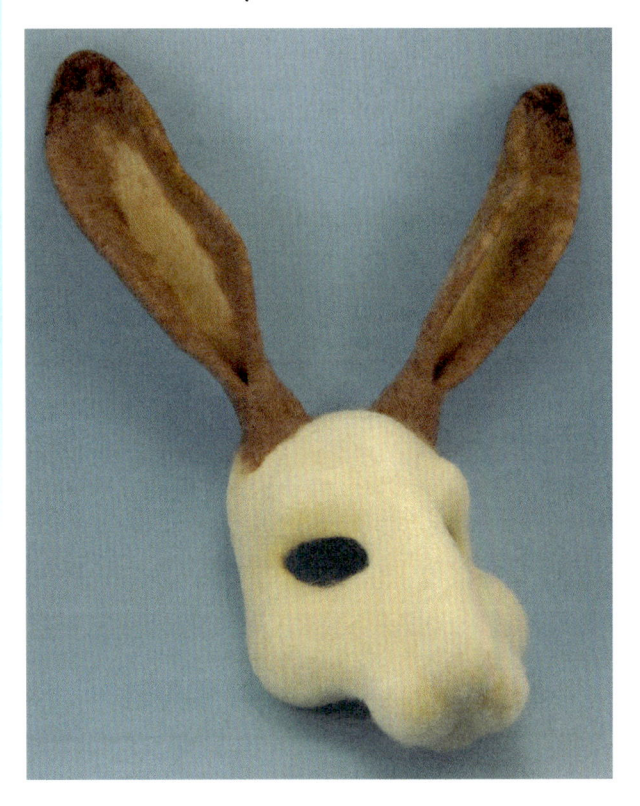

Use the nose template as a guide for the size of the nose. Lay a piece of brown wool on the foam. Poke a curved line as shown on the template. Fold the wool over on the line and felt the fold. Leave the rest of the nose fluffy.

Attach the nose with the folded end toward the bottom. Roll a very thin strip of dark brown between the palms of your hands. (*Refer to Felting Ropes on page 26*) Poke the strip under the nose. Add some dark brown between the lips and between the muzzle.

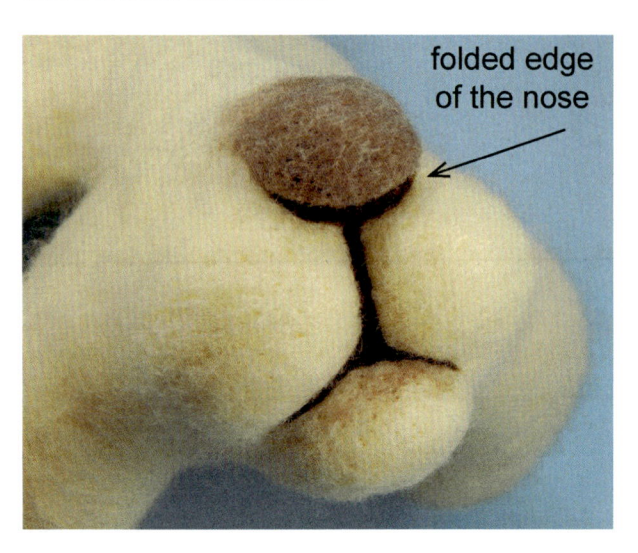

folded edge of the nose

If you have not read **Blending Colors As You Felt** *on page 22* take a moment and read that section before the next step.

Cover the entire mask with the brown base color except for the muzzle under the nose and the chin. The edge of the brown against the off-white muzzle is very thin and wispy so it creates an irregular line. This makes a gradual transition from one color to the next. It has a softer more realistic look than a hard line of color.

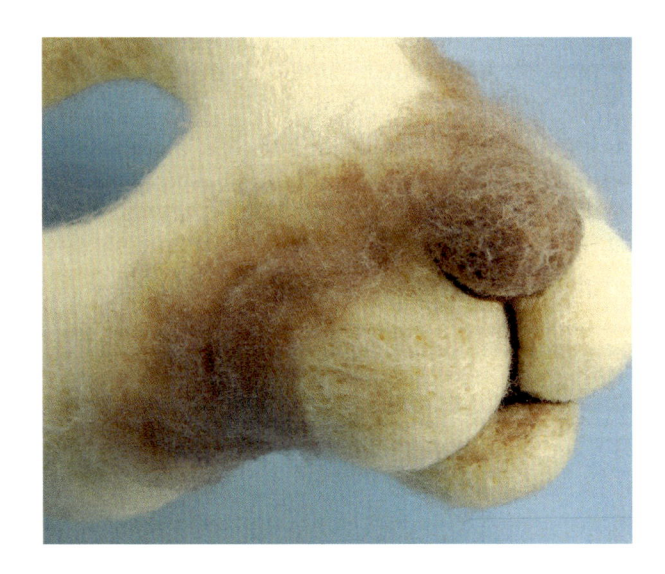

Poke the brown just enough to attach it but not completely felt it. Add small amounts of medium brown, dark brown, and off-white on top of the base color. Add the colors in thin layers so the base color will show through. Shade the nose, under the eyes, the cheeks, brows, and the forehead. The light brown is still fluffy so the other colors will mix with it as you felt. Felt the entire mask.

Put a bit of hair in each ear. Poke some white or off-white roving into his ears. Leave the ends of the roving uneven.

A craft or button weight dark brown thread is used for the hare's whiskers. A 5" or 7" sewing needle will be long enough to reach from one side of the muzzle to the other. Insert the needle on one side of the muzzle and come out in the same area on the opposite side. Put a small dot of white craft glue on the thread and pull the thread until the glue is inside the wool. Once the glue is dry the whiskers will not pull out of the wool. Cut the whiskers about 2 1/2" long. Repeat the process until there are 5 or 6 whiskers on each side of the muzzle.

Notice the hare's The forehead is bui gently slopes dow

On the back of the mask you can see how the ears were attached on the edge of the mask. The inside of the chin is out far enough so it will not touch your mouth as you wear the mask. The mask is more comfortable to wearer if it is not pressed against your nose and mouth. *Refer to* **Attach Elastic Strap To The Mask** *on page 29.*

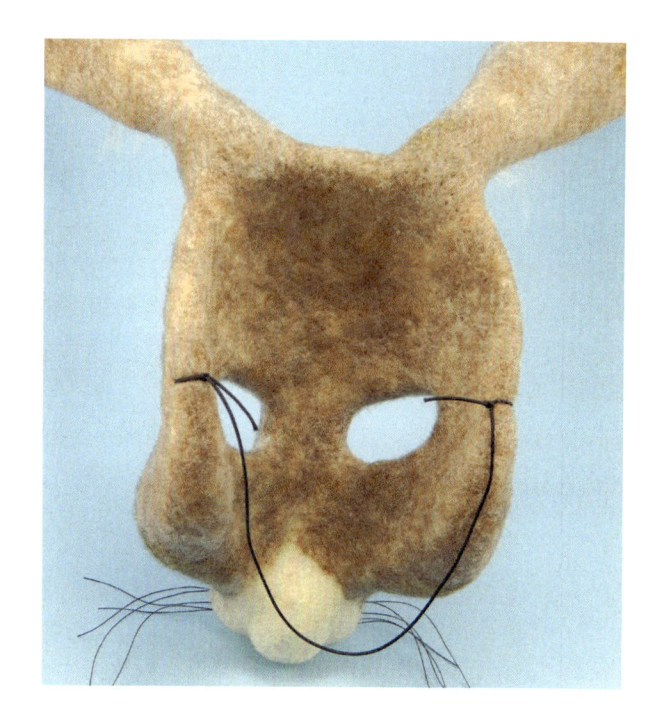

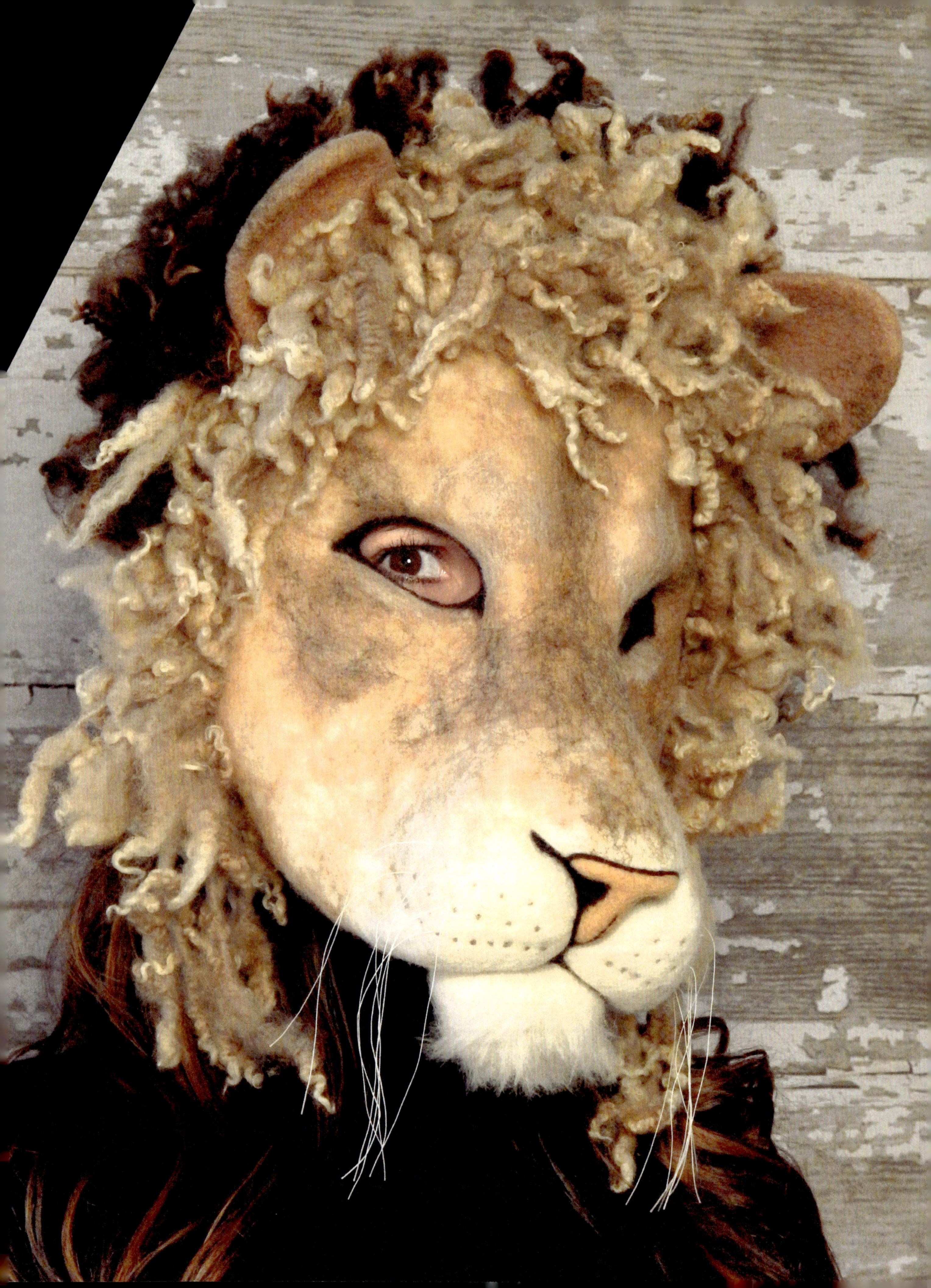

King Of The Jungle
Lion Mask

The lion template is a large size mask. When you look at the template you will notice how large and tall the forehead is. Darts cut into the top of the mask will allow it to curve onto the top of the head of the person wearing the mask. This creates space for the ears and mane to be attached on top of the head.

This mask is large with a subtle yet strong shape. I always look at photos of real animals when I am sculpting them. Get the shape right and the animal will be instantly recognizable. The first thing you may notice about a lion is their wide, flat nose. Masks require eye holes that will allow the person wearing it to be able see easily. Some animals have eyes that are set far apart or on the side of their head. This means that you need to pay special attention to the space between the eyes on the mask. Even though the eyes of the mask need to be closer together than a real lion's eyes, make the nose flat and you will achieve the right look.

While looking at a photo of a real lion there are several areas to notice on the face. The top of the lion's head is wide. There is a distinct indentation in the center of the forehead from the top of the head to the center of the browline. The temple area, on the side of the head behind the eye, is hollow. A hollow area is lower than the area around it. There is also a hollow area on the sides of the nose under the tear duct of the eyes. If you pay attention to these details, the finished mask will be spectacular.

Supplies

core wool for the mask base
white wool for the nose and chin and shading the face
light brown wool for the face and ears
medium brown wool to shade the face and ears
dark brown wool to shade the face and outline the eyes and nose
medium peach wool for the nose

hand spun wool used for the mane (see **Resources** on page 155)
or you may also use:
dark brown curly locks for the mane
light to medium brown curly locks for the mane

felt fabric for the mask base and the ears
craft or button weight white thread for the whiskers
straight white roving for the chin hair
1/4" wide elastic for the strap on the back of the mask

Create A Base For The Mask

Use the **King Of The Jungle template** to cut a mask from felt fabric. *Refer to page 18 for information about using **Felt Fabric** or how to create a base without it.* Cut slits in the forehead using the dotted lines on the template as a guide.

Overlap the cut edges and poke to hold them in place. This will shape the forehead so it will curve over the top of the head. Try the base on your face as you are making it. The curve of the forehead should reach to the middle of the top of your head.

*Overlapping the edges of the mask are the same as shown for the **wild hare** on page 52 and the **ram** on page 72.*

Cover the entire mask on the inside and outside with core wool. A tool that holds several needles will make the felting go quicker. Once both sides of the mask are covered, wrap core wool around the edge of the mask and the edge of the eye openings.

As the wool becomes felted you will notice the mask will begin to stiffen. At this point the mask is very flimsy. Handle it gently. Bend the mask at the center and the nose area will stick out. Hold the mask in this position on your foam work surface and poke on the front and then on the back of the mask. Curve the sides of the mask and poke the area. Keep it in the curved shape as you poke and it will eventually hold the shape on its own.

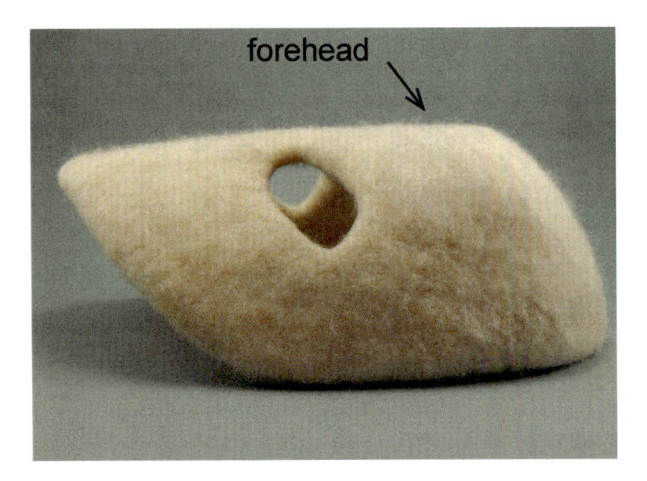

When you put the mask on you should feel it resting on the top of your head.

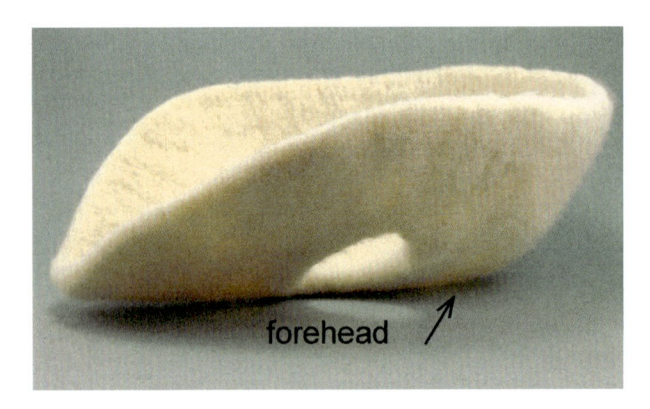

Shaping The Mask

Make two logs that are 5" long and about 1 1/2" wide. Fold over one end and poke it in a rounded shape. Leave the other end fluffy.

Lay the logs side by side and poke to attach them together. From the rounded end of the logs they are attached for about 3". Separate the fluffy ends.

The fluffy ends will be attached to the mask. These attached logs will become the lion's snout. Do not be concerned with the size. They are just meant to be the base for the snout. Once they are attached to the mask they will be shaped as you add more wool to them.

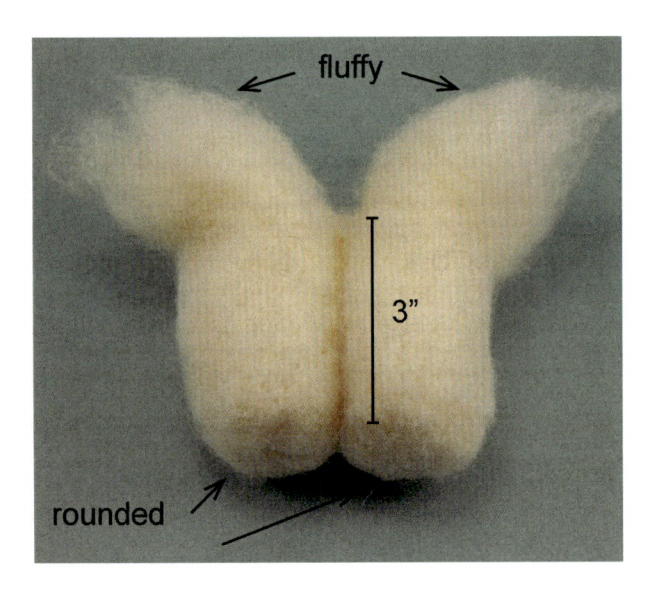

Make a third log for the nose that is about 7" long. Poke three flat sides to create a triangle shape for the nose. The nose is 2 1/2" across the top and 1 1/2" tall at the center. Attach the nose to the snout.

Attach the snout to the mask with a coarse needle. Poke from the front and the back of the mask until it is secure. The snout is at the bottom edge of the mask and the fluffy ends are under the eyes. The fluffy end of the nose log goes up the center of the mask between the eyes.

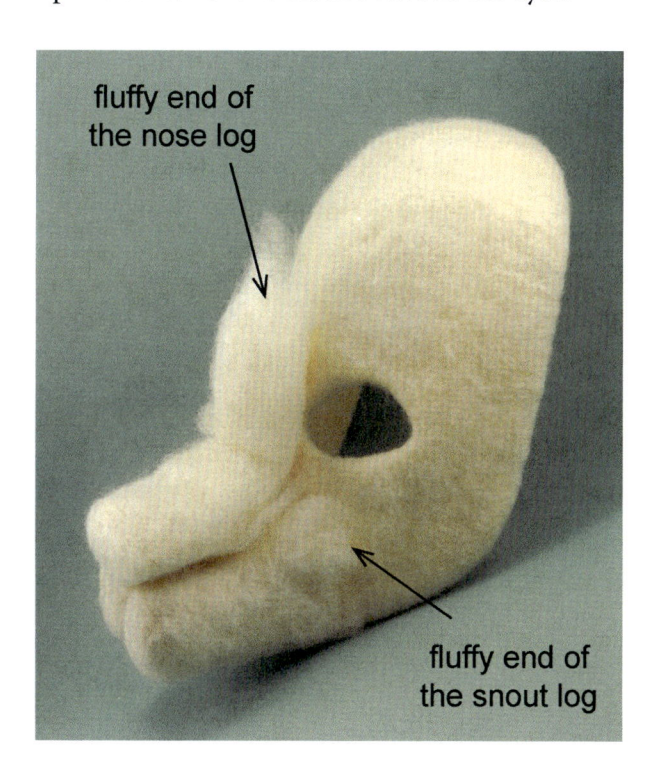

Right now everything seems a bit awkward. Things will start to come together as you begin to shape the features.

The lips on the snout need to be longer on the sides. Make a thin log to add around the bottom edge of the snout. Wrap wool from the outside of the mask, over the log, and onto the inside of the mask to attach the log securely.

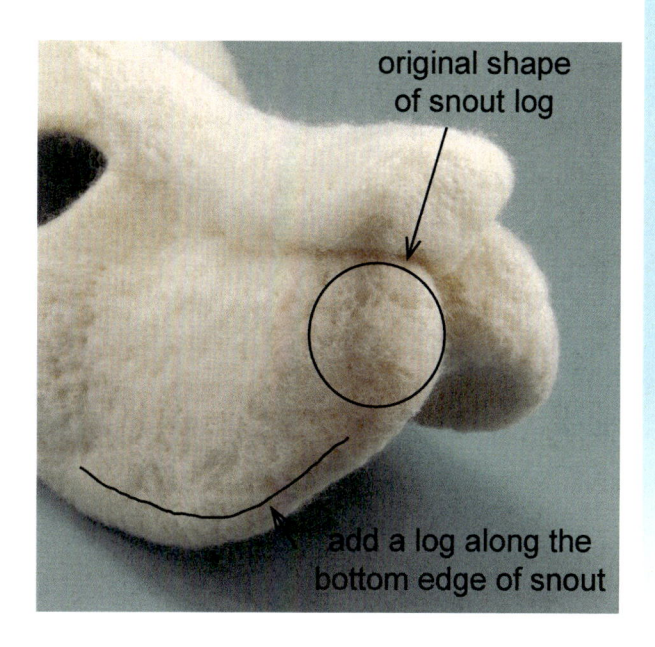

Roll a large ball of wool for the chin. *Refer to Shaping The Sculpture on page 28.* Stop rolling just before the end and leave a fluffy tail. The ball should be 2 1/2" across and 2" tall. The ball needs to fit between the lips under the snout. Add more wool if the ball is not large enough.

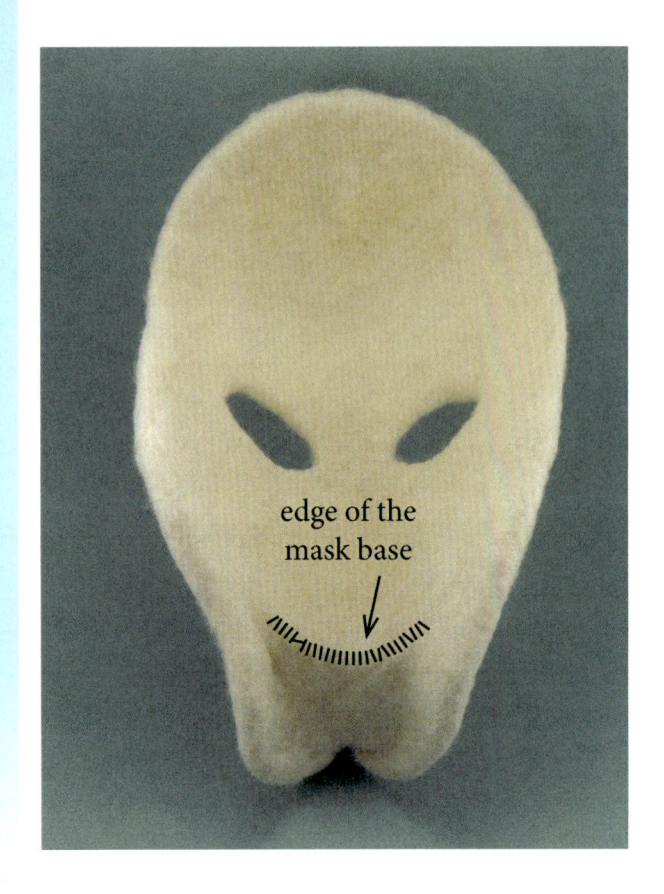

Poke to attach the chin between the lips under the snout. The photo (*top left*) shows the inside of the mask. You can see the bottom edge of the mask base. The chin is attached between the lips and should not extend past the edge of the mask base. This leaves a space between the mask and *your mouth* when you are wearing the mask. The fluffy tail that was left on the chin is wrapped over the edge of the mask base (*photo bottom left*). Poke through the lips and snout into the chin to secure it to the mask.

Add wool to build up and shape the snout. In the photo (*below*) wool has been added on the right side.

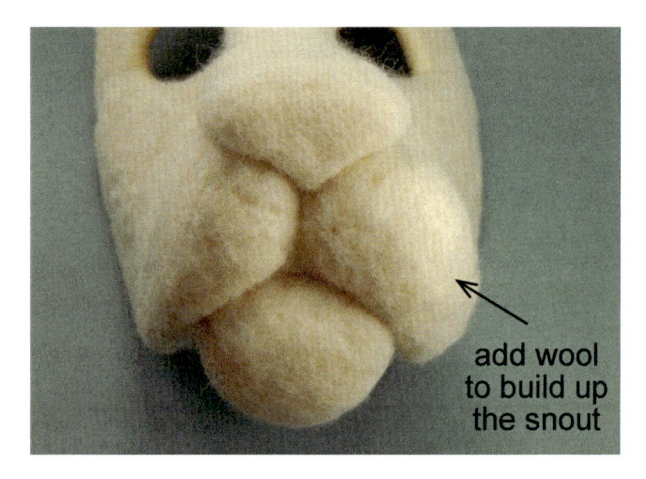

Add wool to the side of the nose to cover the line of the nose log and create a smooth transition from the side of the nose to the snout.

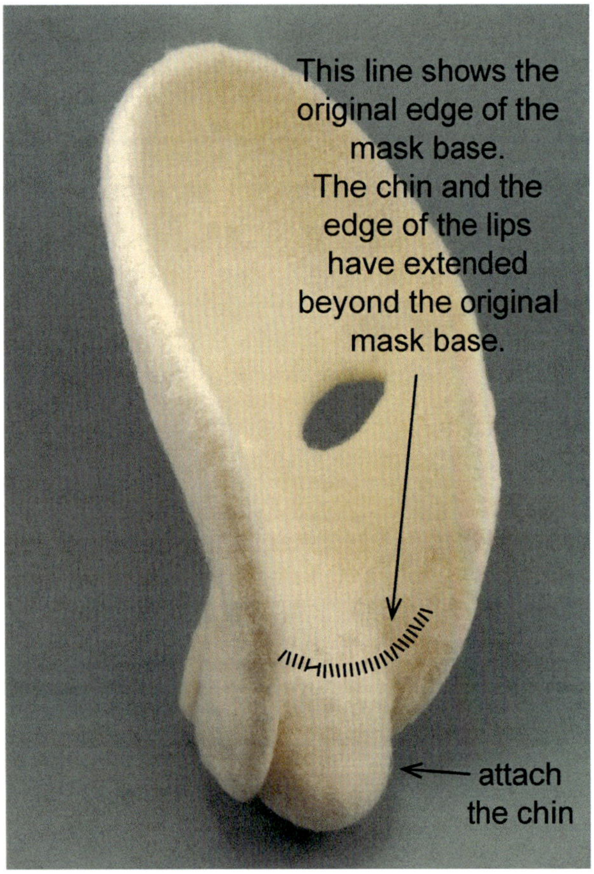

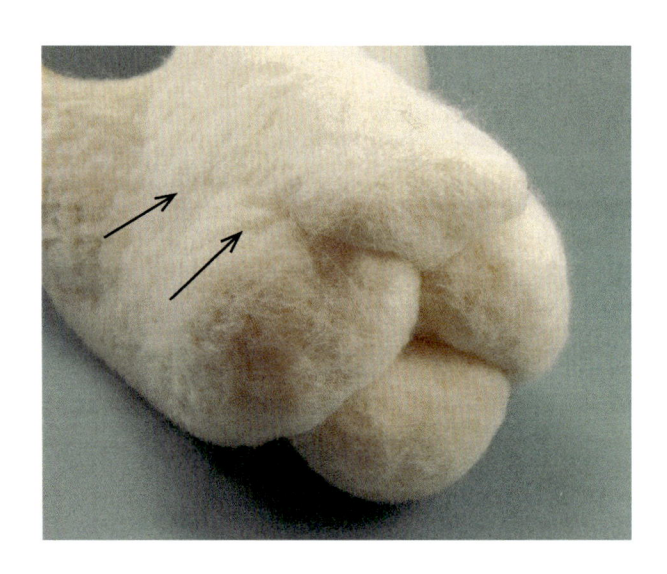

Add fullness under each eye. Pull off two pieces of wool that are the same size. Fold the fluffy edges under. *Refer to **Shaping The Sculpture** on page 28.* Place the wool under the eye and poke around the perimeter of the wool in a triangle shape.

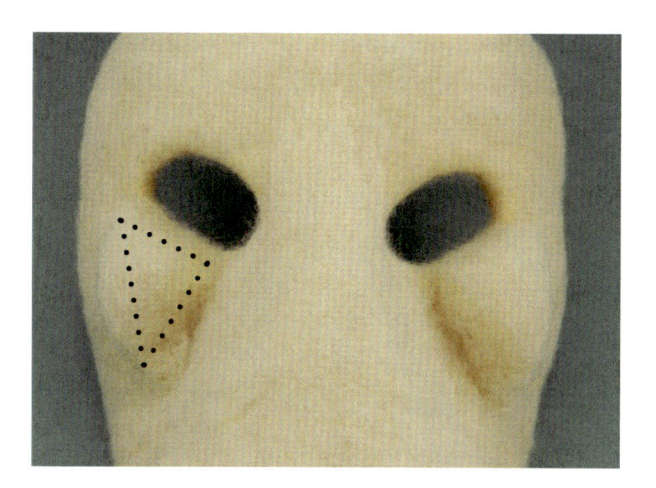

When you poke around the perimeter of the wool it will keep the bulk of the wool inside the area you are building up. Poke to felt the wool under each eye. You may find that once the wool is felted it has become too flat. You may not have added enough wool. If this is the case, simply repeat the process and add more wool on top of the area. Work on both sides at the same time so that you can felt identical shapes. When you are happy with the shape, add wool around the outer edges to hide the seam lines.

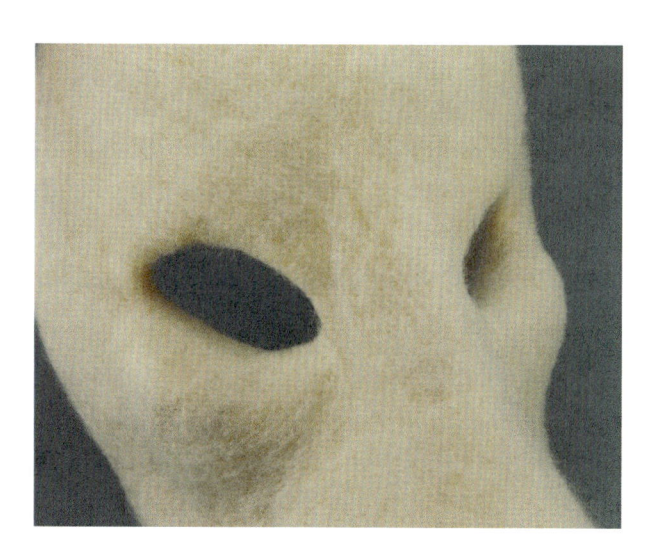

Add fullness to the forehead leaving an indentation in the center of the forehead. Add fullness to each side of the head. Lions have a broad head. Work on both sides of the head at the same time to keep them the same size.

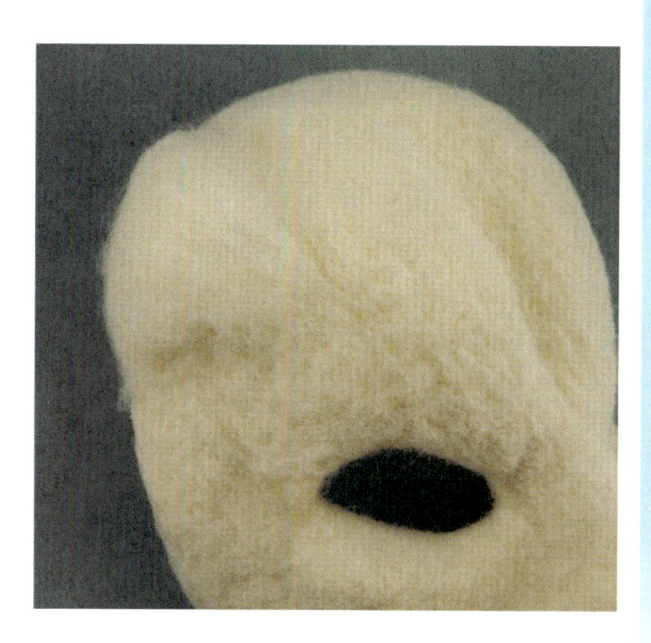

Make a log and attach it over the eyes to build up the brow area. Bring the end of the log down to the nose to keep it wide between the eyes.

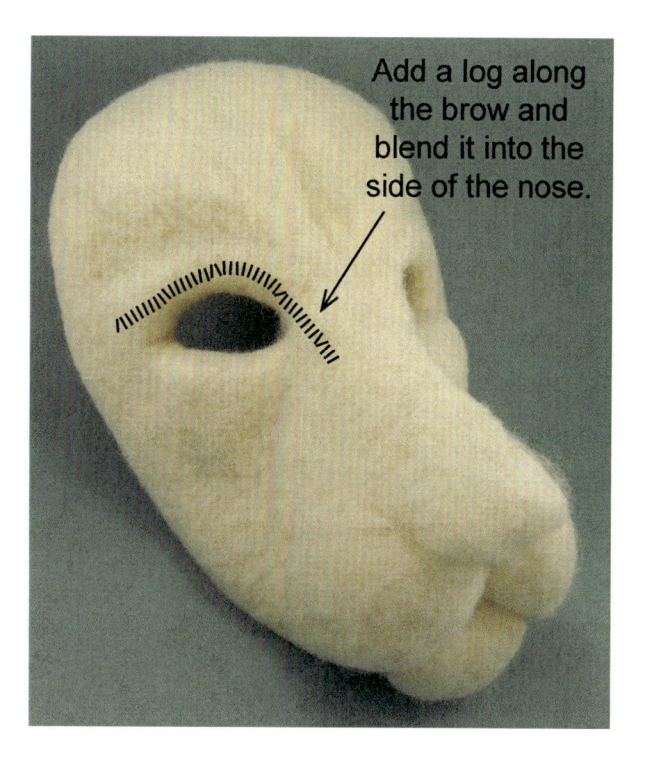

Add a log along the brow and blend it into the side of the nose.

63

Use the end of a sharpened dowel to make the nostril holes. The dowel will slide easily between the nose and the snout. Twist the dowel to create the holes. Poke inside the nostril holes so they become firm.

Poke across the top of the nose to flatten it. The next step will be covering the mask with color. Before moving on make any adjustments to the shape of the mask. You can still add wool if needed. The mask should also be firm at this point. Felt any areas that are not firm.

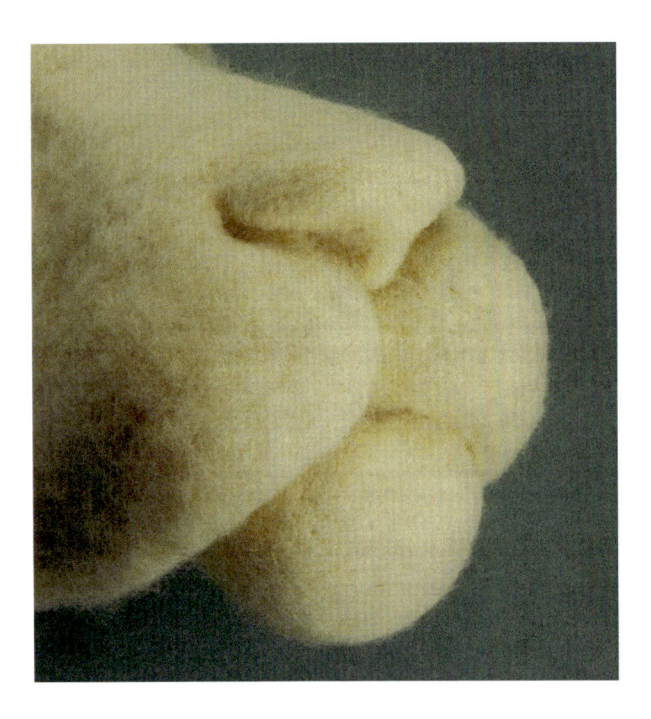

Use the **lion's ear template** to create the ears. You may use the template to cut two ears from felt fabric or shape your own from wool. *(Refer to page 18 for more information on using templates to help shape the wool.)* Make two ears and felt them on the front and back. Leave the bottom edge fluffy for attaching to the head.

Add a bit of dark brown wool to shade the ears.

Open the fluff at the bottom of the ears and poke to attach them to the head. Do not attach them to the edge of the mask. Leave room to add some of the lion's mane behind the ears.

If you have not read **Blending Colors As You Felt** on page 22, take a moment and read that section before the next step.

Cover the muzzle, chin, and top of the nose with white. Cover the sides of the face and half of the nose with a light brown. The edge of the brown against the white muzzle is very thin and wispy so it creates an irregular line. This makes a gradual transition from one color to the next. It has a softer more realistic look than a hard line of color.

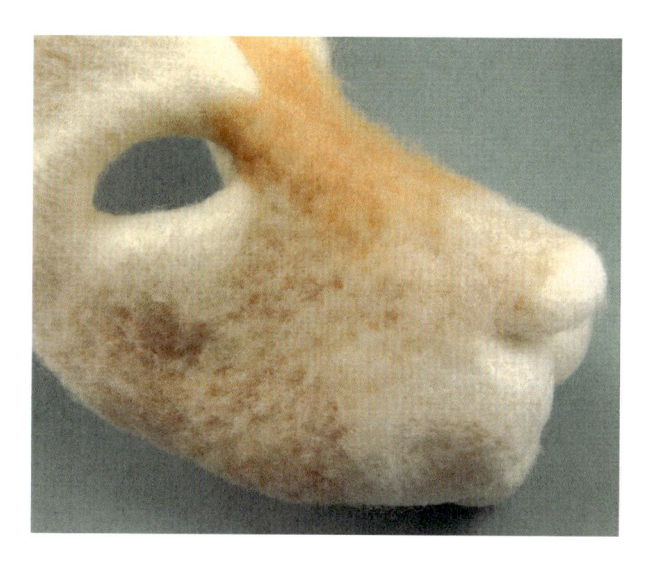

Cover the rest of the mask with a medium brown. Poke the brown just enough to attach it but not completely felt it.

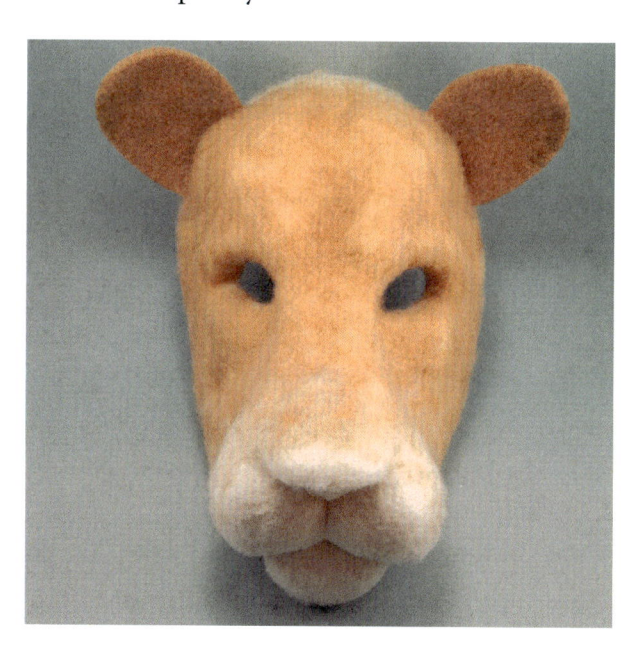

Add small amounts of medium brown, dark brown, and off-white on top of the base color. Add the colors in thin layers so the base color will show through. Shade the nose all the way up to the top of the head. Shade around the eyes. The light brown is still fluffy so the other colors will mix with it as you felt. Felt the entire mask.

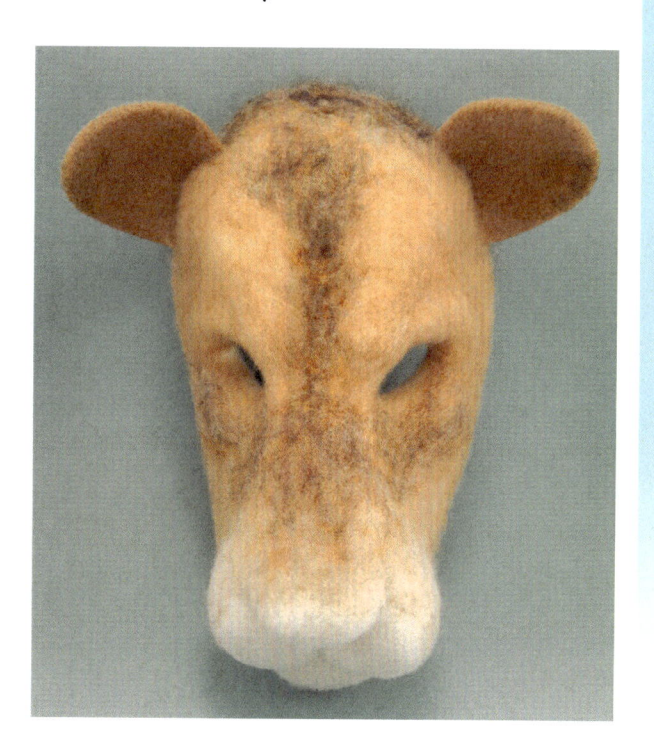

Wrap dark brown wool around a stick or dowel to make a rope for adding color to the eye openings. You may choose to use black for the eyes. The color you use for the eyes will be the same color you use to outline the nose later. *Refer to page 27 for more information on using dowels to make ropes.* Using the dowel method will allow you to control the thickness of the rope. It will also give you a more defined edge. It is more difficult to produce a rope with consistent thickness when you are rolling it in your hands.

Poke the rope around the eye opening. Simply pull off the excess rope when you get to the end. Add a tear duct shape at the inside corner of the eye with a small bit of wool. Then add a point to the outside corner of the eye. Completely felt the dark brown wool neatly around each eye.

Add some white wool around the eyes.

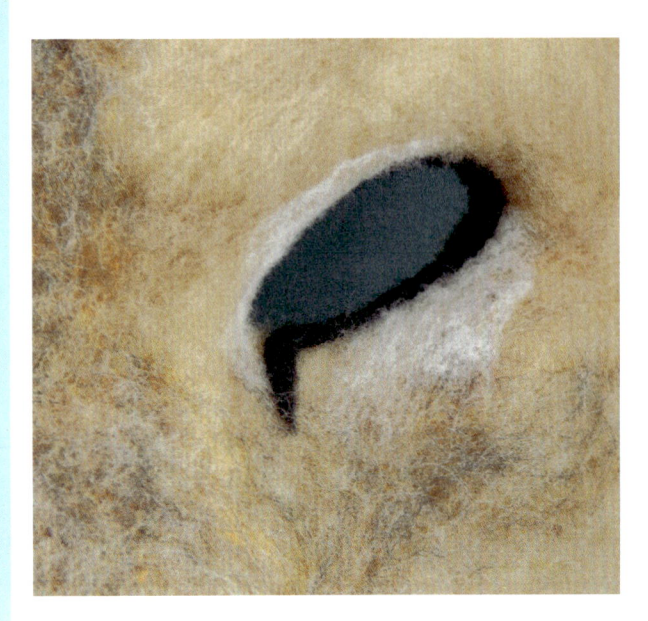

Tip: The ears look a bit plain, however, the lion's mane will cover all of the ear except the top edge. Make sure the color of the mane is not a close match to the color of the ears, or they will not be noticeable sticking out of the mane.

Completely felt the entire mask.

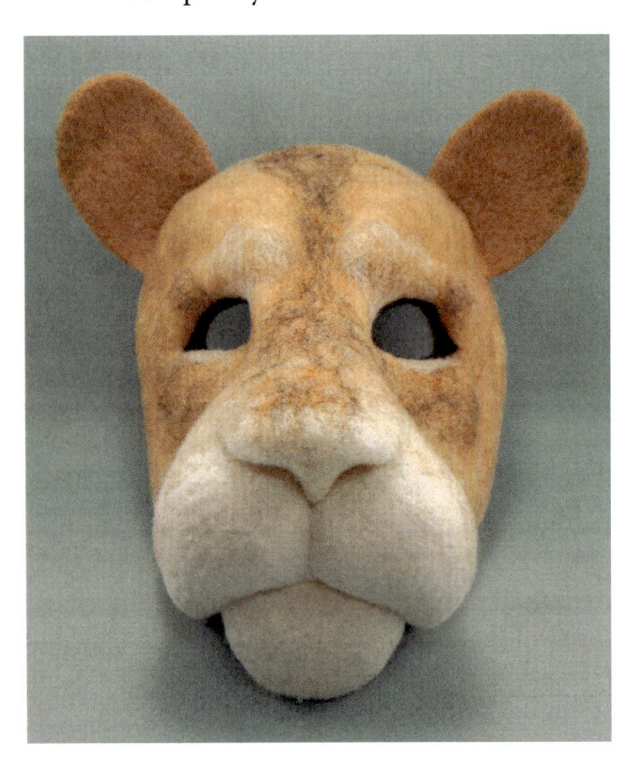

Felting The Nose

Use the **lion's nose template** to shape the nose. *Refer to the **cat's nose** on page 36 for additional photos.* Lay a piece of peach colored wool on the foam work surface that is larger than the nose template. Place the template on top of the wool. Stick a few straight pins through the template and into the foam to hold the template in position. Use a slow and controlled poke to outline the nose template on the wool.

Remove the template. Fold over the fluffy edge along the outline and poke. Pull the nose off the foam carefully so the shape is not distorted. Lay the nose on the mask.

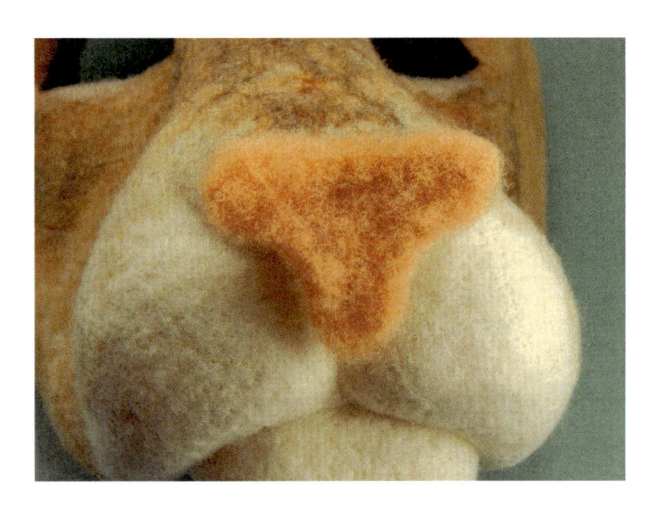

Poke around the perimeter of the nose to secure it in place. The nose shape on the mask is wider than the peach colored nose you are attaching.

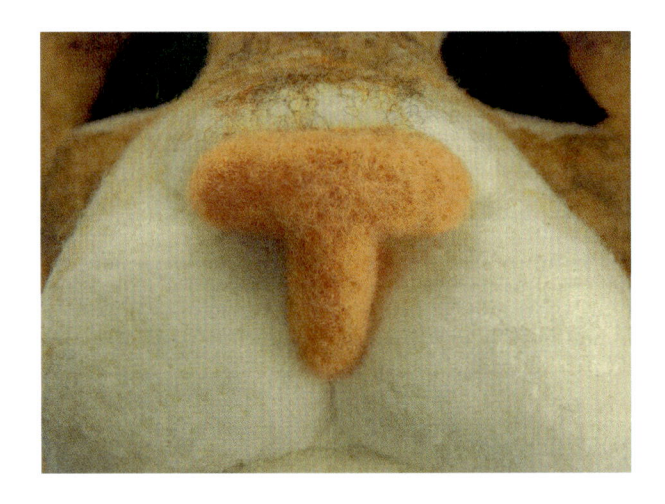

The peach colored part of the nose does not extend onto the top flat part of the nose. When you look at a photo of a real lion you will notice that the nose sticks out like a ledge. You can see into the dark nostril holes. Felt the peach wool.

Roll a strip of brown wool between the palms of your hands. This rope is thicker than the one used to outline the top of the nose. Outline the nostril with the brown rope. Tuck the brown under the ledge at the corner of the nose.

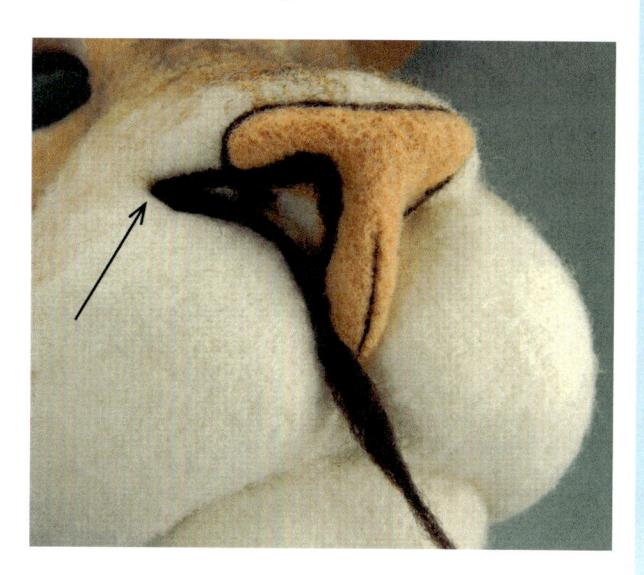

The nose is outlined with the same color wool that was used to outline the eyes. The sample in the photo uses a very dark brown wool. Roll a very thin strip of wool between the palms of your hands. *Refer to **Felting Ropes** on page 26.* Poke the brown strip around the outline across the top of the peach nose. Start at the bottom of the nose and poke a straight line halfway up the nose. Fill the line with a small amount of brown wool.

Bring the brown wool around the bottom of the nose and between the separation of the lips. If you run out of brown just roll another strip and overlap it on top of the other piece. As you are poking between the lips, the brown may get tucked in deep and not be visible enough. If this happens, add another strip of brown on top of it. Fill in the nostrils completely with the brown wool and felt. If the white starts to show through the brown as you felt, add more brown.

While looking at lion photos you will notice that they have lines of dots along the muzzle where their whiskers are. Pull off a very small bit of dark brown wool. Roll the wool in your fingers to make a tiny ball. Poke the ball into the muzzle. Make several rows of tiny dots.

Adding The Mane

Some lions have a light brown mane while others have a dark brown underneath the light brown. I chose to use the dark and the light brown together. The mane is made from curly locks wool. These are natural curls just as they were sheared off the sheep. I chose the curly locks for two reasons. First, I like the way it looks and the variation of color looks natural. Second, you can handle it without messing up the curls. This is great for a mask that will certainly be handled. Simply omit the mane to make a female lioness.

The end of the locks where they were cut from the sheep are blunt and thick. The other end is the natural end of the curl so it has a thin, tapered end. Poke to attach the blunt cut end of the locks to the mask. As you attach them close together they will stand up on the mask. Attach a row of dark wool locks along the back edge of the mask. Then attach lighter brown wool locks in front of the dark locks.

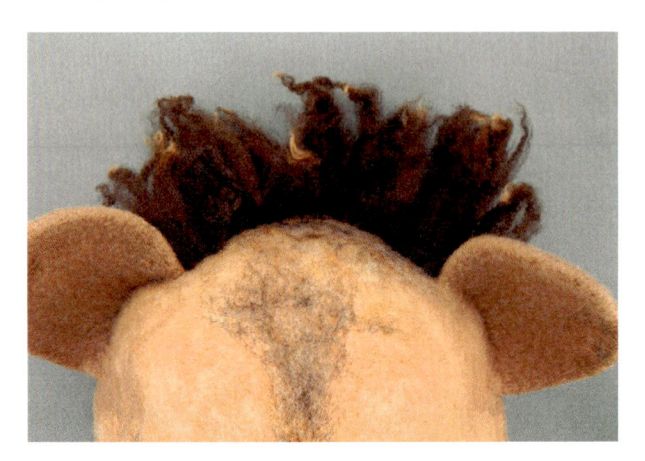

I found curly locks that were spun into a very loose yarn. The end of the locks are hanging freely from the hand spun yarn. I attached the yarn to the mask in loops. The loops are not visible on the finished mask because of the locks that are hanging off the yarn. I used a 2 yard length of yarn (about 2 oz.) to create the light brown mane on the lion. *Refer to the* **Resources** *(page 155) to find these novelty hand spun yarns.*

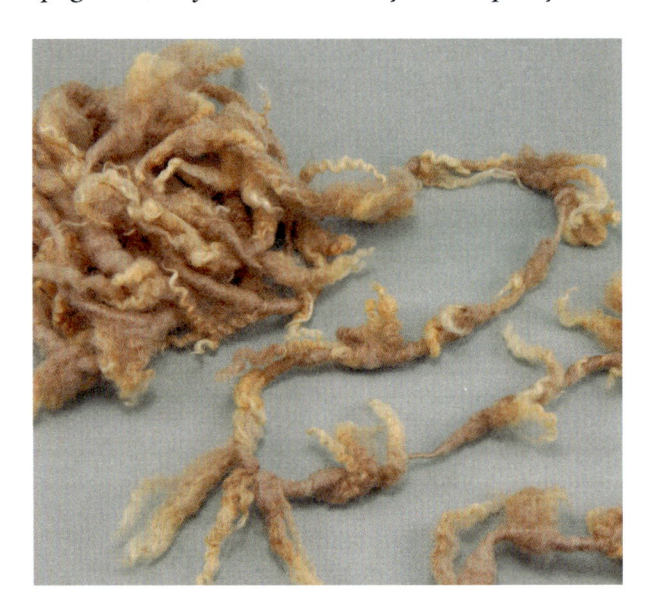

Attach An Elastic Strap To The Back Of The Mask

In the **Techniques** on *page 29* it explains how to attach elastic cord to the back of the mask. The wool masks are unbelievably light weight so the cord works well. However, this lion mask is quite large and calls for a thicker strap. 1/4" wide elastic is used for the strap on this lion mask.

To help locate the area for attaching the elastic, try the mask on. The elastic should be above your ears. The elastic is too large to pull through the wool without creating a hole first. Use a sharpened dowel to make a hole in the edge of the mask. Twist the dowel while pushing it into the wool.

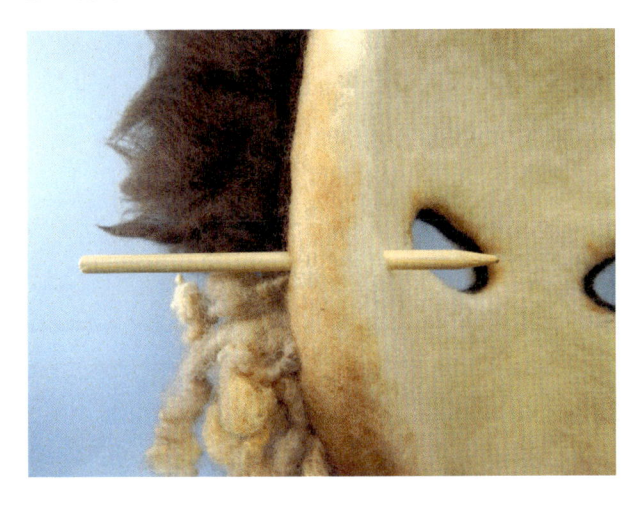

A doll needle or upholstery needle will have an eye large enough for the elastic. Insert the needle into the prepared hole and pull the elastic through the mask edge.

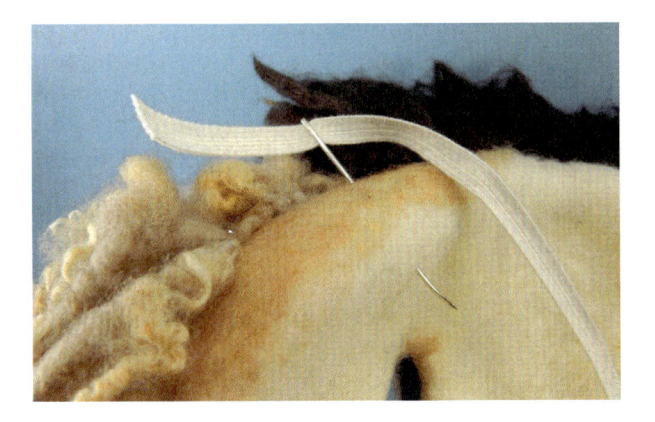

Tie the elastic in a knot. Put the mask on and stretch the elastic around the back of your head to the other side of the mask. Add 1 1/2" for tying the knot and cut the elastic.

For a neat appearance you can sew the cut end of the elastic to secure it. I used an ordinary sewing needle and white thread to whip stitch the edge of the elastic.

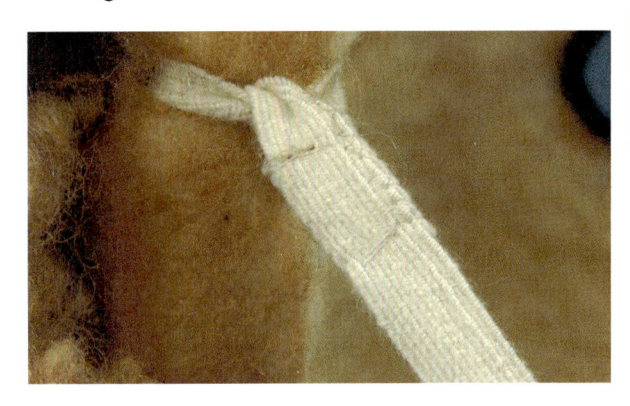

A craft or button weight off-white thread is used for the lion's whiskers. On smaller masks I use a 5" or 7" sewing needle because it is long enough to reach from one side of the muzzle to the other. The lion's muzzle was too wide so I used a curved sewing needle. (*See step 26 on page 45*) Insert the needle next to one of the dots on the muzzle and come out next to another dot. Put a small dot of white craft glue on the thread and pull the thread until the glue is inside the wool. Once the glue is dry the whiskers will not pull out of the wool. Cut the whiskers about 4" long. Repeat the process until there are 9 or 10 whiskers on each side of the muzzle.

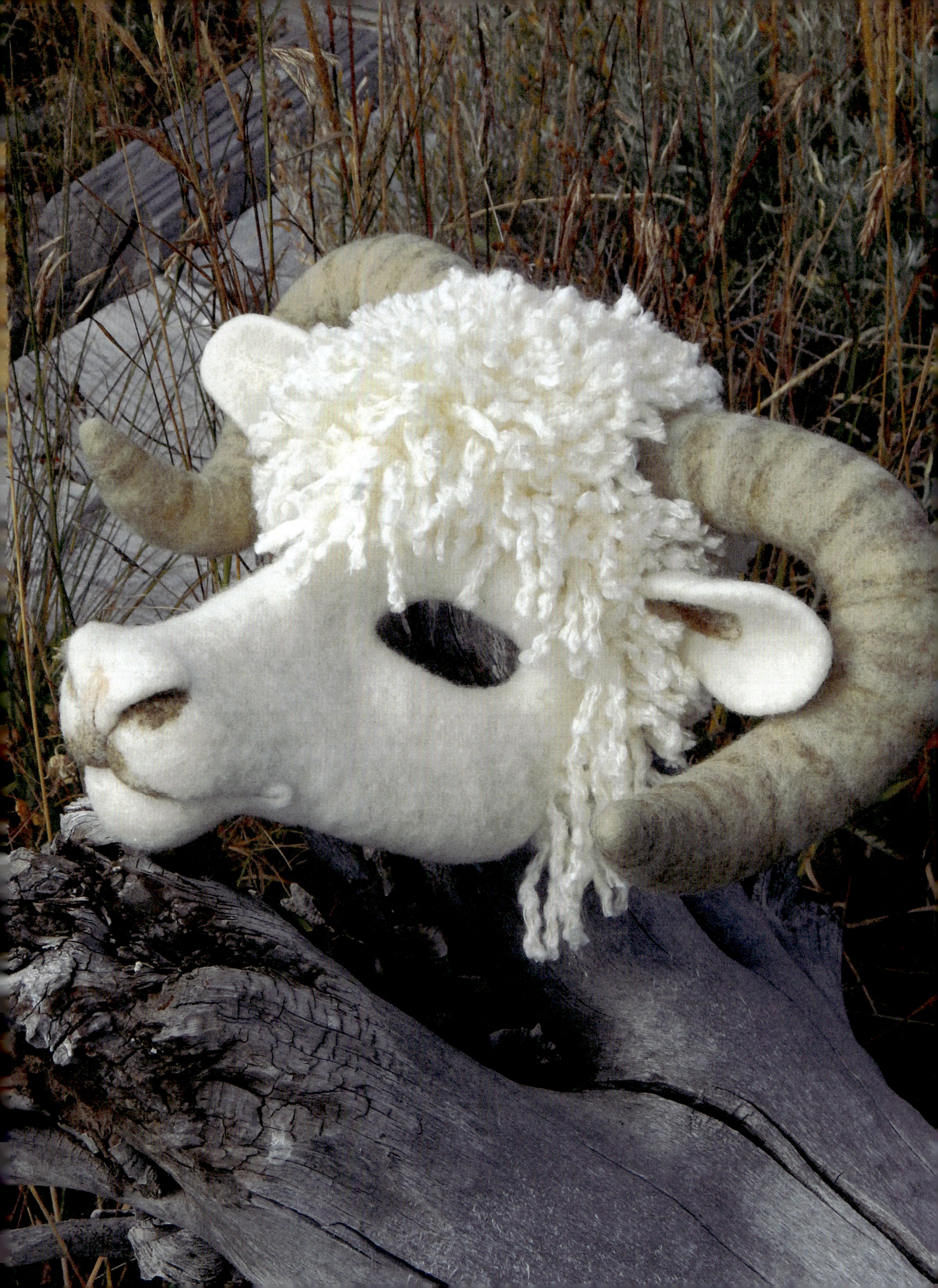

Ram Mask

The **ram template** is a medium size mask. When you look at the template you will notice how large the forehead is. Darts cut into the top of the mask will allow it to curve onto the top of the head of the person wearing the mask. This creates space for the horns to be attached on top of the rams head.

The majority of the wool used to construct this mask is core wool. You may make the choice to give your sheep a stark white, brown, or black face. If you decide to use a different color on the face, you would create the base shape from the core wool and then cover it with another color of wool.

I chose to use a wool blend yarn for the ram's fleece. The yarn is off-white to match the core wool. The yarn is lumpy and adds a lot of texture to the mask. There are many irregular or lumpy yarns available and off-white is a common color that is easily found. If you would like to take the time, you could certainly felt your own strands to use in the fleece.

Supplies

core wool for the mask base
light brown wool for the horns
medium to dark brown wool for shading
medium peach wool for shading the nose

Very small amounts of light, medium, and dark brown wool are needed to shade the horns, nose, and inside the ears. Aside from that, this mask is made entirely from core wool.

felt fabric for the mask base and the ears
a wool blend yarn for the ram's fleece
1/4" wide elastic for the strap on the back of the mask

Create A Base For The Mask

Use the **ram template** to cut a mask from felt fabric. *Refer to page 18 for information about using **Felt Fabric** or how to create a base without it.* Cut slits in the forehead using the dotted lines on the template as a guide.

Overlap the cut edges and poke to hold them in place. This will shape the forehead so it will curve over the top of the head.

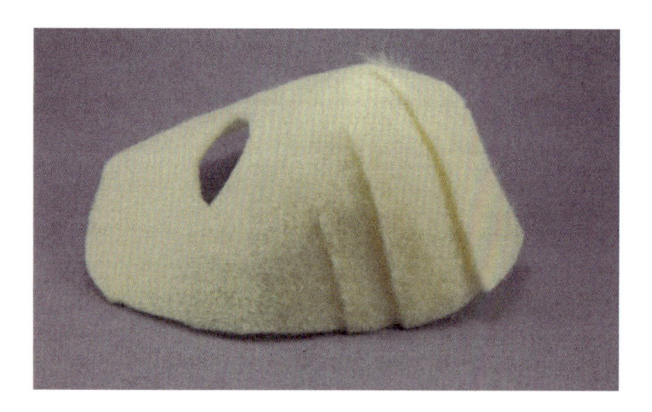

Cover the entire mask on the inside and outside with core wool. Pull off small pieces of wool and poke to attach. A tool that holds several needles will make the felting go quicker. Once both sides of the mask are covered, wrap core wool around the edge of the mask and the edge of the eye openings.

As the wool becomes felted, the mask will begin to stiffen. Each layer of wool that is added will continue to stiffen the mask. The top of the forehead is curved because of the overlapping wool. Make sure to bend the sides of the mask as you poke so they will curve also.

Shaping The Mask

Make a log that is about 5" long. Add wool to one end so that it is 2" to 3" thick. Let the other end taper down and become thin. Lay the log between the eyes with the thick end at the bottom of the mask. Poke along the edge of the log to attach and then poke the center.

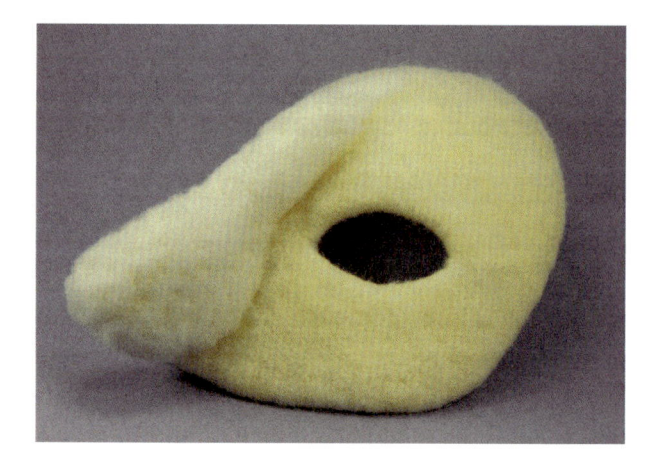

Tip: You don't need to add the shape of the snout all at once. The basic shape is attached to build up the area first. Then you continue to add more wool as you sculpt and refine the shape.

Make a log about 4" long. The center of the log should be 1" thick and each end of the log is thinner so that it may be blended into the side of the face. Poke the center of the log so that it is firm before you attach it to the face. Attach the log to the side of the face as shown in the photo below. If there is a dip in the center add more wool to build up the area.

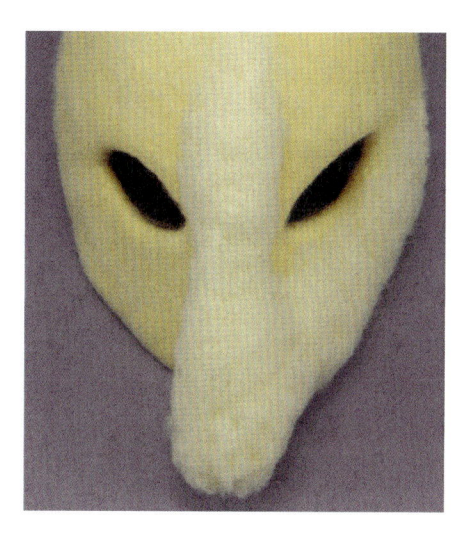

Make two logs that are 3" long. Attach a log above each eye to build up the brow area.

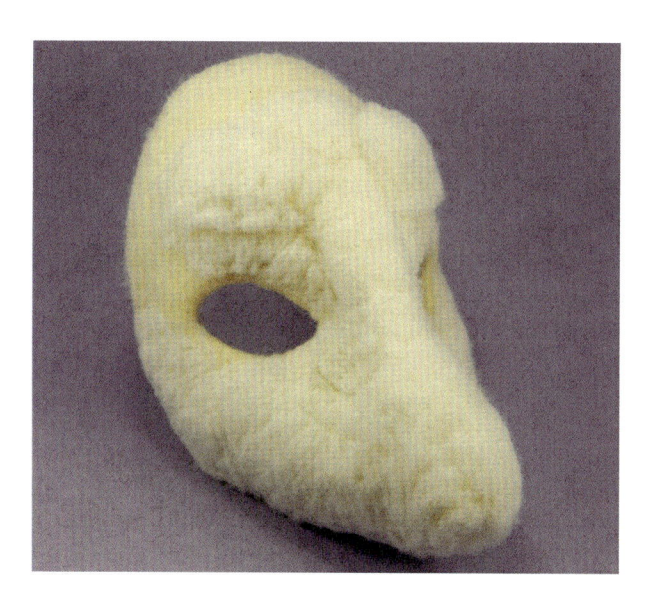

Add some wool to the sides of the forehead to create a broad, flat area rather than one that is rounded. Poke the entire front of the mask adding wool as needed to refine the shape of the face.

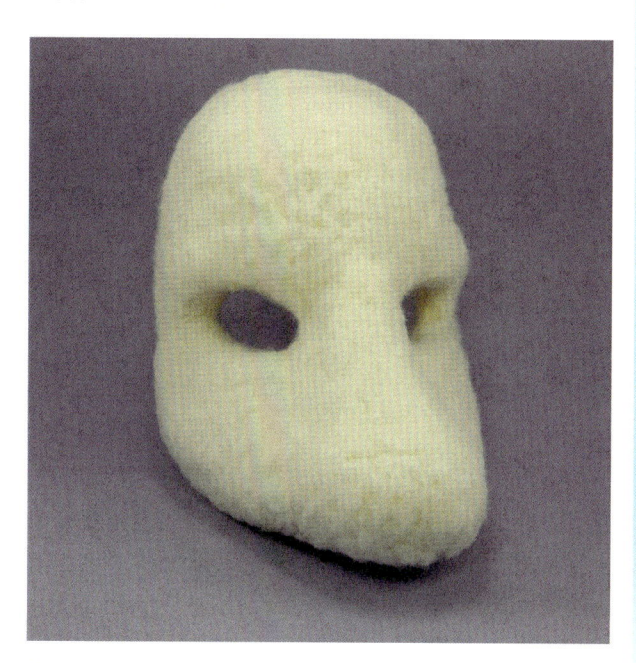

The curve of the mask creates an open area behind the snout. When you wear the mask the wool will not be touching your nostrils or your mouth. This makes it comfortable to breathe and talk while you are wearing the mask.

The chin is attached to the bottom side of the snout. Do not make is so large that it fills in the open area on the inside of the mask. Make a log that is 3" long. Roll one end over to make a thick rounded end poking as you roll. Leave the other end of the ball fluffy.

Poke one side of the chin to create a flat surface. Attach the flat surface of the chin against the bottom of the snout. Poke around the edge of the chin and in the center to attach it to the snout. Pull out the fluffy edge of the chin toward each side to create the line that is the separation between the upper and lower lips. Add wool (if needed) until you have the size and shape desired for the chin. Felt the chin completely until it is firm. The front of the chin should stick out as far as the nose. When the nose and upper lips are attached it will bring out the snout a bit more and then the chin will be slightly indented.

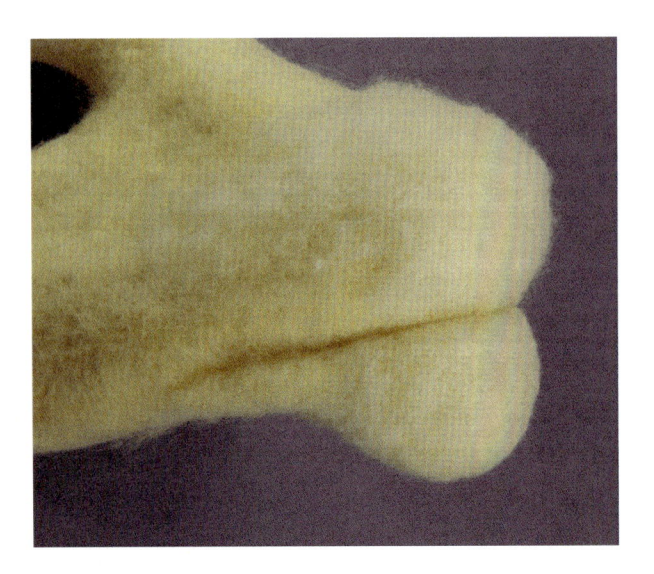

Adding Detail

The upper lips are felted on the foam work surface and then attached to the snout. Pull off a piece of wool about 3 1/2" long by 2 1/2" tall. Poke a straight line about 1/2" from the end of the wool and then fold over to create an edge. *Refer to page 24 for more information about creating edges.* Create a second edge on the adjoining side of the wool. Leave the other edge of the wool fluffy.

The longest edge will be the bottom of the lip. Felt a small bit of medium brown wool to the corners created by the straight edges.

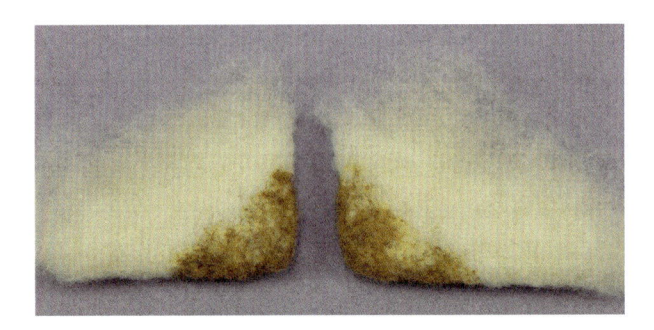

Lay the lips on the end of the snout making sure that they are centered. Poke just enough to hold them in place. Then poke around the edges to secure them. The bottom edge of the lips should cover the separation line where the chin and snout meet. Notice in the photo (*at the top of the next page*) how the corners where the lips meet have become rounded now that they are felted to the snout. If you find that the lips are not full enough or not rounded enough, pull back the lips and add wool behind them. The snout should be slightly wider than the chin. Curve the end of the lip down onto the side of the chin to create the corner of the mouth. Now that the lips are attached, felt the entire area to blend all the fluffy edges.

Use the template for the **ram's nose** to help shape it. Pull off a piece of wool that is larger than the nose template. Lay the wool on your foam work surface. Lay the template on top of the wool. You may use a few straight pins to push through the template and into the foam to hold the template in place. Use a slow, controlled poke to outline the shape of the nose around the template. Leave the top edge fluffy for attaching to the face. Remove the template and fold over the wool along the poked line to create an edge.

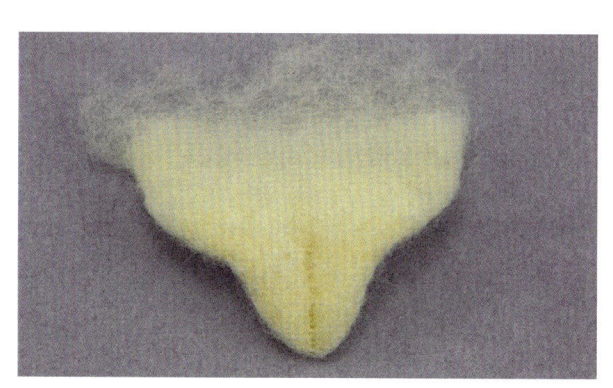

Refer to page 20 for more information on using templates to help shape the wool.

You may add just a hint of pink or peach colored wool to shade the nose. Felt the nose completely, but leave the top straight edge of the nose fluffy. Shade the end of the snout with the same brown wool used to shade the lips. Hold the nose up to the snout to make sure you have enough brown peeking out.

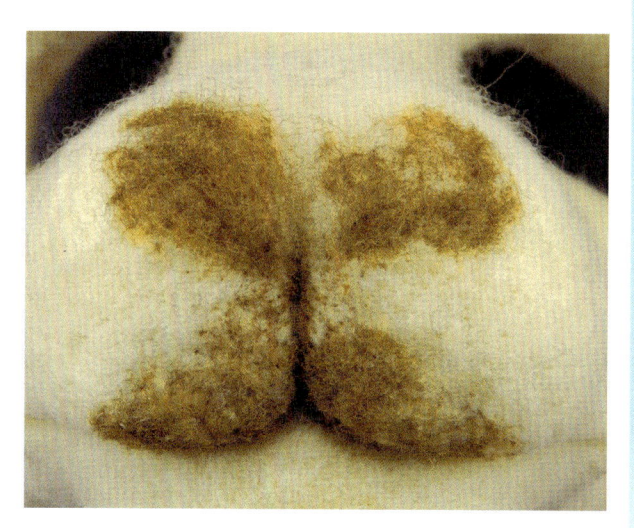

Poke a straight line into the nose. Start at the tip and poke up the nose 1/2" to 3/4".

Attach the nose. Poke along the line you made at the bottom of the nose and around the tip. Turn under the top edge of the nose on each side and poke the fluff in the middle on the top of the snout. Add a small bit of wool to the top of the nose so there is a smooth transition from the nose to the snout. Poke the center of the nose leaving the edge of the nostrils open.

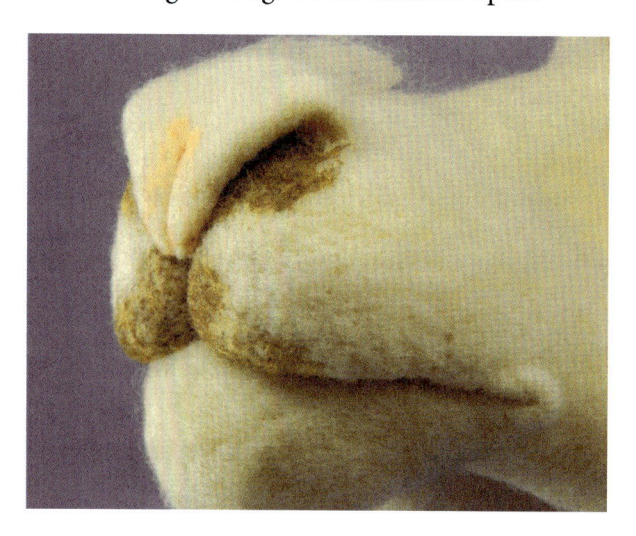

75

Roll a long, skinny log from dark brown. *Refer to page 26 for more information on outlining to define details.* Poke the brown into the separation between the upper and lower lips. Add more brown from the poked line in the nose and down to the bottom lip.

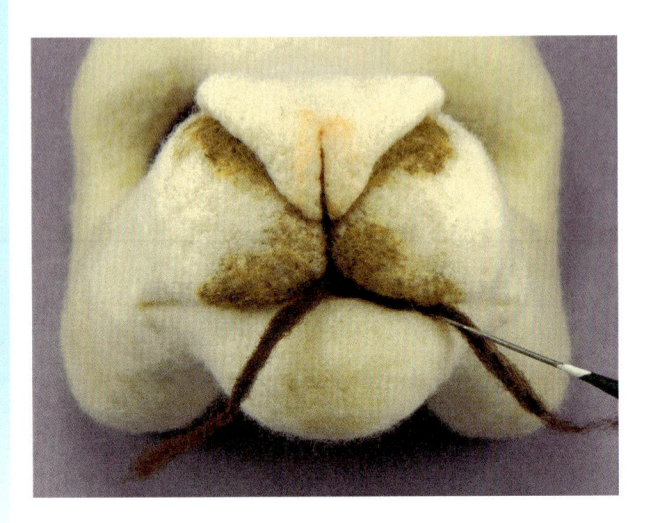

If the brown disappears between the lips as you are poking, do not pull it out. Simply add more brown to that area. Outlining the mouth in dark brown will bring more detail to the area.

Tip: You may certainly choose to add more brown shading to the face than I did on the project sample. If you want to add more shading then do it now before moving on.

Making The Ears And Horns

Make the ears and the horns at the same time. When you are making a matched set it is helpful to work on them together. This will help you keep them similar in shape and size.

Use the **ram ear template** to create the ear. You may use the template to cut two ears from felt fabric and cover them with core wool or shape your own from wool. *Refer to page 18 for more information on using templates to help shape the wool.* Pull off a piece of wool that is larger than the ear template. Lay the wool on your foam work surface. Lay the template on top of the wool. You may use a few straight pins to push through the template and into the foam to hold the template in place. Use a slow, controlled poke to outline the shape of the ear around the template. Poke around the ear leaving the end of the ear fluffy for attaching to the head. Remove the template and fold over the wool along the poked line to create an edge. Completely felt both sides of the ear. Add a bit of brown wool to shade the inside of the ear.

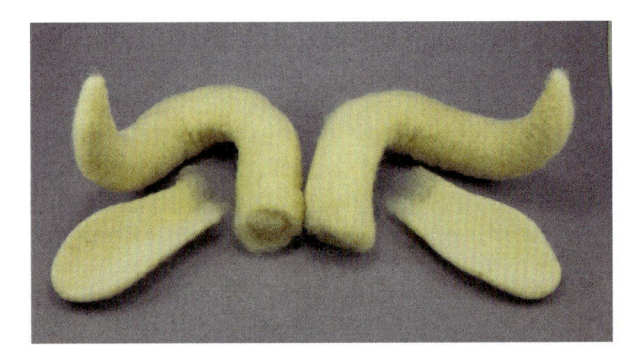

Make two logs that are 14" long for the horns. Wrap layers of wool around the log felting each layer. The horns will become firmer with each layer of wool. Continue adding layers until the horns are 2" across and one end tapers to a point. The points of the horns should be just as firm as the rest of the horn. Twist the horns and poke while holding them in the twisted position. This will make the curve permanent.

Cover the horns with a light shade of brown. Poke the wool to attach it but do not felt it completely. This will allow you to blend more colors into the horn. Do not cover the bottom of the horn with brown wool. The horn will be attached to the head with core wool so you need to leave room for this. It is an option to attach the horn to the head first and then cover it with color. However, you will find it easier to cover the horn before it is attached to the mask.

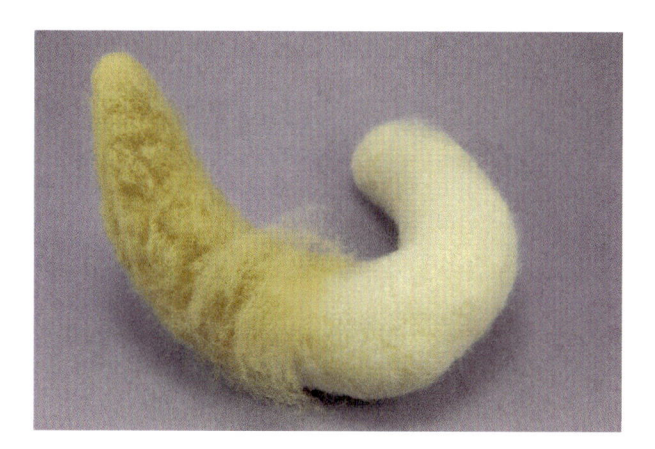

Choose two colors of brown to shade the horns. The wool should be darker than the base color of the horn. Pull very thin strips of the darker brown and wrap around the horn to create rings of shading. **Do not** roll the wool between your palms as if you were making a clay snake. Doing this will create hard lines of color. Keep the wool strips thin and airy and they will blend easily. Poke just enough to attach the rings. Add extremely thin strips of the core wool over the brown to soften the brown rings.

Once all of the rings have been added you can begin to felt the horns. Leave the bottom edge of the brown fluffy so that you can blend the wool after the horns are attached.

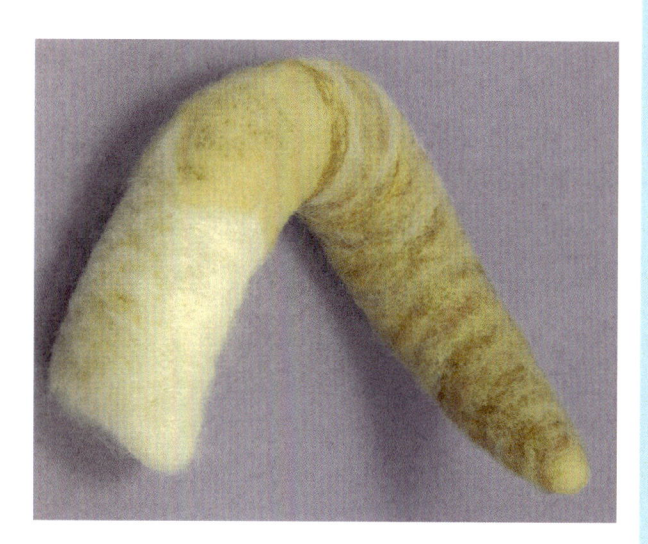

Attach The Ears and Horns

The horns are attached to the top of the head and the ears are below the horns. Hold a horn and ear to the mask to help with placement. If you attach the horns too low you will not leave ample room for the ears. The back of the horn is at the edge of the mask. Use strips of core wool to securely attach the horns. Use a coarse #36 or #38 felting needle to poke through the back of the mask and into the horn. When securely attached, the horns will not bend or wobble at the area of attachment.

Create a clean edge with the base color of the horn. Lay the wool on the foam work surface. Poke a straight line down the center of the wool. Fold the wool over along the poked line to create an edge. Poke the edge on both sides so it is holding together. Wrap the wool around the base of the horn with the clean edge against the mask. *Refer to page 24 for more information about creating edges.*

Cover the remainder of the horn with the base color. Poke just enough to hold the wool in place. Create the color rings around the horn using the same process as explained earlier. Felt the entire horn until it is firm.

Use the fluff at the end of the ear to attach it to the mask. Place the back of the ear near the edge of the mask and curve the base of the ear. Pull off small strips of core wool and poke them around the base of the ear on the inside and outside to secure the attachment.

Attaching The Fleece

A wool blend yarn is used for the sheep's fleece. Cut the yarn into 3" pieces as needed.

Tip: As an option you may choose to make wool dreadlocks instead of using yarn. They may be made using a dowel or stick. Refer to page 27 for more information.

Hold the two ends of the yarn creating a loop. Poke the center of the loop into the mask.

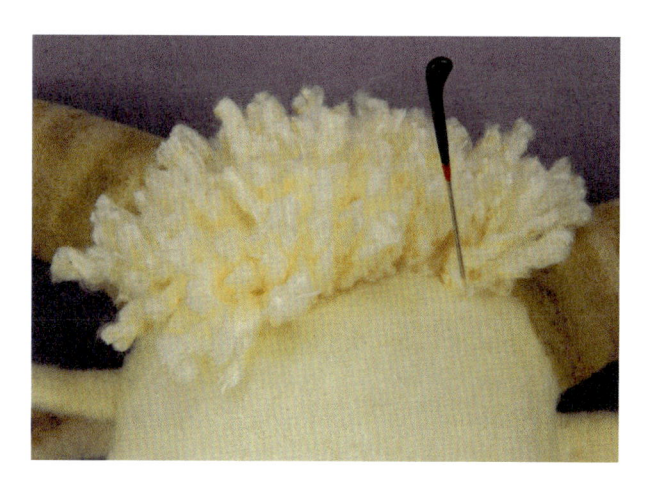

Cut yarn in 4" and 4 1/2" lengths to attach above the eyes and on the sides of the mask.

Do not attach the yarn in neat rows. Fill in the top of the head, around the ears and horns, and up to the back edge of the mask.

Refer to page 29 for instructions on attaching an elastic strap to the mask.

79

Giraffe Mask

The basic shape of the giraffe mask is the same as the ram mask. Both masks have a large forehead to accommodate their horns. One of the major differences is that the snout of the giraffe is much more narrow and a bit longer than that of the ram. The entire mask is made from core wool and then the shading on the nose and the spots are added. A giraffe's spots are like human fingerprints. No two giraffes have exactly the same pattern. This makes felting the spots fun. Both males and females have hair covered horns called ossicones. Brown roving is felted to the top of the horns for hair. If you look at photos of giraffes you will notice that they have bumps on their head that are made of bone, so I have made a bump in the middle of the forehead. Giraffes also have a large upper lip and nostrils much like a horse.

MASKS

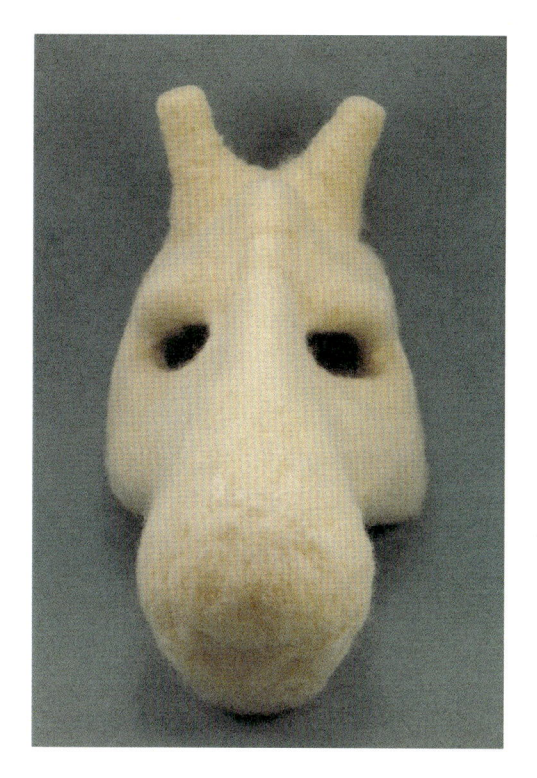

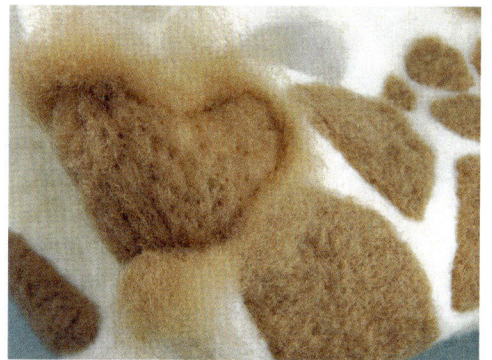

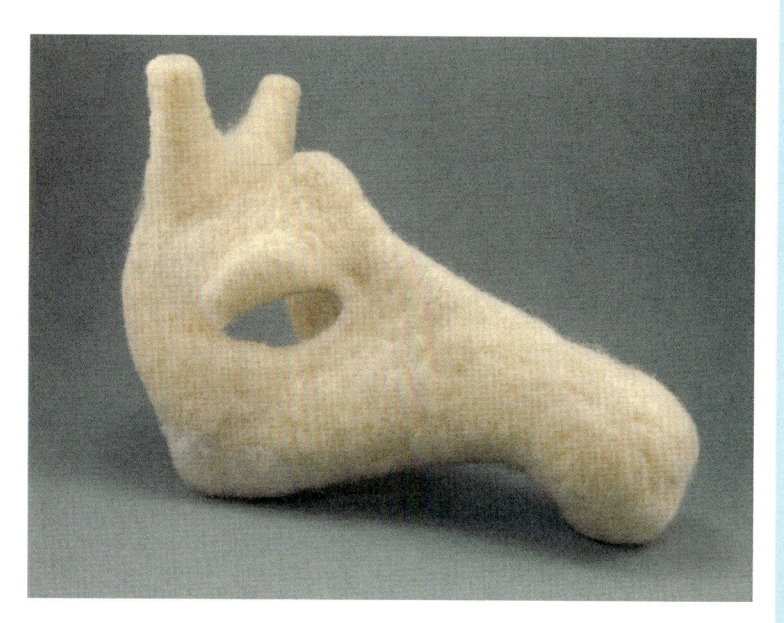

On *page 24* it explains how to **Felt An Edge On The Sculpture**. The giraffe's spots were used as an example in the directions because it is the perfect instance to use this technique.

When I look at a giraffe it is their eyes that stand out. They are large with long eyelashes. If you duplicate these details it will help to capture the likeness of the giraffe. The eye holes on the mask are outlined with a dark brown. Then eyelashes are added with black roving. Once the lashes are all attached, they are trimmed with scissors.

The giraffe is one of my favorite masks. When you see this mask you are compelled to pet his nose.

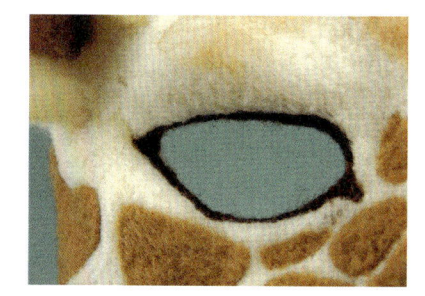

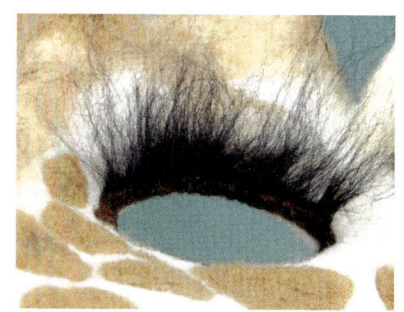

MASKS

82

Displaying Masks

On The Wall

When you make a mask you are creating a beautiful piece of art that should be displayed. A mask may be hung on a wall alone or as part of a group. A thin nail is all that is needed to hang these light weight masks. Push the nail through the wool at the top edge of the mask and hammer the nail into the wall. Don't worry about making a hole in the mask. A few pokes with a felting needle and the hole is gone and the mask is ready to wear.

On A Stand

As I was preparing the masks to be photographed for this book I realized that simply setting them on the table didn't work well. After making the first stand I knew immediately it was a perfect way to display the masks.

The base of the stand is a wood cutout that is available at craft supply stores. I use a variety of shapes that are 4" to 6" wide. Drill a 1/2" hole in the base for a 1/2" wide dowel. The length of the dowel depends on how large your mask is. In most cases a 10" to 12" length works well. For an exceptionally large mask (*like the lion on page 58*) cut a 16" long dowel. Use a pencil sharpener to sharpen one end of the dowel. Glue the dowel into the hole in the base with the sharpened end at the top. Let the glue dry and paint the stand with acrylic paint. I like to use an off-white paint so it doesn't distract from the mask.

Use core wool to felt a triangle or wedge shape. Insert the sharpened end of the dowel into the felted wedge. Twist the dowel as you push it into the wool. Do not push the dowel all the way through the wedge. Remove the dowel and put a small amount of glue into the hole and then insert the dowel back into the hole. Make sure the wedge is positioned the way you want and let the glue dry. Set the mask on the wedge and insert a few straight pins to hold it in place.

84

MAKING
Animal Finger Puppets

Puppets need friends to help tell their stories so you can not make just one. Make a set of puppets that will encourage a child's imagination. Prompt their storytelling by giving them a group of puppets that follow a theme or feel like they are a set. If the puppets have something in common they will feel more like a set. It could be all zoo animals or all forest animals. It could be animals that would not go together in the wild but perhaps have a similar eye shape or body shape that make them feel related. You can make the animal's entire body or just the head and you can make the animals with or without legs. Oddly enough animals can be made without legs and still be appealing. It is fun to make a group that are all the same species such as bears with individuals from around the world. Give thought about the recipient of the puppets and what might spark their imagination.

Every puppet begins by making a tube. On *pages 86-87* it explains the steps to making a finger puppet base. The height of the tube may be adjusted to fit the animal you are making. Make the finger hole so that it is snug on your finger. The wool will shrink when you wear it and be a better fit for a child's small finger. When the puppet is complete, your finger may not slide all the way through the hole but a child's finger will.

On *page 141* it talks about making a stand to display your finger puppets. I love this idea for several reasons. The finger puppets are functional art and art should be displayed. You can make the stand in any size to accommodate a set of three puppets or a larger group. After you have put *your* time and imagination into creating these puppets you will want to give them their own special place. When the puppets are not being played with, they make a delightful decoration on the shelf in a child's room.

You should not give these puppets to a very young child that will put them in their mouth. Adding small plastic eyes or beads for the eyes is a **choking hazard for young children**. You can omit plastic eyes and beads and use wool to felt the eyes.

Making A Base For Finger Puppets

Each finger puppet you make will begin with the 7 steps explained here. The base of the finger puppet begins with a tube. I like to start with a felt fabric rectangle to make the tube. If you choose to make your own felt rectangle refer to **Felt Sheets And Prefelt** on page 18 and **Making Ears Without A Felt Fabric Base** on page 20. I choose to use the felt fabric because the felting is done and I can cut a rectangle in the exact size I need. It makes building the base quicker and easier.

1. You will need a piece of foam the size of your index finger to insert into the base while you are felting. **Do Not** cut foam from your foam work surface. You may have a piece of foam around the house or from packing materials used to ship a package. If you don't have foam you can use a soft sponge. Some sponges get hard when they dry out and others remain soft. Look for a soft sponge.

Cut the foam or sponge about 4" long. Trim the corners off so the shape is more rounded. It does not have to be perfectly shaped.

Tip: The foam you choose for a work surface is dense so that it will last longer than a softer foam. The foam you choose for inserting into the finger puppet tube does not have to be as dense as the foam used for the work surface. Any foam will work. It just means that a softer foam may not last as long as a more dense foam. I was able to use a soft foam to make a dozen puppets before throwing it away and cutting a new one. When your foam or sponge begins to fall apart just throw it away and cut a new one.

2. Use the template (*on page 144*) for the finger puppet base to cut a rectangle or use the template to felt your own rectangle. The rectangle measures 2 1/2" tall by 3 1/2" wide.

3. Wrap the 3 1/2" width of the rectangle around your finger to fit for size. Notice how much the ends overlap. Wrap the rectangle around the foam or sponge you prepared. Poke along the overlapped edges of the rectangle until they hold together. The foam is longer than the tube and should stick out both ends of the tube. Pull one end of the foam to move it inside the tube. This will keep the wool fibers from getting embedded into the foam. Keep pulling the foam back and forth as you work so it will not become attached to the base. If you do not reposition the foam as you are felting you will end up pulling the foam out in pieces.

4. Wrap core wool around the tube. The wool is thin at this point so shallow pokes is all that is needed to begin felting. Poking deeply into the foam will just embed the wool fibers quicker. Wrap a layer of wool around the entire tube, poke as you wrap.

5. Pull the foam so it is just inside one end of the tube. Fold the edges over to close the end of the tube and poke.

close one end of the tube

6. Lay some wool over the closed end of the tube and poke. This will secure the closed end.

Now that one end of the tube is closed you will not be able to pull the foam back and forth inside the tube. However, it is still very necessary to move the foam as you are working. Pull the foam about 1/3 of the way out of the tube. Then use the end of a stick or dowel to aid in pushing the foam back into the tube.

7. Pull the foam out of the tube completely. Lay the tube on the foam work surface and poke inside the tube. Poke the inside wall of the tube, as well as, the inside of the closed end of the tube. As you move on to felt the head and body repeat this step several times. By the time you are finished with the puppet the interior of the tube will be firmly felted.

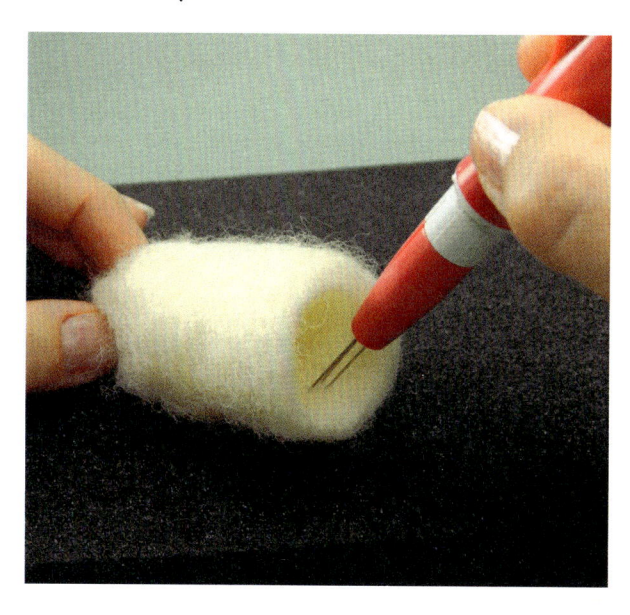

PUPPETS

MAKING THE
Red Fox
finger puppet

Supplies

core wool
dark orange wool for the body and ears
white wool for the eyes, cheeks, chin, belly
brown wool for the eyes
black wool for the nose and ears

2 1/2" x 3" piece of felt fabric for base
two 4mm black beads for the eyes
black thread to sew beads
button weight black thread for whiskers
straight white roving for ear hair

The red fox is 4" tall.
The body is 2" wide.
The face is 2 1/2" wide across the cheeks.

Red Fox Finger Puppet

1. Begin by following steps 1 through 7 of *Making A Base For Finger Puppets* on *pages 86-87*.

2. Wrap wool around the middle of the head and the middle of the body to begin building them up. Do not build up the neck area.

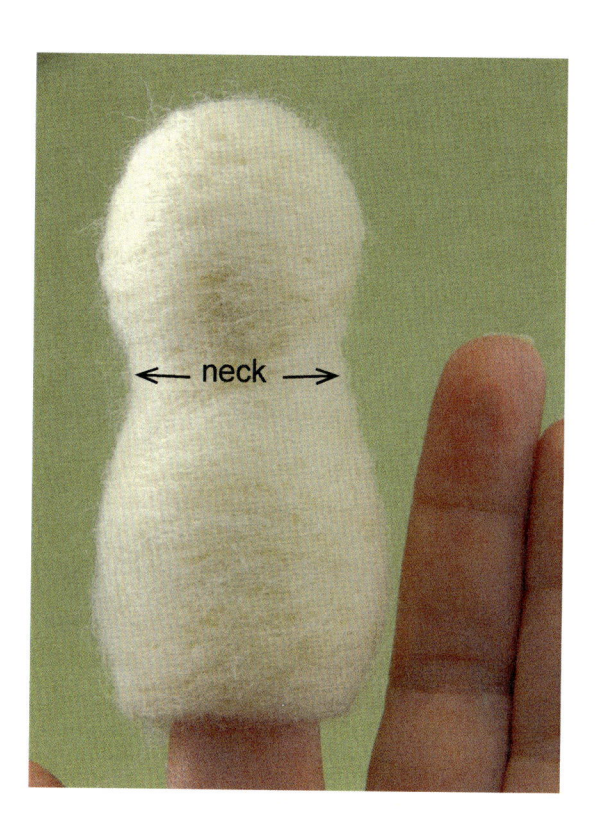

The widest part of the body at the center is 2" across. Poke as you wrap the wool. Do not let the neck get wider than 1 1/4" across.

3. The finished width of the head from cheek to cheek is 2 1/2". Add a triangle shape to each side of the head. Add a bit of wool to the top of the head so it is also pointed.

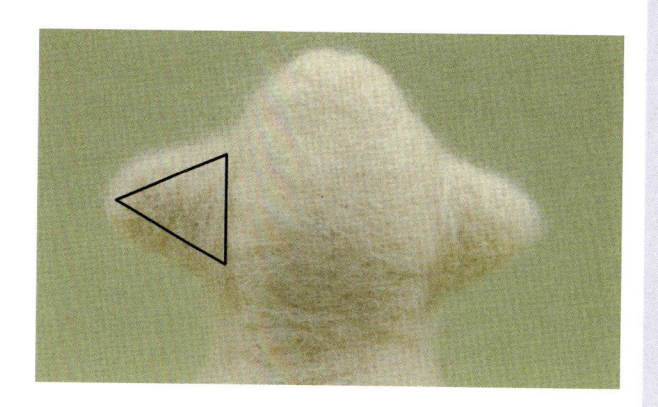

4. Add wool to make a smooth transition from the point of the cheek down to the neck. Then from the cheek to the top of the head. Wool has been added to the right side of the photo below.

5. Make four balls that will be the nose, muzzle, and chin. *Refer to Shaping The Sculpture on page 28*. Roll a ball shape and leave a fluffy tail. Lay a piece of wool on your foam work surface and start rolling one edge poking as you roll. Tuck in the sides as you roll. The face is small so the balls are only 1/2" wide. Stop rolling the ball when it is the right size and just pull off any excess wool leaving a short tail.

6. Put the two balls for the muzzle next to each other and poke to hold them together. Attach the fluffy tails to the face. Add the nose on top of the muzzle and the chin below the muzzle.

7. Add wool to make a smooth transition from the muzzle to the face. Build up the cheeks below the eyes and the nose to the top of the head.

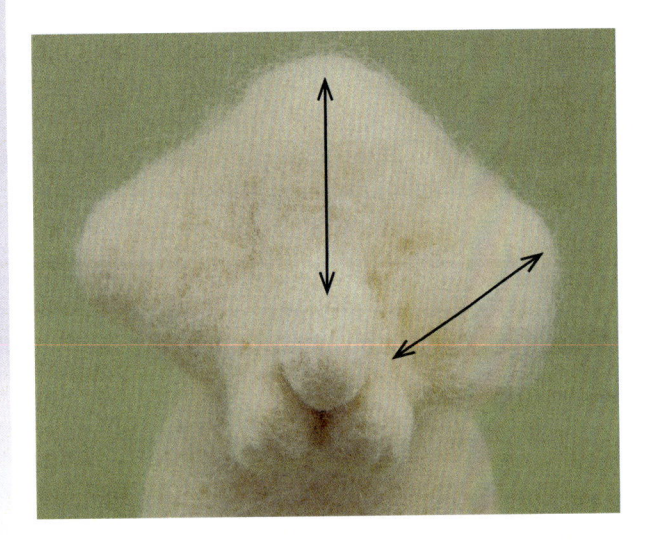

8. Poke a tear drop shape for each eye. Then poke inside the outline. Notice how this makes the wool around the eyes push out and the bridge of the nose between the eyes is defined.

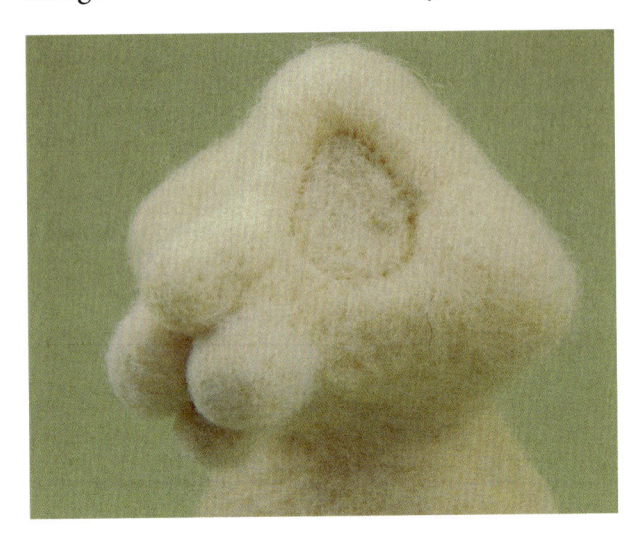

9. Make a circle that has the same thickness all the way across. Pull off two pieces of white wool that are the same size (one for each eye). While holding one in your hand, fold under all the fluffy edges. Lay the piece inside the outline of the eye and poke around the perimeter of the eye. Poke along the same eye outline you made previously. Once the edge is attached you can poke the entire eye. This gives the same thickness across the entire white of the eye. Repeat for the other eye.

10. Half of the eye will be covered by an eyelid so the iris will be placed low on the white of the eye. Lay a small piece of brown wool on the eye. Poke the outline of the iris. Fold the fluffy edge of the wool over the outline and poke to felt the wool inside the circle of the iris.

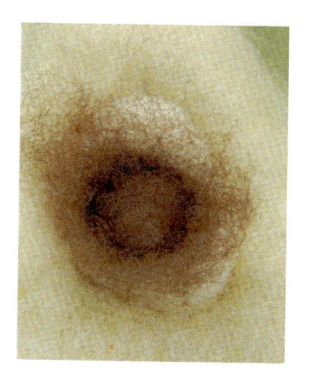

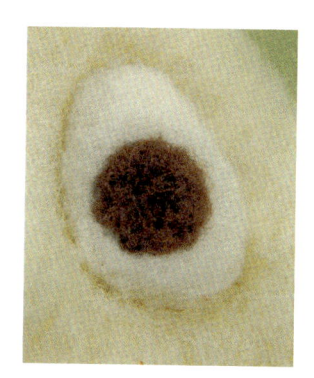

11. The pupil can be a 4mm or 5mm black glass eye on a wire loop (*on the left below*) or a black bead (*on the right*). Choose a gloss finish.

12. Attach the pupil with a sewing needle and thread. A bit of the thread may be seen if you are using beads so choose black thread. Insert the needle at the back of the head and come out in the eye. Go back into the eye and out the back of the head and tie a knot. The thread will get covered with wool later.

13. Make two eyelids from the orange wool you will use for the body. Create an edge that is 1" long with 1/2" of fluff. *Refer to* **Felt An Edge On The Foam Work Surface** *on page 25.*

14. Lay the eyelid over the eye with the folded edge against the iris. Poke to hold the lid in place. Use a large sewing needle to tuck the eyelid into the groove around the white of the eye. Felt the eyelid to the eye.

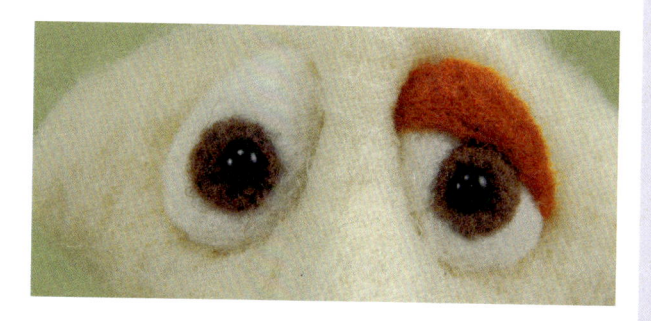

15. Make a long folded edge of orange wool for the body that is 6" long. Lay the wool on the fox with the folded edge against his stomach. Create a rounded shape and poke. Do not attach the ends of the wool yet.

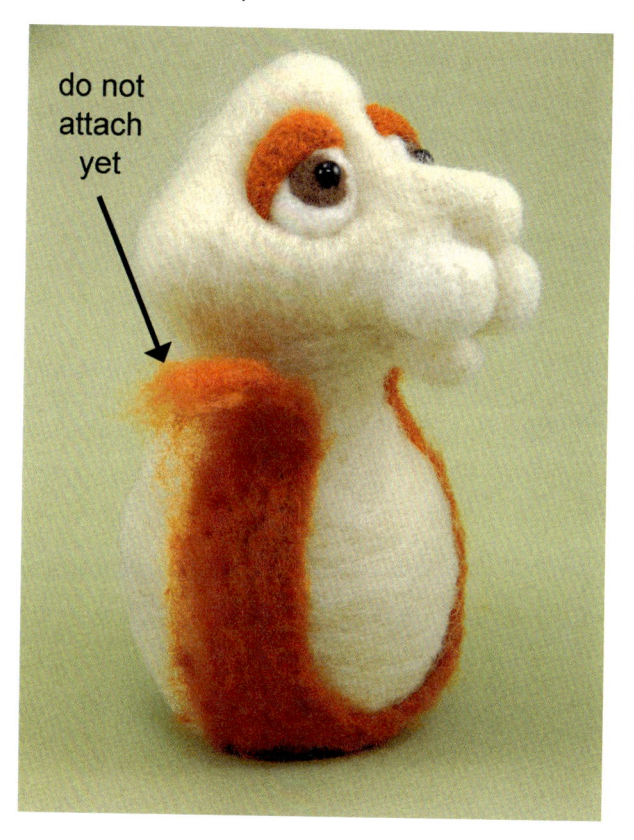

do not attach yet

91

16. Cover the back of the body and the top of the head with orange wool. Tuck the wool in the groove around the eyes. Poke in the groove to secure the wool. Cover the entrance to the finger hole with orange for a neat appearance.

17. Make another orange folded edge to go across the top of the nose, under the eye, and around the back of the cheek. Join this edge with the edge you attached to the body previously. Cover the stomach and face with white wool. Felt the white and orange wool to the body.

18. Make a black folded edge for the nose that is 1 1/4" long. Lay the folded edge of the black against the folded edge of the orange on top of the nose. Felt along the perimeter of the nose.

Felt the wool inside the perimeter of the nose.

19. Pull off a thin strip of brown wool. Roll the wool between the palms of your hands to condense the loose fibers. Poke the strip in the groove between the muzzle and the lips.

20. Use the template (*page 144*) for the fox's ears. The ears are small so they do not require a core wool base. Make the ears from the orange wool. *Refer to **Making Ears Without A Felt Fabric Base** on page 20.* Make black tips on each ear with a small amount of wool.

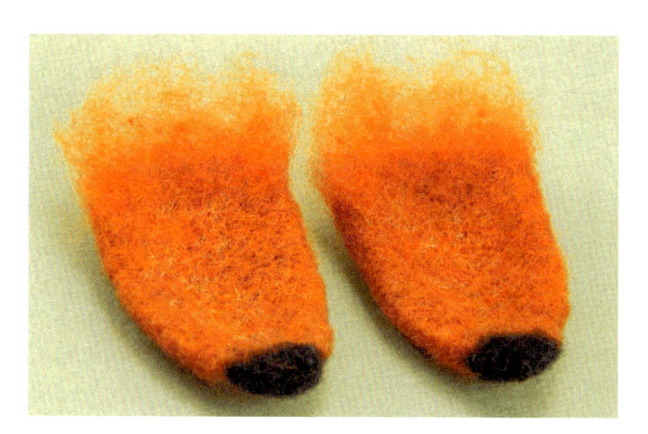

21. Spread open the fluff at the bottom of each ear to attach it to the head. The ear is attached to the back of the head (*see the photo below and the photo above right*). Curve the edge on each side of the ear so it does not lay flat against the head. This creates a little pocket inside the ear. Felt the ears to the head. Add a bit of orange wool to smooth the attachment if needed. Poke a little bit of white roving (straight fibers) into the pocket of each ear.

22. Wrap wool around a stick to make a 3" long tail. Add a white tip to the tail. *Refer to **Felting Ropes** on page 26 for more information.* Attach the tail in the center at the bottom of the back.

23. Thread a sewing needle with black thread for the whiskers. Insert the needle on one side of the muzzle and come out in the same area on the opposite side. Put a small dot of white craft glue on the thread and pull the thread until the glue is inside the wool. Once the glue is dry the whiskers will not pull out of the wool. Cut the whiskers about 1" long. Repeat the process until there are 4 or 5 whiskers on each side.

MAKING THE
Raccoon
finger puppet

Supplies

core wool
gray wool for the body and ears
black wool for the eyes, nose, and tail
white wool for the eyes, snout, and chin

2 1/2" x 3" piece of felt fabric for base
two 8mm brown plastic animal eyes
button weight white thread for whiskers

**The raccoon is 4" tall.
The body is 2" wide.
The face is 2 1/2" wide across the cheeks.**

Make The Red Fox First And Then The Raccoon

If you make the red fox first the directions for the raccoon will seem repetitious, and they are. The red fox and the raccoon have identical shapes. The only differences between them are the wool colors used and the markings on their coats. Having the same body shapes make these puppets feel like they are part of a set. I recommend that you make the red fox first, then the raccoon, and then the bear.

Raccoon Finger Puppet

1. Begin by following steps 1 through 7 of *Making A Base For Finger Puppets* on pages 86- 87.

2. Follow steps 2 through 9 of the **Red Fox** on *pages 89 and 90*.

3. The raccoon's eyes are 4.5mm brown acrylic animal eyes. Use a sharpened dowel or candy apple stick to make a hole for the eyes. Position the hole slightly below the center of the white of the eye. Twist the dowel while pushing it into the wool.

Twist while pushing the stem of the eye into the hole.

4. Make two eyelids from black wool. Create an edge that is 1" long with 1/2" of fluff. *Refer to* **Felt An Edge On The Foam Work Surface** *on page 25*.

5. Lay the eyelid over the eye with the folded edge against the acrylic eye. Poke to hold the lid in place. Use a large sewing needle to tuck the eyelid into the groove around the white of the eye. Felt the eyelid to the eye. Be careful that you do not hit the acrylic eye with the felting needle.

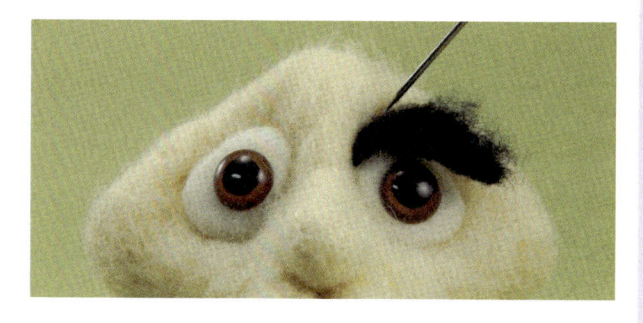

6. Make a 3" long folded edge of black wool for the black ring under the raccoon's eyes. Lay the wool under the eye with the folded edge facing away from the eye. Create a rounded shape that starts on the inside corner of the eye and ends on the outer corner of the eye. Tuck the fluffy edge of the black wool into the groove around the white of the eye. Felt the wool to the face.

7. Make a 4" long folded edge of gray wool to make a ring over the eye. As an option you could

95

felt the edge right on the sculpture. *Read **Creating Edges**, **Felt An Edge On The Sculpture** on page 24.* The gray edge starts at the nose, goes over the top of the eye, and meets under the chin. Cover the back of the head, the body, and the entrance to the finger hole with gray wool. Cover the muzzle, chin, and ring over the eye in white wool. Felt the entire puppet.

8. Make a black folded edge for the nose that is 1 1/4" long. Lay the folded edge of the black against the top of the nose. Felt along the perimeter of the nose. Felt the wool inside the perimeter of the nose in an oval shape.

9. Pull off a thin strip of brown or black wool. Roll the wool between the palms of your hands to condense the loose fibers. Poke the strip in the groove between the muzzle and the lips.

10. Use the template (page 144) for the raccoon's ears. The ears are small so they do not require a core wool base. Make the ears from gray wool. *Refer to **Making Ears Without A Felt Fabric Base** on page 20.* The ears are completely shaped and felted before they are attached to the head. Leave the bottom edge of the ear fluffy.

11. Spread open the fluff at the bottom of each ear to attach it to the head. The ear is attached to the back of the head. Curve the edge on each side of the ear so it does not lay flat against the head. This creates a little pocket inside the ear. Felt the ears to the head. Add a bit of gray wool to smooth the attachment if needed. Poke a little bit of black or white roving (straight fibers) into the pocket of each ear.

12. Wrap gray wool around a stick to make a 3" long tail. Add three stripes of black to the tail. *Refer to* **Felting Ropes** *on page 26 for more information.* Attach the tail in the center at the bottom of the puppet.

13. Thread a sewing needle with white thread for the whiskers. Insert the needle on one side of the muzzle and come out in the same area on the opposite side. Put a small dot of white craft glue on the thread and pull the thread until the glue is inside the wool. Once the glue is dry the whiskers will not pull out of the wool. Cut the whiskers about 1" long. Repeat the process until there are 4 or 5 whiskers on each side.

Make The Bear Last

If you make the red fox and the raccoon first, the bear will be easy. The directions are the same with the exception of different wool colors and markings on his coat. You may even come up with your own ideas for other animals you can make to include in this set.

The bear has the same type of plastic eyes that were used on the raccoon, but you could also use beads or felt them with wool.

97

MAKING THE
Lion
finger puppet

Supplies

core wool
light brown wool for the body and ears
white wool for the eyes and snout
peach wool for the nose
brown wool to outline eyes, nose, mouth
brown curly locks for the mane

2 1/2" x 3" piece of felt fabric for base
two 4mm black beads for the eyes
black thread to sew beads
button weight white thread for whiskers

**The finished lion is 4" tall.
The face is 2 1/4" wide across the cheeks.
The body is about 2" wide and 2" tall.
The neck of the lion is 1 1/4" wide.**

PUPPETS

Lion Finger Puppet

1. Begin by following steps 1 through 7 of **Making A Base For Finger Puppets** on *pages 86-87*.

2. Wrap wool around the middle of the head and the middle of the body to begin building them up. Do not build up the neck area. The widest part of the body at the center is 2" across. Poke as you wrap the wool. Do not let the neck get wider than 1 1/4" across.

3. Add a bit of wool on each side at the top of the head to widen it. Roll a log that is 1 1/2" long for the nose. Felt one end of the log and leave the other end fluffy.

Open the fluffy end of the log and felt it to the center of the face. The snout of the lion will extend 1" out from the face.

4. Make two more logs for the snout. Felt one end and leave the other end fluffy. Open the fluffy end of the two logs and felt them to the face under the nose. Use your fingers to squeeze together these three logs that make up the snout and felt them together.

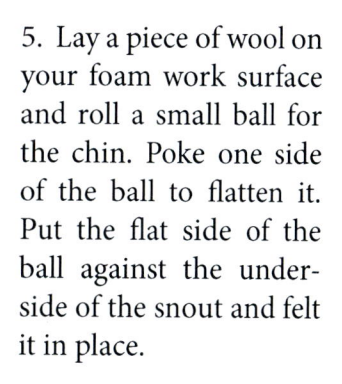

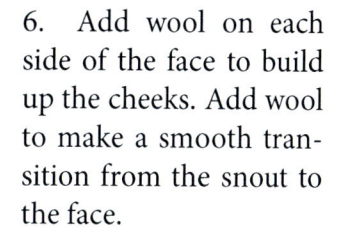

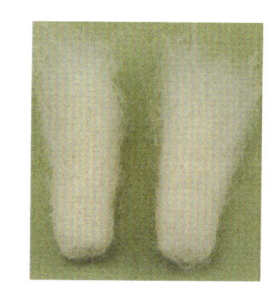

5. Lay a piece of wool on your foam work surface and roll a small ball for the chin. Poke one side of the ball to flatten it. Put the flat side of the ball against the underside of the snout and felt it in place.

6. Add wool on each side of the face to build up the cheeks. Add wool to make a smooth transition from the snout to the face.

99

7. The snout may be left in the core wool or you may cover it in white wool. Cover the entire body with light brown wool. Leave just the end of the snout uncovered.

8. Refer to **Felting A Firm Ball** on *page 23*. Make two white 1/2" balls for the eyes. Sew a 4mm black bead on each eye knotting the thread on the back of the ball. Felt the eyes to the face.

9. Make four eyelids from the brown wool. Create an edge that is 1 1/2" long on each eyelid. *Refer to* **Felt An Edge On The Foam Work Surface** *on page 25*. Wrap the bottom lid around the bottom of each eyeball and felt. Wrap the top lid around the top of each eyeball and felt. Let the top lid cover more of the white eyeball than the bottom lid.

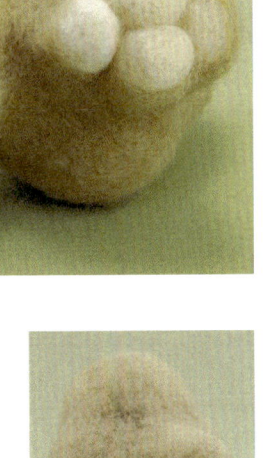

10. Make a mushroom shaped nose from peach wool on the foam work surface. Felt it until it is holding its shape. Place the peach wool on the tip of the nose and finish felting it on the face.

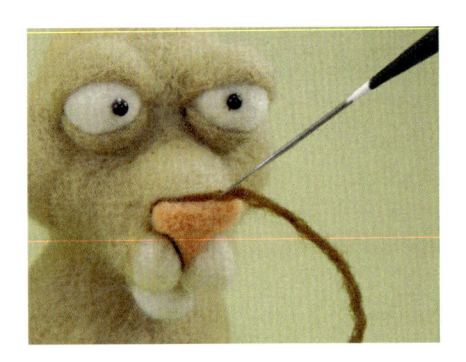

11. Pull off a thin strip of dark brown wool. Roll the wool between the palms of your hands to condense the loose fibers. Refer to **Felting Ropes** on *page 26*. Outline the nose and poke the strip in the groove between the muzzle and the lips. Then outline the eyes at the edge of the eyelids.

12. The ears are small half circles. Make the ears from light brown wool. *Refer to **Making Ears Without A Felt Fabric Base** on page 20.* The ears are completely shaped and felted on the foam work surface before they are attached to the head. Spread open the fluff at the bottom of each ear to attach it to the head. Curve the edge on each side of the ear so it does not lay flat against the head. Felt the ears to the head.

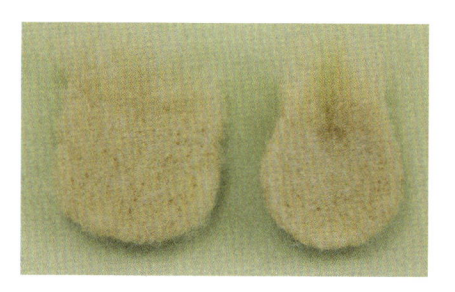

13. Choose medium brown curly locks for the lion's mane. Pull off a curl and poke the center of it to attach it to the head. This leaves both ends of the curl hanging free for a fuller mane.

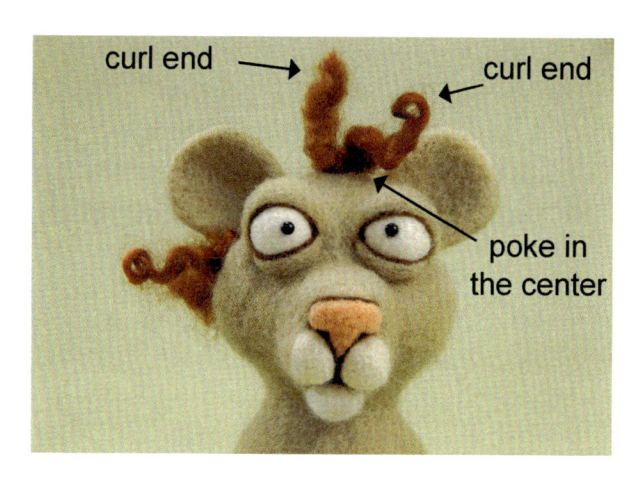

14. Thread a sewing needle with white thread for the whiskers. Insert the needle on one side of the muzzle and come out in the same area on the opposite side. Put a small dot of white craft glue on the thread and pull the thread until the glue is inside the wool. Once the glue is dry the whiskers will not pull out of the wool. Cut the whiskers about 1" long. Repeat the process until there are 4 or 5 whiskers on each side.

15. Wrap light brown wool around a stick to make a 2" long tail. *Refer to **Felting Ropes** on page 26 for more information.* Leave one end of the tail fluffy to attach it to the body and poke a curl into the opposite end of the tail. Felt the tail completely before attaching it to the body. Attach the tail in the center back at the bottom of the body.

Make a second lion and omit the mane to make a female.

MAKING THE *Elephant* finger puppet

Supplies

core wool
light gray wool for the body and ears
medium gray wool for the eyelids
dark gray for the tail, eyebrows, and mouth
white wool for the eyes and tusks

2 1/2" x 3" piece of felt fabric for base
two 4mm black beads for the eyes
black thread to sew beads

*There is a very small amount of medium and dark gray used for the elephant. You could blend these colors yourself if you don't have them on hand. Refer to **Blending Colors** on page 22. You can use the light gray from the body to blend with a dark gray. You can also blend varying amounts of black to the light gray for different shades of gray.*

**The elephant is 4" tall.
The face is 2" wide across the cheeks.
The body is about 2" wide and 2" tall.
The neck of the elephant is 1 1/2" wide.**

Elephant Finger Puppet

1. Begin by following steps 1 through 7 of *Making A Base For Finger Puppets* on *pages 86-87*.

2. The size and shape of the elephant's body is identical to the lion on *page 98*. Wrap wool around the middle of the head and the middle of the body to build them up. Do not build up the neck area. The widest part of the body at the center is 2" across.

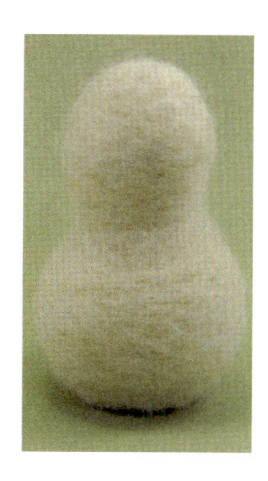

3. Roll two balls and attach them to the top of the head to make the forehead taller. Then add two more balls of wool to build up the cheeks. Cover the face with core wool to smooth the edges of the ball shapes.

4. Refer back to *page 27* in the **Techniques** chapter. It explains how to wrap wool around sticks to make a rope or thin log. This technique is used to make the elephant's trunk. Usually, when this technique is used, the hole from the stick will disappear as the piece is felted. In this case you want to retain the hole at the thin end of the trunk. The hole only needs to be deep enough to suggest that there is a opening through the trunk. The inside and outside of the hole is felted **before** you felt the entire trunk. If you lose the shape of the hole, insert the stick into the hole while twisting it.

Pull off thin strips of gray wool and wrap them around a stick or dowel. It is better to wrap several thin layers of wool than to wrap one thick layer. The trunk is 3" long. Wrap more wool around one end of the trunk and less wool as you get to the opposite end. Slide the wool carefully off the stick. Poke inside the opening of the hole at the thin end of the trunk to felt it and then felt the entire trunk. The hole will compress but you will retain the felted opening.

elephant's trunk

chin

5. Roll a small gray ball and poke it until it is flat and somewhat oval for the chin. Add dark gray on one side to shade the inside of the mouth.

6. Roll a tiny gray ball and felt it at the edge of the hole in the trunk. This will help to make the hole firmer and resemble the shape of a real elephant. Curve the trunk and felt it so the bend is permanent. The trunk should be completely felted on the foam work surface before attaching it. Felt the thick end of the trunk in the center of the face with the tiny ball on the tip of the trunk pointing up. Add additional gray wool around the base of the trunk until there is a smooth transition from the trunk to the face.

felt a tiny ball at the edge of the trunk

7. Cover the entire elephant with gray wool. As you are felting the head, you can define the cheeks and indent a line on the forehead. Attach the chin under the elephant's trunk.

8. Refer to **Felting A Firm Ball** on *page 23*. Make two white 1/2" balls for the eyes. Sew a 4mm black bead on each eye knotting the thread on the back of the ball. Felt the eyes on top of the trunk with no space between them.

9. Make one eyelid from medium gray wool. Create an edge that is 2 1/2" long. *Refer to* **Felt An Edge On The Foam Work Surface** *on page 25*. Start at the bottom of one eye and wrap the eyelid around both eyes. Poke a line in the eyelid between the eyes.

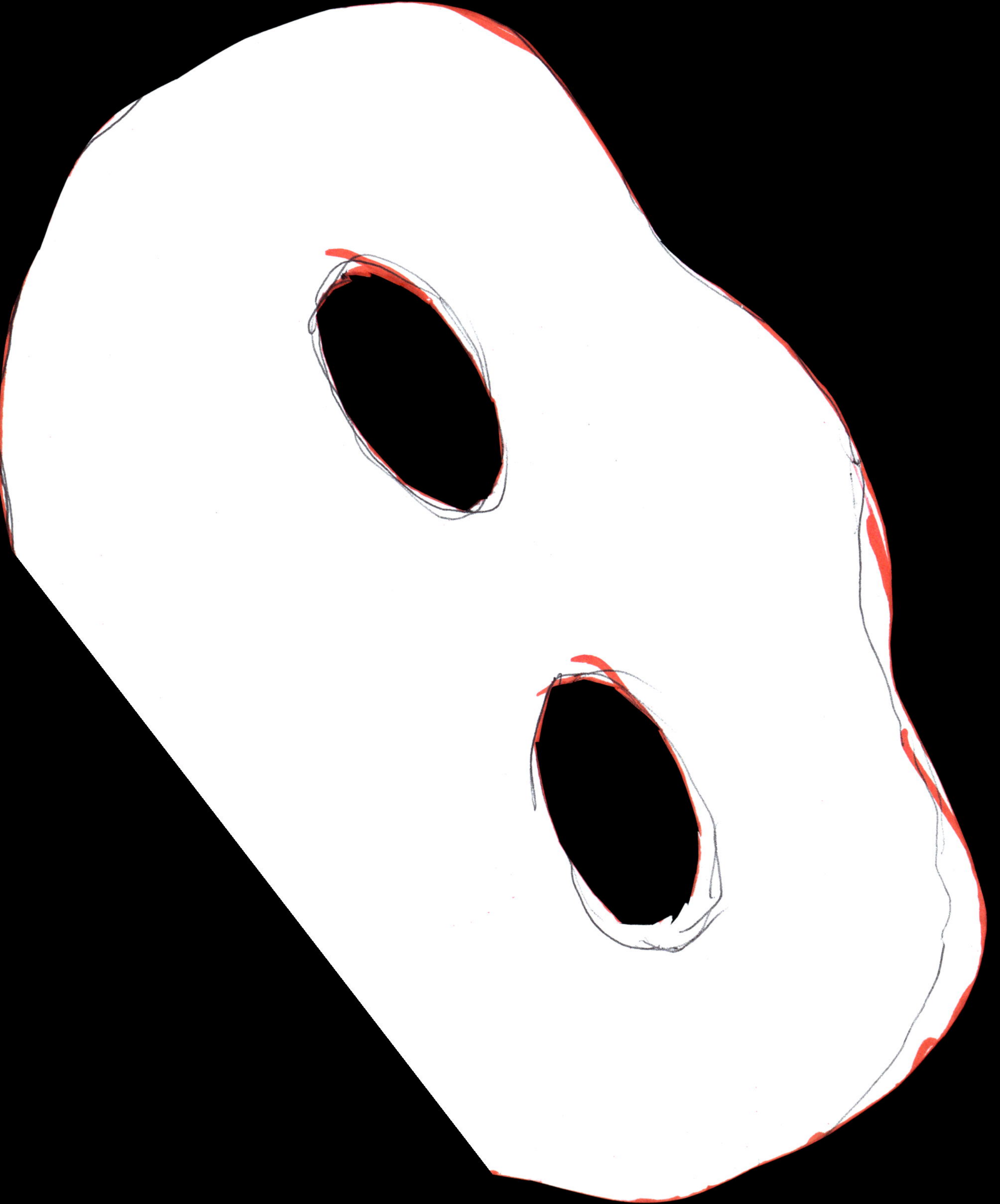

Terms of Use (/terms-use/) (/privacy-policy/)

10. The ears are 2" circles. A 1" wide portion of the edge of the circle is left fluffy for attaching. Felt the ears completely before attaching them. Felt a curve in the ear so it does not lay flat on the head. Felt the ears to the sides of the head.

11. Make two tusks from white wool. The tusks are made by wrapping wool on a stick like the trunk. You can make one on each end of the stick at the same time to help keep them the same size. Each tusk is 1 1/2" long. Slide the tusks off the stick and felt them with one blunt end and one pointed end.

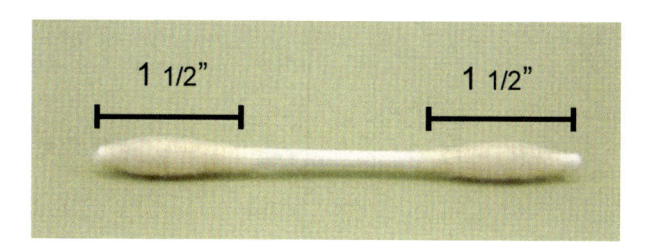

12. Felt the tusks to the elephant on each side of his trunk. The thick end of the tusk is blunt without any fluff for attaching. This creates a clean edge between the white and gray wool. Poke through the tusk into the face to attach.

13. Wrap gray wool around a stick to make a thin tail that is 2" long. Add a bit of dark gray at the tip of the tail. Felt the tail to the back of the elephant at the bottom of the puppet. Use dark gray wool to make triangle shaped eyebrows above the eyelids.

105

PUPPETS

MAKING THE
Horse
finger puppet

Supplies

core wool
medium brown wool for the body and ears
white wool for the eyes
dark brown wool for the eyes
gray wool for the nose
light tan roving for the mane

2 1/2" x 3" piece of felt fabric for base
two 4mm black beads for the eyes
black thread to sew beads
button weight brown thread for eyelashes

**The horse is 5" tall.
The face is 1 1/2" wide across the cheeks.
This puppet does not have a body. The neck of the horse is the area that has the hole for your finger. The neck is about 1 1/4" wide and gets slightly larger at the bottom. It is just wide enough to accommodate the finger hole.**

Horse Finger Puppet

1. Begin by following steps 1 through 7 of **Making A Base For Finger Puppets** on pages 86-87.

2. Pull off a piece of core wool and roll it up on your foam work surface. Make two log shapes. One end is felted and the other end is left fluffy for attaching. One log is the head. The head is 2" long and 3/4" thick. The second log is the snout. The snout is 1 1/2" long and 3/4" thick.

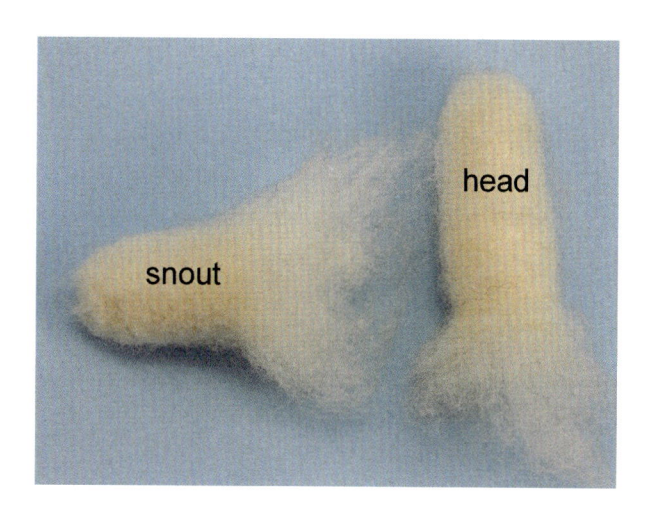

3. Spread open the fluffy end of the snout and push it against the head just above the fluffy end of the head piece. Felt the snout to the head.

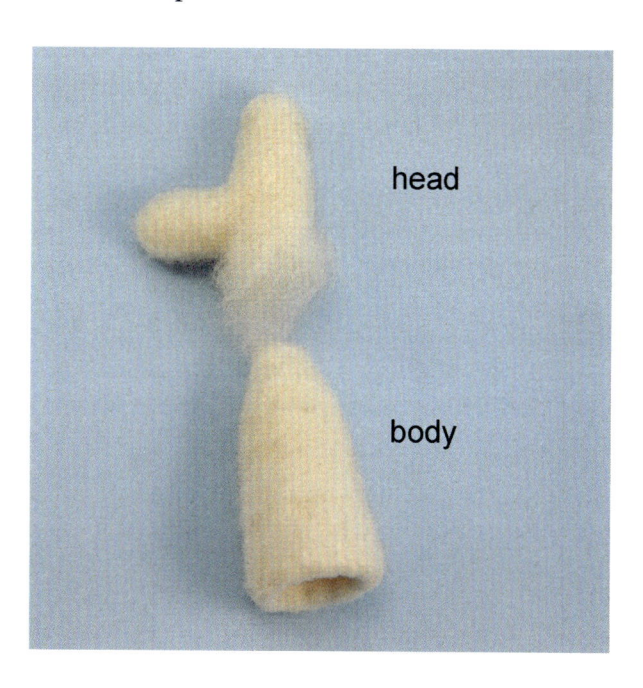

4. Spread open the fluffy end of the head and put it on top of the puppet base. Felt the head to the puppet base.

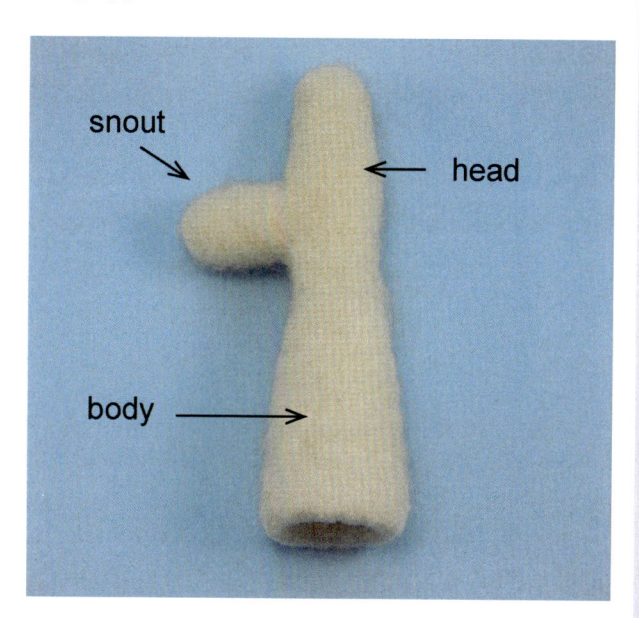

5. Add wool to each side of the face to build up the cheeks.

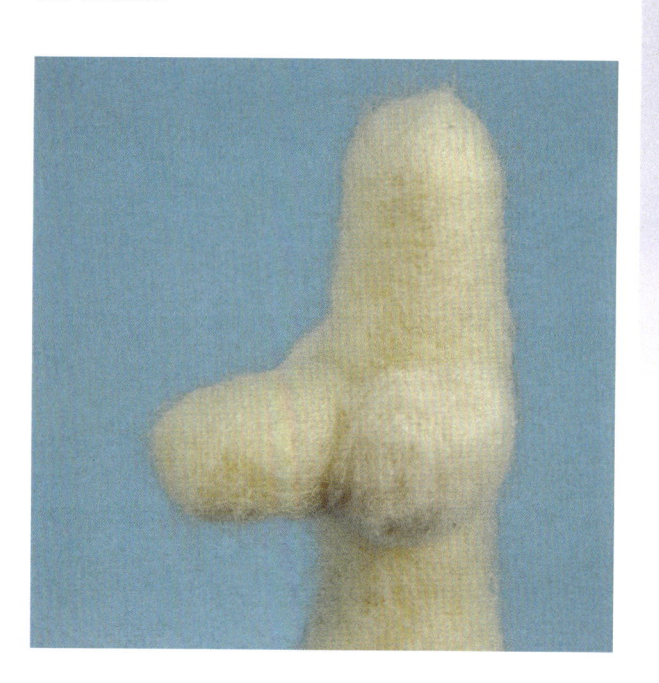

6. Add wool to the puppet to define the shape. Add wool to the cheeks to smooth out the edges. Add a bit of wool in the throat area where the snout meets the head. You can also add some wool to the back of the head just behind the

107

cheeks. I also added more wool to the bottom of the neck to suggest a broad chest. Felt the entire puppet. Also felt the bottom edge and inside the finger hole.

7. Cover the entire puppet with brown wool. Leave a bit of core wool showing on the neck for a white spot.

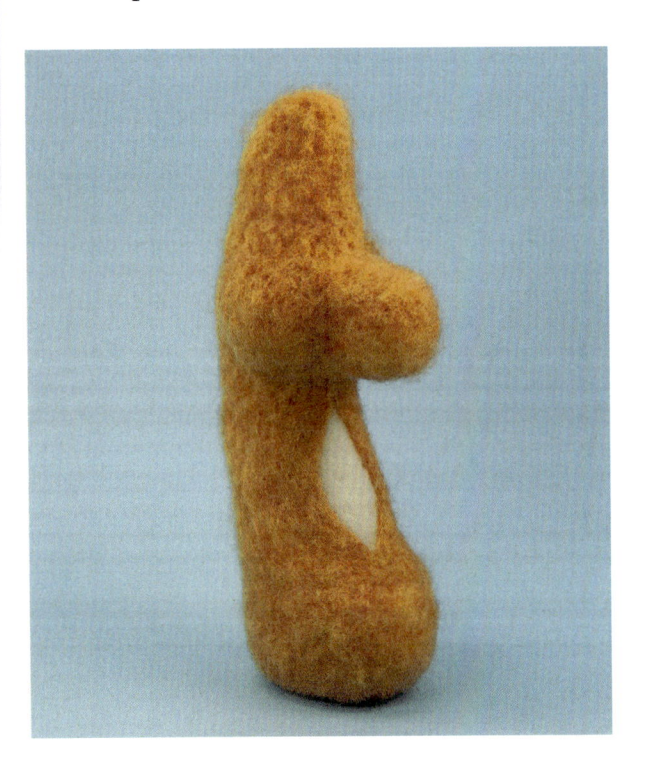

8. Choose a gray or light brown wool for the nose and mouth. Felt an edge on the foam work surface (*page 25*). Wrap the wool around the end of the snout so it is about 1" long and felt it to the snout. If you feel that the snout is too short, add wool to the end before covering it with gray wool.

9. Felt an edge on the foam work surface that is 2" long for the line of the mouth. Felt two edges that are each 1" long for the nostrils. Felt the 2" edge below the center of the snout to create the line of the mouth. Felt the 1" edge on the side of the snout to create the nostrils. The edge of the nostril is completely felted on the foam work surface before attaching it to the puppet. This allows you to let the edge stick out and form the nostril. Put a bit of dark brown wool inside the nostril and in the line of the lip.

10. Use the ear template to shape two ears. Refer to *pages 18-20* for details on making ears with or without a felt fabric base. I prefer to cut the ears from felt fabric because they will felt quickly and it is easy to make a matched set the same size. If you poke in the center of the ear repeatedly with a tool that holds multiple needles, the ear will indent and the edges will curve up quickly.

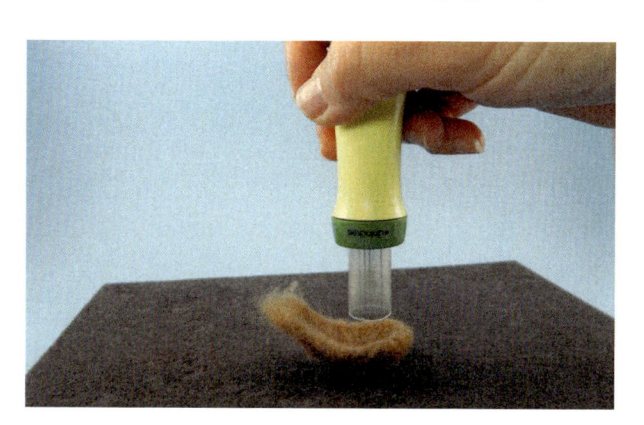

11. Eyes can be made directly on the sculpture or made completely on the foam work surface and then attached to the sculpture. I have shown it both ways on the projects in this book. I chose to make these eyes completely before attaching them so I could hide the knots on the thread of the eyelashes behind the eye. Use white wool to make an egg shape that is 1" long and 1/2" wide for each eye. Use brown wool to make two eyelids that have a 1 1/4" edge.

Wrap the eyelid around half of the eye and felt. Use dark brown wool to make a round iris below each eyelid. Use a sewing needle with black thread to attach a 4mm or 5mm bead to the center of each iris. Insert the needle on the back of the eye and come out on the brown iris. Push the needle through the eye and tie the thread on the back of the eye.

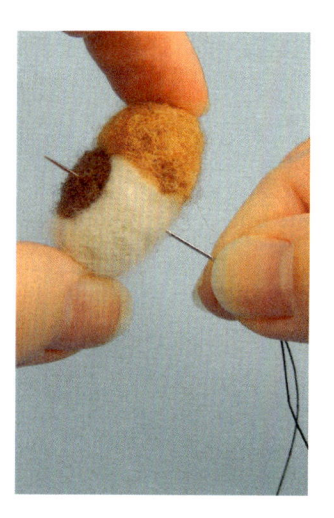

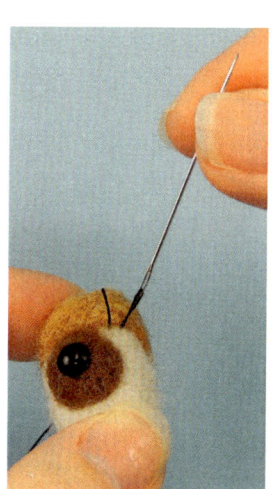

12. Use a heavy weight black thread to make the eyelashes. Thread a sewing needle with black thread and knot the end of the thread. Insert the needle in the back of the eye and come out on the front of the eye at the edge of the eyelid. Pull the thread until the knot catches at the back of the eye and cut the thread. Cut the thread longer than needed. Wait until all the eyelashes are in place and then trim them. Add as many eyelashes as you like. Keep all the thread knots in the same area on the center of the back of the eye. When you attach the eye to the head you should avoid poking the felting needle through the area where the knots are located.

13. Attach the ears and eyes to the head. Poke around the outer edge of the entire eye to make sure it is completely attached. Pinch together the lower part of the ear where it attaches to the head and poke.

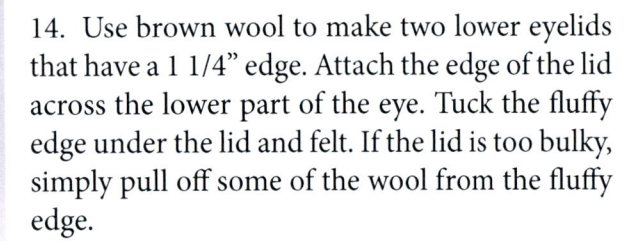

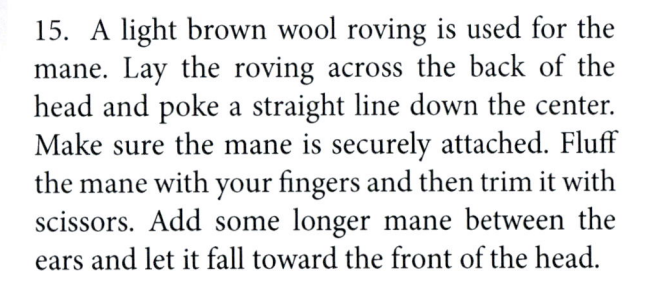

14. Use brown wool to make two lower eyelids that have a 1 1/4" edge. Attach the edge of the lid across the lower part of the eye. Tuck the fluffy edge under the lid and felt. If the lid is too bulky, simply pull off some of the wool from the fluffy edge.

15. A light brown wool roving is used for the mane. Lay the roving across the back of the head and poke a straight line down the center. Make sure the mane is securely attached. Fluff the mane with your fingers and then trim it with scissors. Add some longer mane between the ears and let it fall toward the front of the head.

16. The puppet should be firmly felted at this point. Use a fine felting needle to poke the surface of the wool and get rid of any fibers that may be sticking out. Dip the end of a toothpick into white paint and put a very small white dot on each black bead on the eyes.

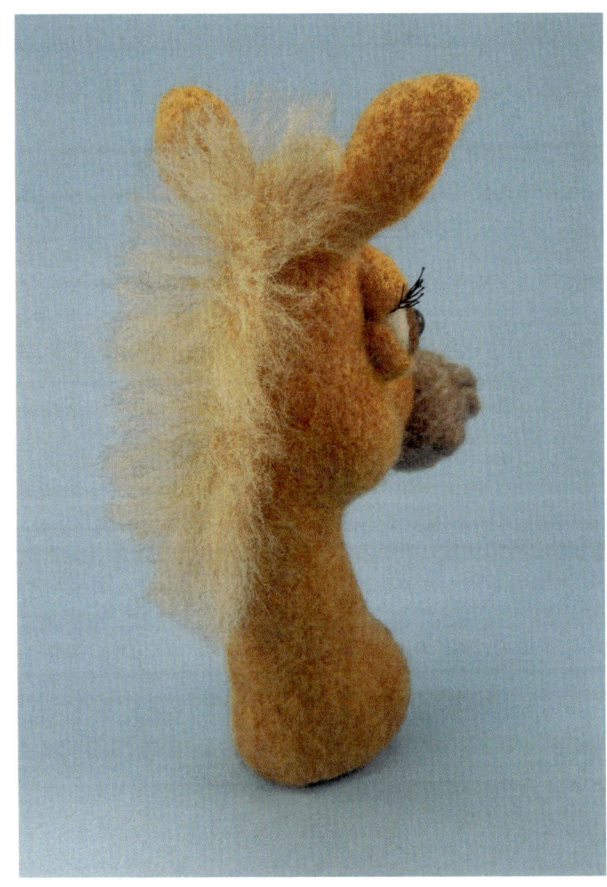

MAKING THE *Zebra* finger puppet

The zebra is made as part of a set with the **lion** (*page 98*) and the **elephant** (*page 102*). The lion, elephant, and zebra all have the same plump body. They also have the same big, round eyes and eyelids.

The horse puppet does not have a body but you could easily give him one like the zebra. The zebra puppet is more round and plump than the horse but the features of the face are the same. The zebra is made of core wool and then covered with white wool. His stripes, nose, tip of the ears, and eyelids are all made of black wool.

The zebra's mane is made from straight black and white roving. Lay the roving across the back of the head in a stripe pattern and poke a straight line down the center. Make sure the mane is securely attached. Fluff the mane with your fingers and then trim it with scissors.

Poke a straight line (shown in red) down the center of the back of the head to attach the roving.

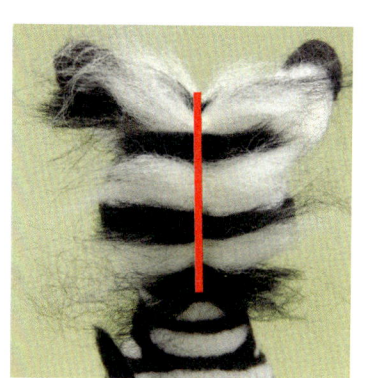

111

Farm Animal Finger Puppets

I made additional puppets to complete my set of farm animals. All of the puppets begin with the same base shape. With the exception of the rooster and hen, I made all of their eyes in a similar shape. Some of the eyes I made completely on my foam work surface and then attached them to the puppet. Other eyes where made on the puppet. You can make the black pupil of the eye from wool. I chose to sew on tiny buttons or beads because I liked the way they shine when the light hits them.

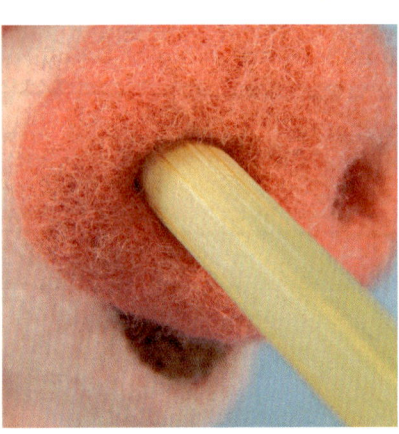

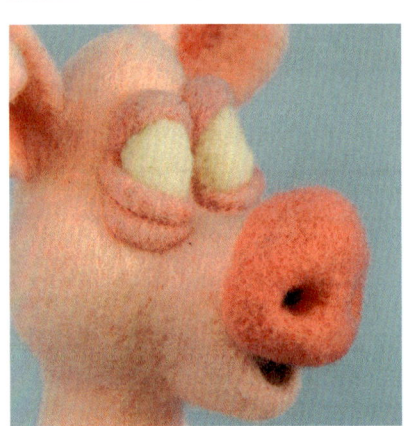

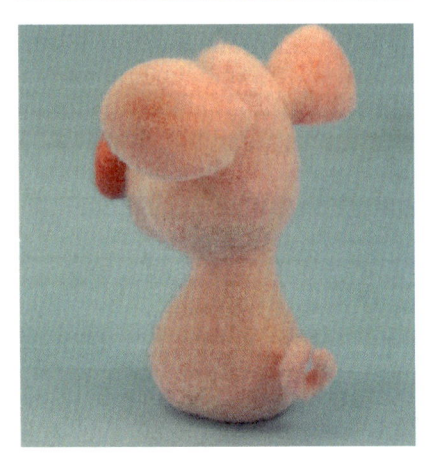

Pig Finger Puppet

I used three shades of pink wool for the pig. Light pink for the body, medium pink for the eyelids, and dark pink for the nose. I put dark brown inside the nostrils and the mouth. A sharpened dowel was used to make holes for the nose. After attaching the nose to the puppet, twist the blunt end of the dowel in each nostril to keep the round shape. Wrap light pink wool around a 2" length of pipe cleaner for the tail. After the pipe cleaner is covered in wool, wrap it around a dowel to curl it.

Sheep Finger Puppet

To add color I decided to make a black faced sheep, but you could also choose to make the face white. I used a dark charcoal color for the face so the black nose would stand out. The rich black used for the nose is also poked in the groove created by the lips. The sheep has upper and lower eyelids like the horse but they are made on the sheep's face instead of the foam work surface. The knotted thread from the beads (pupil) and the eyelashes are on the back of the head. The sheep's fleece will cover the knots.

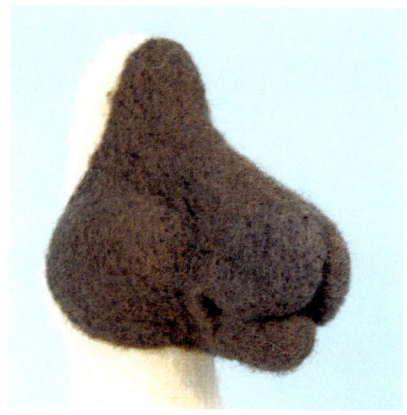

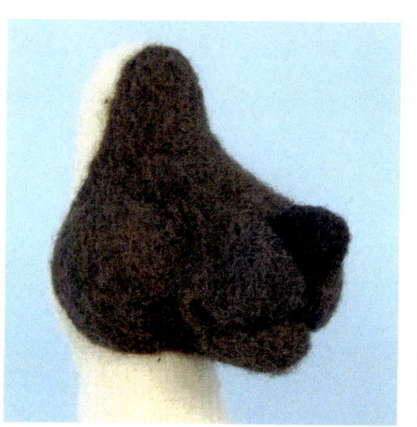

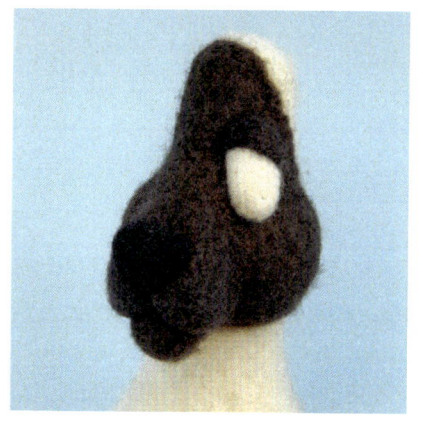

The ears are attached before the fleece. It requires a large amount of tiny balls to cover the puppet but the end result is well worth the effort. Make a batch of balls and then attach them. Making the balls in batches will give you a break from the tedious work. Don't be concerned with making each ball exactly the same size. The variation in size actually looks better. The photo on the *left* shows wool being poked as it is rolled up into a ball. A sharpened dowel is used to hold the ball and keep your fingers away from the needle. Stack up balls on the top of the head and behind the cheeks to shape the head.

113

Goat Finger Puppet

The snout of the goat is attached in a downward angle rather than straight out like some of the other puppets. The nose and mouth look very similar to that of the sheep. The horns are made by wrapping wool around a dowel or stick. I have made most of the puppets with a pleasant or happy expression on their face so I thought I would give the goat an angry look. Attaching the eyelids high on the outside and lower on the inside give an angry appearance. A beard or goatee is made from a small piece of white roving.

Cow Finger Puppet

The cow's horns are made like the goat but are a bit longer with a curve in them. The nostrils are made like the horse's except they are attached in a round shape. The eyes may be made on the foam work surface or on the puppet. If you make the eyes on the puppet, cover the thread knots from the eyelashes with the black spot on the back of the head. Finishing touches include, a tuft of white roving between his horns and a tiny bell tied around his neck with a short scrap of ribbon.

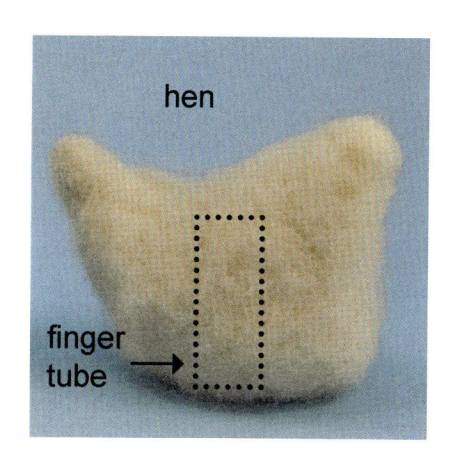

Rooster and Hen Finger Puppets

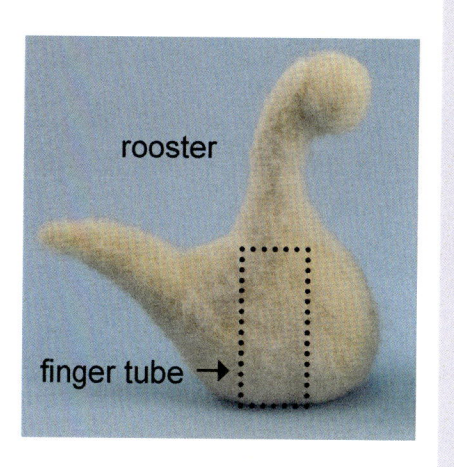

The finger puppets all begin with the same finger tube. There are times when you need to shorten the length of the finger tube or the puppet will end up being larger than you intended. The rooster and hen are a good example of this. The finger tube is reduced to 1 1/2" deep.

Core wool is used for the base shape on both of these puppets. With the exception of the detail on the head, the hen is made entirely of core wool. The rooster has a layer of green wool over the body and yellow wool over the head and neck. A simple wing shape is made on the foam work surface and then attached to the body. The beak, the red comb on the top of the head, and the red wattles dangling under the beak are also felted first and then attached to the birds. The eyes are 4 mm beads that are sewn on.

A ball is felted to the end of a rope (*refer to* **Felting Ropes** *on page 26*) to create the 16 tail feathers for the rooster. The feathers are made in four different shades of blue. The feathers at the base of the tail are 1 1/4" long and increase to 5" long at the top of the tail. Felt each feather completely and then attach to the base.

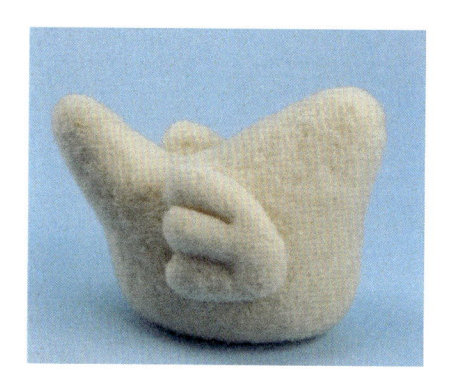

115

It is amazing to watch
a puppet come to life
in the hands of a child.

116

MAKING *People Finger Puppets*

Originally, I was focused on animals for this book. After I created the animal finger puppets I could not stop myself from creating people puppets also. Making a set of puppets to encourage a child's imagination may be all animals, all people, or a combination of the two. I enjoyed creating these tiny people and I love the way the gang looks all grouped together on a stand. They just make me smile.

I made all of the people puppets with a body. Some of the animal puppets are a head without a body and you could make people heads without bodies if you choose to. The list of characters you can create are endless, like the sheriff, pirate, and elf. Once again it is about prompting a child's storytelling by giving them a group of puppets that follow a theme or feel like they are a set. Knowing the interests of the recipients of these little works of art will help you decide what to make.

The people puppets begin by making a tube just like the animal puppets. On *pages 86-87* it explains the **7 steps to making a tube**. The height of the finger tube may be adjusted to create short and tall people.

The next step is **Making A Base For People Finger Puppets** on *page 118*. The process for building a base is always the same. It is the shape of the head and body that will change to create different characters. The head may be round, oval, or any shape in-between. The body may be slender or plump with a round belly.

The third step that is consistent among the people puppets is **Making Arms And Hands For People Finger Puppets** on *page 119*. Again, the process will remain unchanged but the size and shape may change.

After you have made a couple of puppets you will be able to build the base and implement your own ideas for characters.

I would not give these puppets to a very young child that may put them in their mouth. Adding small plastic eyes or beads for the eyes is a **choking hazard for young children**. You can omit plastic eyes and beads and use wool to felt the eyes.

Making A Base For People Finger Puppets

The base of the finger puppet begins with a tube and follows the same **7 steps** explained on *pages 86-87* for the animal puppets. I used the base template to cut a rectangle from felt fabric for all of the finger puppets in this book.

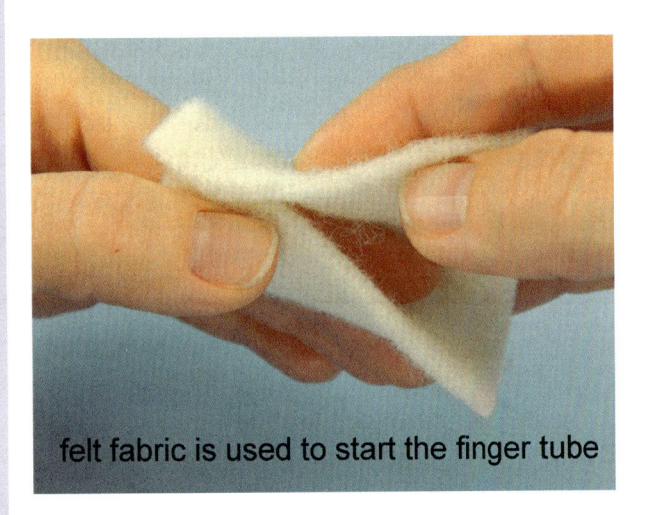

felt fabric is used to start the finger tube

One decision I had to make when I created the first puppet was how big to make the finger hole. It needs to be a *one size fits all*, but there is a large difference in the size of a child's finger compared to an adults. The template used for the finger tube will make a puppet that may be a bit snug for an adult. Wool does have a natural elasticity so you are able to push an adult finger into the tube. A large finger may not fit all the way to the end of the tube (*and it really doesn't need to*) but a child's finger will.

All of the people finger puppets begin with the same basic base. You may make changes in the shape or height, but the construction of the base will not change. The directions that follow are meant to be basic instructions and do not give measurements. Directions for individual puppets will give you measurements.

Core wool is used on the finger tube and head shape. Colored wool is felted over the core wool base.

1. Follow the directions on *pages 86-87* for making a finger tube. You can also lengthen or shorten the finger tube to change the height of your puppet, but do not change the width of the tube. The sample below shows a round head, but a long narrow head will add height to a puppet.

2. Felt a ball shape for the head using core wool. Refer to **Felting A Firm Ball** on *page 23*. The head should be felted until it is firm.

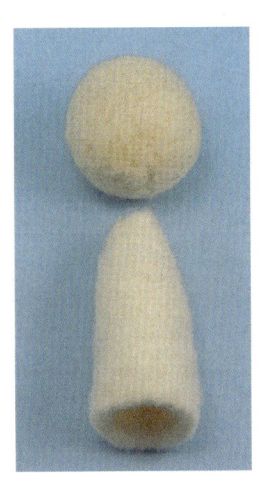

3. Make the neck using the wool you have chosen for the skin tone. Wrap the wool tightly around the top of the finger tube. Felt the neck firmly. You can also stick your felting needle inside the tube opening and poke the neck from the inside.

4. Hold the head firmly against the neck and poke to attach. Poke through the head and into the neck. Also poke inside the tube through the neck and into the head.

Tip: As you are making the puppet it is important to continually stick your finger into the tube. You want to be sure that you are not closing the hole as you felt. You can stick foam in the hole but remember to pull it in and out often so it does not become embedded in the wool.

5. Cover the head in a flesh tone wool. Add wool where the head meets the neck so the connection is smooth and seamless.

6. Build up the shoulder area on each side of the neck. The shoulders should be firm so that the arms can be attached to them later.

7. Add wool over the chest and back area and felt the upper torso and head until they are firm.

The base is now ready to be transformed into a character.

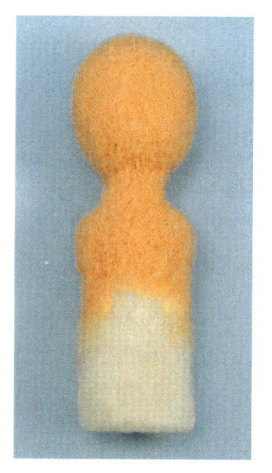

Making Arms And Hands For People Finger Puppets

The hands are the shape of mittens. Lines are poked on both sides of the hand to suggest fingers. The 10 steps that follow show hands that are wearing mittens. For the sake of clarity, the demonstration uses two wool colors. The hands are shaped like mittens so I will actually make red mittens on the hands.

1. Cut a piece of pipe cleaner in a length called out by the pattern you are following. Pull off a thin strip of flesh tone wool and wrap it tightly around the pipe cleaner until it is thick enough for the arm. Lay the arm on the foam work surface and poke slowly so you do not poke the wire in the pipe cleaner. Roll the arm quickly between the palms of your hands to facilitate the felting process.

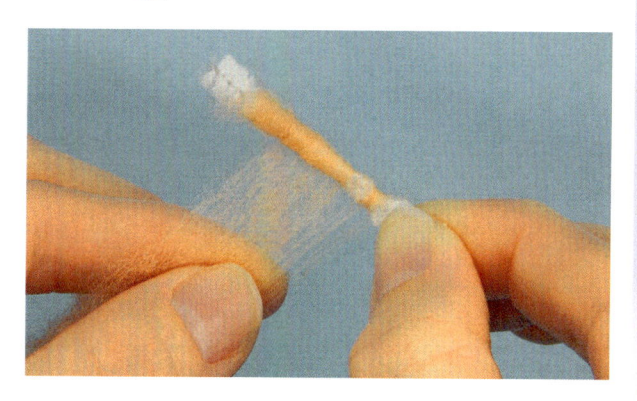

2. Lay wool on the foam work surface that is a bit larger than the hand template. Lay the template in the center of the wool. Stick straight pins through the template and into the foam.

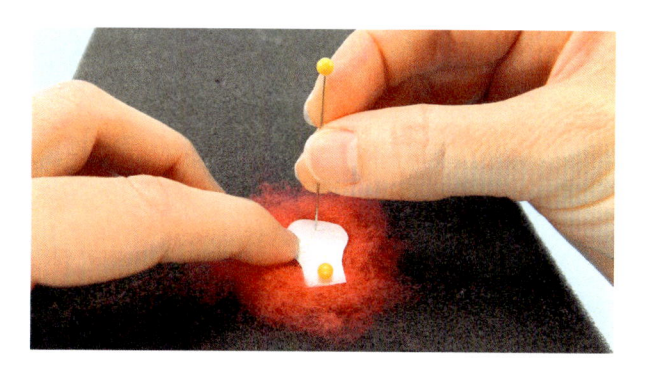

119

3. Poke into the wool around the outline of the template. Poke in a slow, controlled manner. Do not poke across the wrist area of the template.

4. Pull out the straight pins and remove the template. Lay the arm over the wrist area.

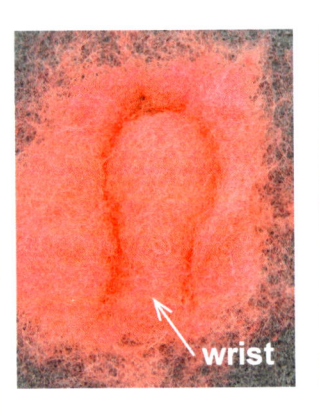

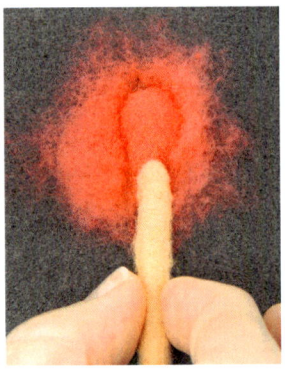

5. Gently fold over the wool along the hand outline and poke. Poke the wool to attach the arm to the hand.

6. Poke the hand so it is holding together. Try not to poke to deeply into the foam as this will make it difficult to pull the hand off the foam. You can poke at an angle so more of the needle is penetrating the wool and not the foam.

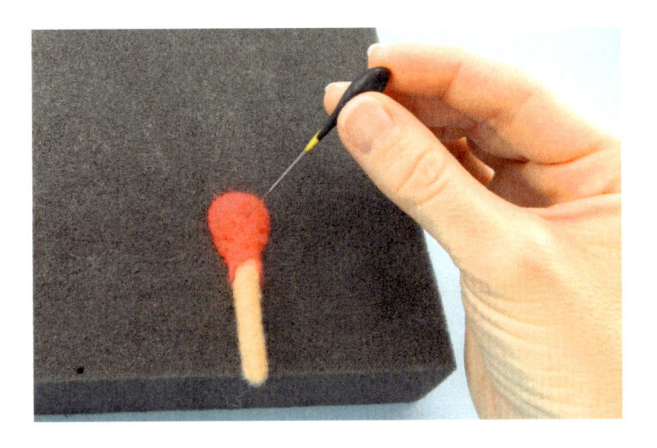

7. Pull the hand off the foam. Do this gently so you do not distort the shape of the hand.

8. Fold a piece of cardboard in half. Put the arm inside the cardboard and squeeze with your fingers to hold the arm firmly. This will allow you to keep your fingers away from the needle while you poke the edges of the mitten. Poke around all the sides of the red mitten. Reposition the arm inside the cardboard so you can reach both sides. If the flesh tone arm needs more felting you can also work on that. Remember that there is a wire inside the arm and poke carefully around it.

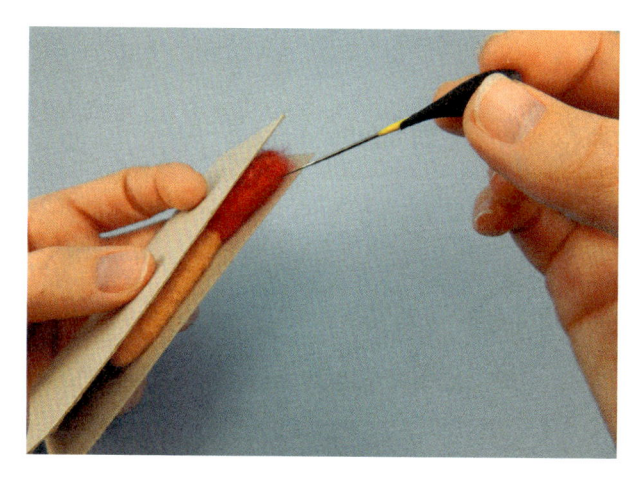

9. Make two thumbs. *Refer to **Felting Ropes** on page 26*. Hold the thumb with the folded cardboard and poke one end until it is blunt and firm. The other soft end is felted to the hand. Poke the red wool around the wrist to give the mitten a clean edge.

10. Felt the sleeve to the arm before attaching the arm to the body.

Making a flesh tone hand with fingers follows the same steps as the red mitten. Explaining the construction using the red wool allows you to comprehend and actually see the mitten shape. Now make a mitten shaped hand using flesh tone wool. Use a fine felting needle (#40 or #42) to felt the tiny hands.

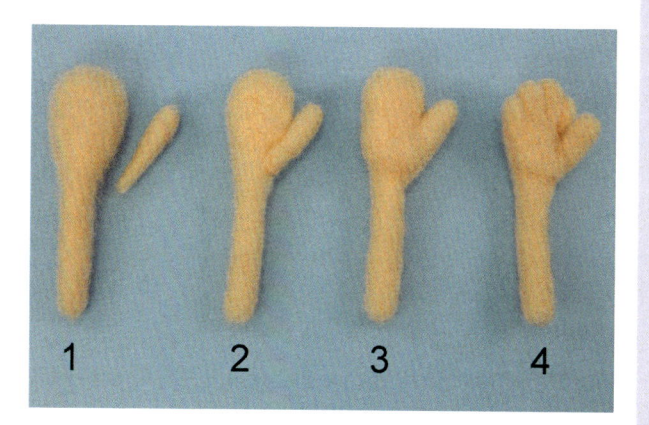

Hand 1 shows the hand attached to the arm and the thumb is felted and ready to attach.

Hand 2 shows the thumb attached to the side of the hand.

Hand 3 shows that wool has been added to the bottom of the palm where the hand connects to the arm. Remember that felting will condense the wool so you need to build up this area before shaping and felting. Add wool to any other area that needs to be built up or seams that need to be covered.

Hand 4 shows the fingers. Poke three lines for the separation of the fingers. Turn the hand over and poke the three lines on the other side of the hand. Poke the edge where the lines meet at the finger tips. This will round the tips of the fingers.

After making the red mittens I thought they were adorable. I decided to make some puppets wearing mittens (page 127). I also gave them hats, sweaters, boots, and scarves.

121

MAKING THE
Mitten Girl
finger puppet

Supplies

core wool
flesh tone wool for the head and arms
white wool for the eyes and hat trim
brown wool for the eyes and eyebrows
pink or peach wool for the cheeks
red wool for the mittens and boots
blue wool for the shirt
gray wool for the pants, scarf, and hat
light brown roving for the hair

2 1/2" x 3" piece of felt fabric for base
white thread for the scarf fringe
3" length of pipe cleaner for the arms

This little girl is 4 1/2" tall to the top of her head and 5 1/2" to the top of her hat. The size of her head is in proportion to her body. The face is 1 3/4" wide across the cheeks. The little boy shown in the photo at the top of page 127 is made identical to the mitten girl. A simple hat change tells you he is a boy.

Follow the *7 steps* for **Making A Base For People Finger Puppets** on pages 118-119. Make a ball for the head that is about 1 1/2" across. When the features are added to the face the size of the head will increase.

Once the head is attached to the finger tube the puppet is 4 1/2" tall. The finger tube is flimsy at this point. As the boots and clothing are felted to the puppet the finger tube will become firmer.

Felt some gray wool around the middle of the body for the pants. The top edge of the boots and the bottom edge of the sweater will overlap the gray pants.

Felt red wool around the bottom of the body for the boots. Make sure to cover the opening of the finger hole with red wool.

Use a #36 or #38 coarse felting needle to poke a straight line down the center on the front and the back of the body. The line starts at the base of the puppet and is 2" long. This line is the separation of the legs and boots. Each time you add wool to the pants and boots, poke the line again. The line will become more defined each time you poke over it.

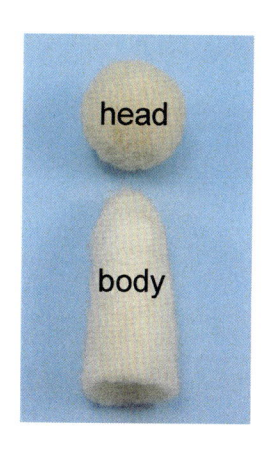

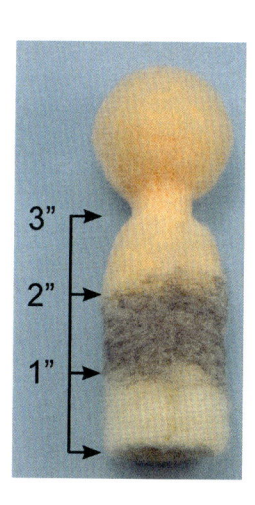

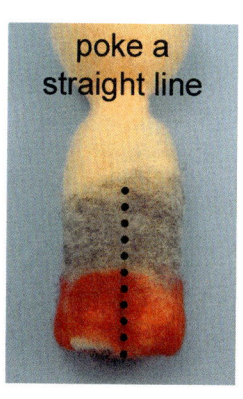

Stop frequently while you are working and stick your finger into the puppet. Twist the puppet back and forth on your finger. This will ensure that you are not distorting the finger hole.

Roll two 1/2" balls from red wool. Attach the balls to the front of the boots.

Felt an edge that is 4" long from red wool. *Refer to* **Felt An Edge On The Foam Work Surface** on *page 25*. Use this edge to make the top of the boots. Wrap the wool around the boots so the top edge overlaps the gray pants. The boots are slightly less than 1" tall. Poke the line that separates the legs and boots again.

Add red wool to the front of the boots to fill in gaps or cover seams where the 1/2" balls are attached. Felt the boots. Round the toe area of each boot. Poke on the line again until the separation of the legs and boots is well defined. Felt the gray pants also.

The puppet should stand up on its own. Poke the bottom edge of the puppet as needed to make it flat and level. The body should be firm.

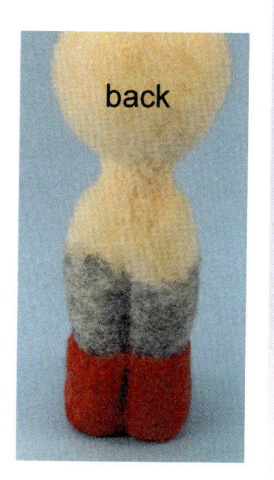

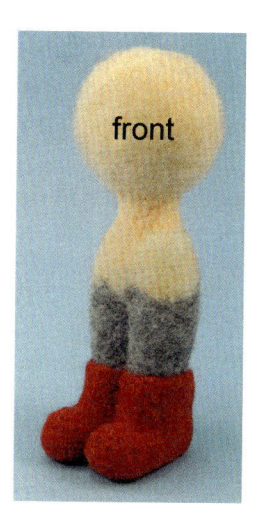

123

Add flesh tone wool to the face to give it some shape. Add a ball of wool at the chin and the cheeks. Add wool across the forehead. As you felt the face the wool will condense. If it turns out that you did not add enough wool, you can add more.

Felt a thin layer of wool over the face to smooth it out and cover any seams.

Add a tiny ball of wool over the mouth area. Make two edges on your foam work surface that are 1" long each. These are the upper and lower lips. Lay the lower lip over the mouth area and poke to hold in place. Attach the upper lip so the straight edge is touching the edge of the lower lip.

Roll a tiny ball for the nose. Do not roll up all the wool. Let the last bit of wool hang off the ball. Attach the nose with the rounded end above the lip.

The features of a child are close together compared to those of an adult. Keep this in mind as you are sculpting. The cheeks and the eyes are low. The photo (right) shows the chubby cheeks and a round chin.

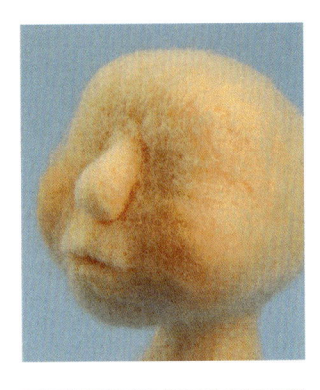

Add a small bit of wool to bring some color into the cheeks. Choose a color that works with the skin tone you are using. It may be a peach, red, or pink color.

Poke 3/8" wide circles for the eyes. Fill each eye with white wool. Poke a smaller dark brown circle on top of the white for the iris. Poke a tiny dot of white on each iris. Roll a thin strip of brown wool between the palms of your hands and use it to outline the top of the eye in the groove around the white. Poke thin eyebrows.

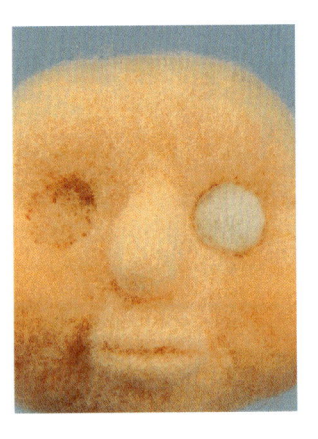

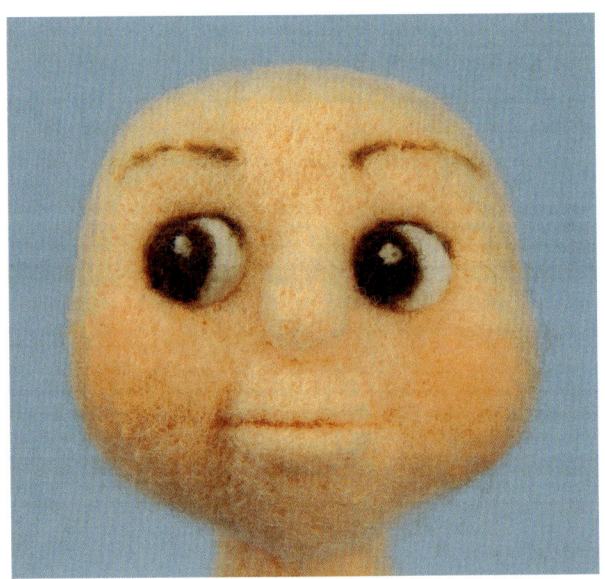

124

Cut two pipe cleaners for the arms that are 1 1/2" long. Follow the directions for **Making Arms And Hands** on *pages 119 - 121*. Felt the sweater sleeves on the arms with blue wool.

Poke through the end of the arm and into the body to attach the arm at the shoulder.

Use blue wool to felt an edge on the foam work surface that is 3" long. Wrap the edge around the puppet's neck and poke to attach. The fluff of the wool is spread out to cover the top of the sweater. The fluff will cover the end of the arm where it attaches to the body.

front

back

Make another edge that is 4" long for the bottom of the sweater. Wrap the edge around the body and poke the edge to attach. Now all the outer edges of the sweater are attached. There may be some areas in the center of the sweater that need additional blue wool. Add wool where needed and felt the sweater to the body. Add wool in the armpit area if the arms are too thin where they attach to the body.

The entire body should be firmly felted at this point. If your puppet needs more poking, do it now before moving on. A shallow poke with the felting needle at a 45 degree angle will tuck in the loose fibers at the surface. Stick your finger in the puppet to make sure the hole is open. Make sure the puppet still stands level.

felt the sweater

Use a 4" to 5" length of straight wool roving for the hair. Fold the roving in half and place the fold on top of the head where the hat will cover it. Poke the fold to attach the roving to the head. Do not trim the bangs until the hat is felted.

Make a 6" long edge on the foam work surface using the same gray wool as the pants. Wrap the wool around the head to create the edge of the hat. Bring the hat edge toward the face as if it is covering the ears.

Roll up a 2" long log from gray wool on the foam. Poke half of the log until it is firm. Leave the other half of the log fluffy.

Make a white ball that is 1/2" wide. Felt the ball to the felted end of the log.

Open the fluffy end of the log and attach it to the top of the head. Add wool as needed to shape the hat. Poke the hat until it is firm.

Gently pull the hair down the sides of the face. Trim the bangs with scissors.

The scarf is 1/2" wide and 7" long. You can cut the scarf from felt fabric and cover it with gray wool to felt it quickly. You can also felt a 7" edge on the foam work surface and make the scarf without the felt fabric.

Thread a needle with two lengths of white thread. Stick the needle through the end of the felted scarf and tie in a knot to create fringe.

Wrap the scarf around the puppet's neck and poke until it is securely attached.

Refer to **Felting Ropes** on *page 26*. Make a white rope about 7" long. Attach the rope around the edge of the hat for added detail. Make a thinner white rope 3" long. Pull the rope in half to make two pieces. Wrap the ropes around the arms at the bottom edge of the sleeves or you could attach them to the edge of the mittens.

You can follow the same directions and create a whole gang dressed for winter fun. Change the colors of the clothing, the hair, and give each one a different hat. You can also make some interesting animal hats.

The little boy has a red sweater with a large turtleneck. The loose neckline is not felted to the body.

A gray jacket is layered over the red sweater. The edge of the jacket is not attached to the sweater. The bottom and front edge of the jacket hang off the body slightly. The rest of the jacket is felted to the puppet. When the clothing hangs off the body it gives the impression that they are separate from the puppet. The edge needs to be felted completely on the foam work surface before attaching it to the puppet.

127

MAKING THE
Pirate
finger puppet

Supplies

core wool
flesh tone wool for the head and arms
white wool for the eye and shirt
brown wool for eyebrows, moustache
blue wool for the pants
dark blue wool for the belt
red wool for the head scarf
black wool for the shoes and eye patch

2 1/2" x 3" piece of felt fabric for base
one 4mm black bead for the eye
black thread to sew bead
jump ring for the earring
3" length of pipe cleaner for arms

The pirate is 4 1/2" tall.
The face is 1 1/4" wide across the cheeks.
He needs friends so make a whole gang of
pirates. Make some tall and some short.
Make some skinny and some chubby.
Refer to the *sheriff* on page 134
for ideas on how to make a pirate hat.
The shape of the hat is different but
the construction is the same.

Follow the **7 steps** for *Making A Base For People Finger Puppets* on *pages 118-119*. Make a ball for the head that is about 1 1/2" across.

Use blue wool to make an edge that is 4" long. Wrap the edge around the waistline for the top of the pants. Add more blue wool to cover the bottom of the pants. Cover the bottom of the puppet and into the finger hole.

Use a #36 or #38 coarse felting needle to poke a straight line down the center on the front and the back of the body. The line starts at the base of the puppet and is 3/4" long. This line is the separation of the legs. Each time you add wool to the pants poke the line again. Add a bit of wool to shape the stomach and buttocks.

Make two 1/2" balls from black wool. Attach them to the pants at the base for the tips of his boots.

Felt the torso, pants, and the boots. Completely felt them before moving on.

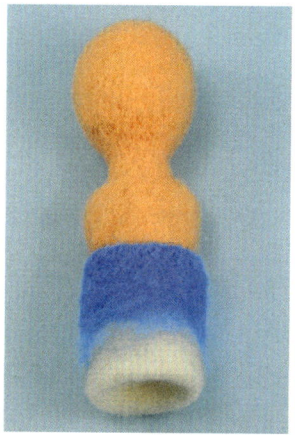

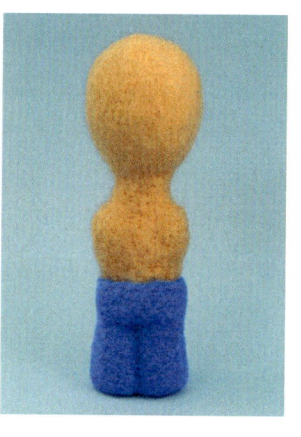

Cut two pipe cleaners for the arms that are 1 1/2" long. Follow the directions for *Making Arms And Hands* on *pages 119 - 121*. Felt the shirt sleeves on the arms with white wool.

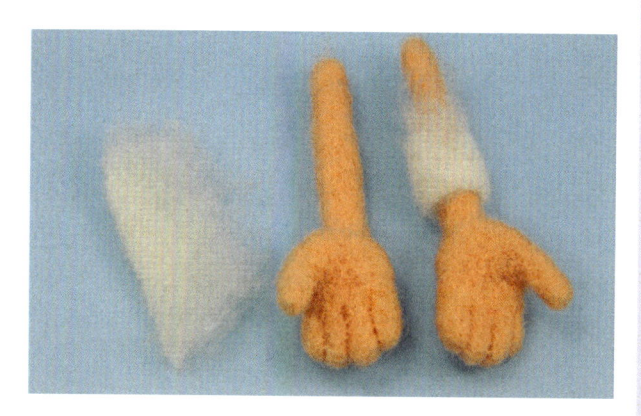

Poke through the end of the arm and into the body to attach the arm at the shoulder.

Make an edge that is 3 1/4" long from white wool for the collar. Fold the ends over to create the point of the collar and felt the entire edge. Wrap the collar around the neck. Poke the collar around the back of the head, but let the front of the collar hang loose from the body.

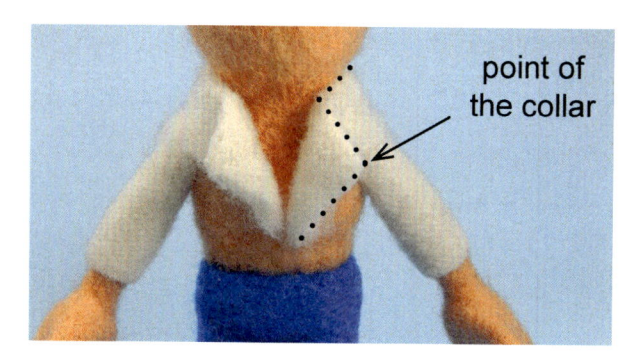

point of the collar

129

The fluff from the collar will cover the end of the arm where it attaches to the body. Cover the rest of the chest and back with white wool. Felt the shirt and let the points of the collar stick out. Use a small bit of black wool to poke an "X" under the collar.

Make a belt that is 1/4" wide. You can make the belt on the foam work surface or directly on the waist.

Roll an oval shape that is 1/4" wide and 1/2" tall for the nose. Attach the nose in the center of the face. Make two tiny balls and attach one to each side of the nose for the nostrils.

Add a ball of wool to the chin to build it up. Blend the chin into the face so there are no seams. This creates an indentation between the nose and chin for a moustache.

Poke a 3/8" circle for the eye. Put the eye close to the nose. The other eye will be covered with a patch.

Fill in the eye with white wool. Make a tiny 1/2" long edge from the skin tone wool for an eyelid.

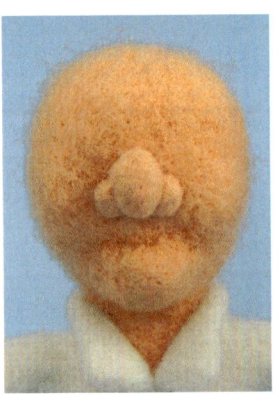

Attach the eyelid over the top of the eye. Use a thread and needle to attach a 4mm black bead to the eye. Knot the thread on the back of the head.

Make a black circle over the right eye. Roll a 3" thin strip of black wool between the palms of your hands to make a strap for the eye patch. Attach the strap over the patch.

Make two flat circles that are 1/2" wide for the ears and attach them to the sides of the head. A jump ring used for jewelry making is perfect for an earring.

Roll a thin strip of brown wool between the palms of your hands and use it to outline the eye. Use the same brown for the eyebrows and moustache. Make a log that is 1 1/2" long and 3/8" thick for the moustache. As you felt the moustache on the foam work surface bend it slightly in the center and round both ends. Attach the moustache between the nose and chin.

Use red wool to make an edge that is 5 1/2" long for the pirate's bandana.

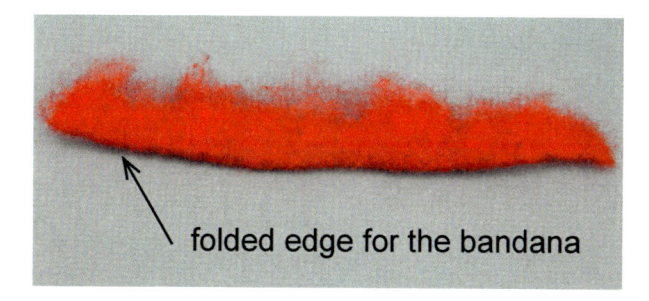

folded edge for the bandana

Wrap the red wool around the head poking the edge to attach it. Felt the bandana to the head adding more wool as necessary.

Make it appear as though the bandana is tied on the side of his head. Make a 3/8" ball for the knot. Make two strips that are about 1" long and 3/8" wide. They do not need to be exactly the same size. Attach the strips behind the ear and place the ball on top.

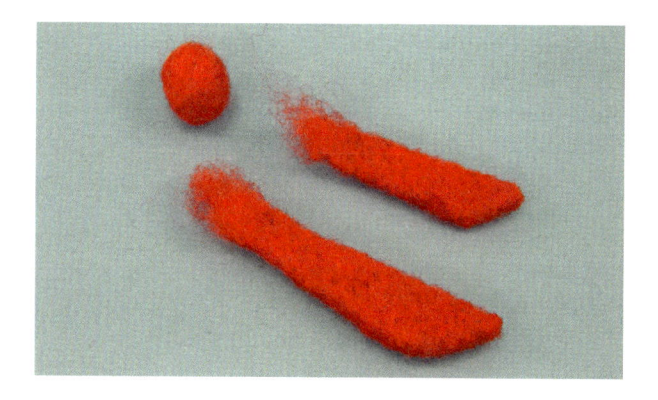

A final surface felting will clean up fibers on the puppet. Use a #40 or #42 fine felting needle. A shallow poke at a 45 degree angle will smooth the surface.

PUPPETS

MAKING THE
Sheriff finger puppet

Supplies

core wool
flesh tone wool for the head and arms
white wool for the eyes and shirt
blue wool for the pants
dark brown wool for eyebrows, moustache
medium brown wool for the hair
light brown wool for the hat tie
black wool for the hat, belt, and shoes

2 1/2" x 3" piece of felt fabric for base
two 4mm black beads for the eyes
black thread to sew beads
3" length of pipe cleaner for the arms
1/2" belt buckle
two 1/8" buttons for the shirt
sheriff's star charm

**The sheriff is 5" tall without his hat
and 6" tall with his hat.
His head and hat make up half
the height of this little guy.
The face is 1" wide across the cheeks.
I found the tiny shirt buttons, belt buckle,
and sheriff star in the scrapbooking
department of the craft store.**

Follow the **7 steps** for *Making A Base For People Finger Puppets* on *pages 118-119*. Instead of a ball shape for the head, this head is tall and thin. Make a log that is 2 1/2" long and 1" wide for the head. Round both ends of the log. The puppet base is 5" tall.

Roll an oval shape that is 1/4" wide and 1" tall for the nose. Attach the nose in the center of the face. Make two tiny balls and attach one to each side of the nose for the nostrils. Blend the top of the nose into the forehead.

Add a ball of wool to the chin to build it up. This creates an area between the nose and chin for a moustache. Blend the seam line of the chin into the face.

Poke 3/8" circles for the eyes. Put the eyes close to the nose. Fill in the eyes with white wool.

Make a 2" long log on the foam work surface for a moustache. Bend it slightly in the center and round both ends. The moustache is thinner at the ends and in the center. Completely felt the moustache and then attach it between the nose and chin. Let the ends of the moustache hang off the sides of the face.

Sew two 4 mm black beads in the center of each eye. Thread a needle with white thread. Stick the needle in the back of the head and come out in the center of the white of the eye. String the bead onto the needle. Stick the needle back in the eye and come out on the back of the head where you started. Knot the thread.

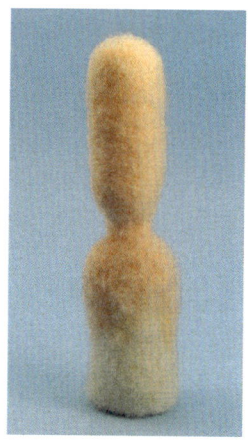

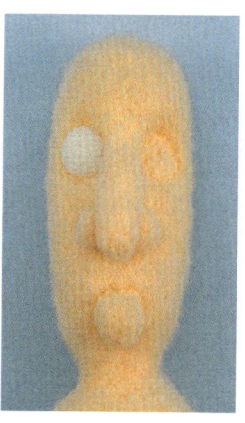

Make two 3/4" long edges from the skin tone wool for eyelids. Lay the lid over the eye so the edge is against the black bead. Felt the lid to the eye. Blend the fluffy edges into the face.

Roll a thin strip of brown wool between the palms of your hands and use it to outline the eyes. Use the same brown for the eyebrows that was used for the moustache. Make thick eyebrows that are placed against the top of the eyelids.

Make two flat circles that are 3/4" wide for the ears. The Sheriff's features are long and thin so make his ears long also. Attach the ears to the sides of the head.

Use a medium brown wool for the hair. You may also add a bit of gray. Make an edge to create the hairline. The hairline goes around each ear with a bit of wool in front of the ear. Felt the hair.

Use the **hat brim template** to cut the brim from black acrylic felt. Cover the brim with black wool. Felt the brim on the foam work surface. Bend the sides of the brim as you felt. Use the folded cardboard to hold the brim while you felt the edge. Attach the brim securely to the top of the head.

Make a 1" square cube for the top of the hat. Round the edges of the square. Attach it to the center of the hat brim.

Use gray wool to make an edge that is 4" long. Wrap the edge around the waistline for the top of the pants. Add more gray wool to cover the bottom of the pants. Cover the bottom of the puppet and into the finger hole.

Use a #36 or #38 coarse felting needle to poke a straight line down the center on the front and the back of the body. The line starts at the base of the puppet and is 3/4" long. This line is the separation of the legs.

Roll two logs 1" long from black wool for the boots. Felt a point on one end and bend the tip up as you felt. Attach the boots to the front of the pants so they are pointing off to the side.

Cut two pipe cleaners for the arms that are 1 1/2" long. Follow the directions for **Making Arms And Hands** on *pages 119 - 121*. Felt the shirt sleeves on the arms with white wool. Poke through the end of the arm and into the body to attach the arm at the shoulder.

Make an edge that is 4" long from white wool for the collar. Fold the ends over to create the point of the collar and felt the entire edge. Wrap the collar around the neck. Poke the collar around the back of the head, but let the front of the collar hang loose from the body.

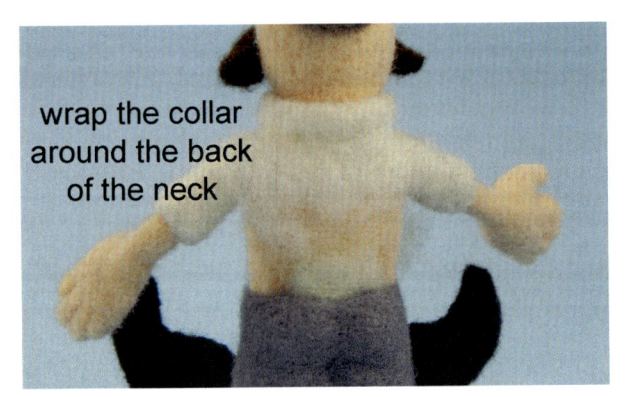

wrap the collar around the back of the neck

134

The fluff from the collar will cover the end of the arm where it attaches to the body. Sew two tiny buttons to the front edge of the shirt opening. Knot the thread on the inside of the shirt. Cover the front of the torso down to the pants with white wool. Do not blend the edge of the shirt that has the buttons attached. Leaving the edge of the shirt visible makes it appear that the shirt is separate from the body. Cover the rest of the chest and back with white wool. Add wool under the arms so they become part of the shirt without a seam. Let the white shirt meet the waistline of the pants. Felt the shirt and let the points of the collar stick out.

The entire puppet should be firmly felted. If not, spend some time poking to firm it up and define the edges.

Cut a belt from black acrylic felt that is 1/4" wide and 5" long. The sample uses a 1/2" buckle that I found in the scrapbooking section of my craft store. If you do not have a metal buckle, you can give him a buckle felted from gray wool. Wrap the belt around the waist. Poke to attach.

A thin rope of tan wool is wrapped around the top of the hat. A small star charm in the shape of a Sheriff's badge is sewn to the shirt.

I love to embellish my projects with details that help to make them special. If you do not have a star charm, work with what you have. You can felt a star to the shirt with yellow wool. Use red fabric or red acrylic felt to cut out a bandana and tie it around his neck. Make another cowboy with a white hat. Make a horse finger puppet and a cowgirl for a complete set. Create a group of characters that will allow a child's imagination to give them a story.

135

PUPPETS

MAKING THE
Forest Elf
finger puppet

Supplies

core wool
flesh tone wool for the head and arms
white wool for the eyes
blue wool for the eyes
brown wool to outline eyes and eyebrows
pink wool for the lips and cheeks
red wool for the hat and sleeves
yellow wool for the shirt
green wool for the shoes
brown curly locks for the hair

2 1/2" x 3" piece of felt fabric for base
two 4mm black beads for the eyes
black thread to sew beads
button weight brown thread for eyelashes
3" length of pipe cleaner for the arms

The elf is 2 1/2" tall at the shoulder
and 6" to the tip of her hat.
Her head and hat make up half
the height of this little elf.
The face is 1 3/4" wide across the cheeks.
The pointed shoes are felted around
the opening of the finger hole.

Follow the **7 steps** for *Making A Base For People Finger Puppets* on *pages 118-119*. Instead of a ball shape for the head, this head is more triangular. Start with a 1" ball and then add wool to the top and two sides to get the triangle shape. The puppet base is 4 1/2" tall.

Add a ball of wool to each cheek to build them up. Add a third smaller ball to the chin. Blend the edges of the cheeks and chin into the face.

Refer to *Felt An Edge On The Foam Work Surface* on *page 25*. Make two edges for the lips that are 1" long. Follow *step 4* on *page 26* to felt the edges of the lips. The edge of the lips are firm before they are attached to the face.

Felt the bottom lip to the face and then felt the upper lip to the face. Add a bit of wool to the corners of the mouth to blend the edges.

Roll a log that is 1/2" wide and 1" tall for the nose. Felt one end of the log and leave the other end fluffy. Use a sharpened dowel to make the nostril holes in the end of the nose.

Attach the nose in the center of the face. Blend the top of the nose into the forehead.

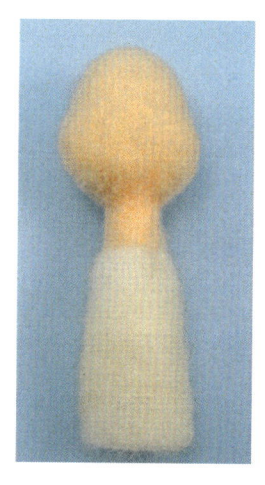

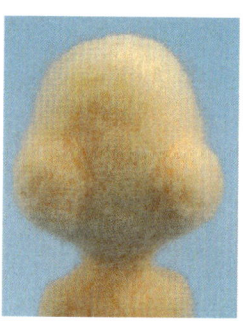

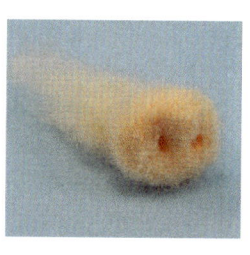

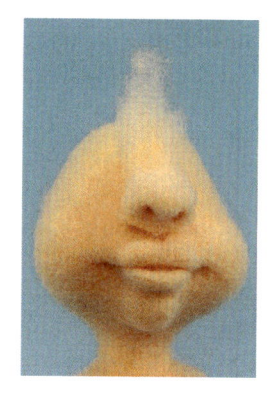

Add wool to the bridge of the nose or the nostrils if needed to shape the nose.

Poke the outline for each eye about 1/2" wide and 1/2" tall. Poke a straight line across the bottom of each eye. This will help define the cheeks.

Fill in the eyes with white wool. Felt the white of the eyes. Poke the white wool around the outline of the eye creating a groove.

Use a medium blue to felt a circle on each eye for the iris.

Thread a long sewing needle with black thread to attach a 4 mm black bead in the center of each iris for the pupil. Insert the needle at the back of the head and come out in the center of the eye. String the bead onto the thread and insert the needle back through the head. Tie a knot in the thread at the back of the head. The hat will cover the knots later.

Make two eyelids the same way you made the lips. Use the cardboard tool to felt the edges. Lay the lid over the eye so it covers the top of the iris. Poke the fluffy edge of the lid into the groove around the eye. Pull off excess fluff if needed.

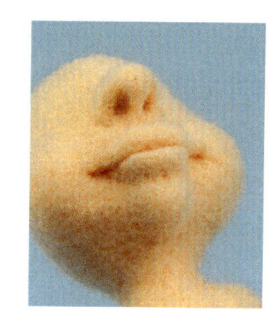

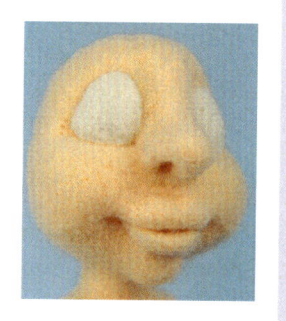

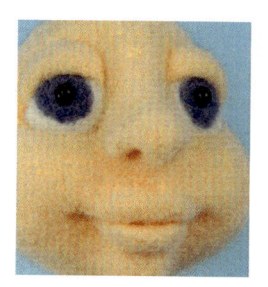

Make two pointed ears that are 1/2" wide and 1 1/2" long. Felt them on the foam work surface leaving one end fluffy for attaching. Add a small bit of dark wool inside the ear to shade it. Spread the fluff open and attach the ears to the sides of head.

Roll a thin strip of brown wool between the palms of your hands and use it to outline the eyes. Use the same brown for eyebrows.

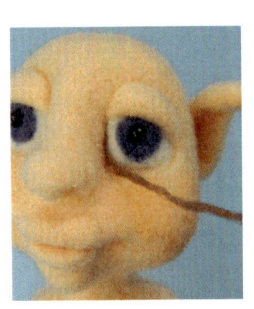

Add a small bit of pink to the lips. Do not define the edge of the pink or cover the entire lip. Just a hint of pink is all that is needed.

A dark brown button or craft weight thread is used for the eyelashes. Thread a long needle and knot the end of the thread. Insert the needle in the back of the head and come out at the edge of the eyelid. Pull the thread until the knot catches and then cut the thread. Repeat until you have 6 lashes on each eye. Dip a toothpick in white paint and put a dot on each black bead.

Use core wool to build up the shape for the hat. Felt the core wool so it is firm.

Use a red berry color wool to make an edge that is 5 1/2" long. Felt the edge on the foam work surface. Wrap the edge of the red wool around the head and overlap the ends. Poke to attach just the edge for now.

Roll a log that is 3 1/2" long from red wool for the top of the hat. Felt one end of the log into a pointed curl for the top of the hat. Build up the other end of the log so it will blend into the base of the hat. Felt the top of the hat to the base. Fill in with red wool as needed to shape the hat.

Poke a 1" line on the front and back of the base for the separation of the legs. Add a bit of wool to give the elf a round belly.

The sample puppet used the core wool for the pants. If you want them a different color you can cover them now before adding the shoes. Moss green wool is used for the elf shoes. Make the pointed shapes for the toes and the back of the shoes on the foam work surface. Also make a rounded flap for the front of the shoe at the ankle. Attach these pieces to the base of the puppet. Fill in around the shapes to join them together and felt. Repeat for the second shoe. Poke between the shoes on the front and back to define the separation.

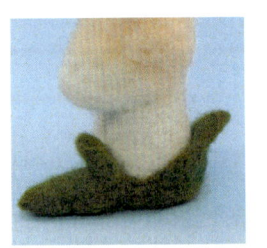

Cut two pipe cleaners for the arms that are 1 1/2" long. Follow the directions for *Making Arms And Hands* on *pages 119- 121*. Felt the sweater sleeves on the arms with yellow wool. Roll a thin strip of red wool between the palms of your hands and attach it to the edge of each sleeve.

Poke through the end of the arm and into the body to attach the arm at the shoulder.

Use yellow wool to felt an edge on the foam work surface that is 3 1/2" long. Wrap the edge around the puppet's neck and poke to attach. The fluff of the wool is spread out to cover the top of the shirt. The fluff will cover the end of the arm where it attaches to the body.

Make another edge that is 4" long for the bottom of the shirt. Wrap the edge around the body and poke to attach. Now all the outer edges of the shirt are attached. There may be some areas in the center of the shirt that need additional yellow wool. Add wool where needed and felt the shirt to the body. Add wool in the armpit area if the arms are too thin where they attach to the body.

Just a few curls are all that is needed for this little elf. Pick out some nice curls from brown curly locks. Poke the curls under the edge of the hat until they are secure.

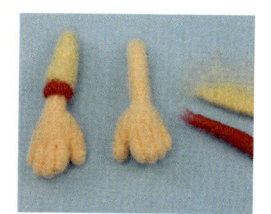

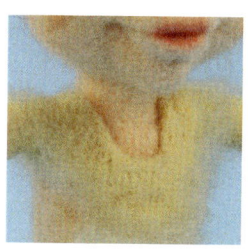

The entire body should be firmly felted at this point. If your puppet needs more poking, do it now. A shallow poke with the felting needle at a 45 degree angle will tuck in the loose fibers at the surface. Stick your finger in the puppet to make sure the hole is open. Make sure the puppet stands level.

139

Make Your Own Finger Puppets

Once you have made a few finger puppets you may notice that the directions are repetitive. The reason is because the basic foundation for each puppet is identical. Changing the shapes and measurements allow you to change the look of each character. The eyes may be round or oval, large or small, but the construction will always be the same. Once you have dressed a few puppets you begin to understand that it is always about the edges. This will make it easy to design your own outfits.

Once you put your tiny works of art into the hands of children, you want to ensure that they will be able to withstand the constant handling. Curly locks and roving are great to use for hairstyles but I like to use them sparingly. A hairstyle that is completely felted will be more durable. The photos (*below*) show felted pigtails. Poking lines create parts in the hair that help add detail. The little girl in the pink dress (*left*) has braids that are felted. Three logs are felted and then braided. The braids are then attached to the head. Ribbon adds the finishing detail to the hairstyle.

Make A Stand For Displaying Finger Puppets

Making a stand to hold the finger puppets will not only give you a place to keep them but it will also be an attractive decoration in a child's room. You can make a stand for a few puppets or one big enough for a large group. The stand is also a nice way to present the puppets if you are giving them as a gift.

If you have minimal woodworking skills you can easily make puppet stands. First you need a piece of wood for the base. It can be a scrap piece of 2" x 2" or 2" x 4" or you can purchase a plaque from the craft store. The plaques come in varying shapes and sizes. Next you will need dowels that will fit into the finger hole of the puppet. A 3/8" or 1/2" dowel is a good size. You will also need sandpaper, a ruler, white craft glue, and acrylic paint. The tools needed are a drill with a bit the size of the dowels and a small hand saw to cut the dowels.

Choose a base large enough to accommodate the number of puppets in the set. Stand two puppets next to each other and measure the distance from the center of each puppet. This measurement will be the distance between the dowels. Use a pencil to mark the placement of the dowels on the wood base. Use a drill bit the same size as the dowels and drill a hole on each mark of the base. Do not drill all the way through the base. A small hand saw will easily cut the dowels. Glue the dowels into the holes. Use a damp cloth to wipe away any excess glue. Let the glue dry completely. Use sandpaper to smooth any rough edges. Paint the base with acrylic paint. A neutral color paint will work best for all your puppets. A white or beige color paint will usually require two coats to cover the raw wood. Let the paint dry completely before putting the puppets on the base.

The stand (*above*) uses a scrap of 2" x 2" wood for the base that is 10 1/2" in length. It is the perfect stand for a set of three puppets.

The stand (*above*) uses an 11" oval plaque. Seven dowels will hold a nice assortment of puppets. The dowels are taller at the back of the stand so you can easily see each puppet in the group.

Puppet Theatre

Originally, I did not have plans to build a puppet theatre. After I started making finger puppets I felt I needed a stage. How can you give the kids puppets without a stage? I knew I couldn't show a photo of the puppet theatre without giving an explanation of how I made it. If you have woodworking skills you could build your own stage from wood. If you are not up to building a wooden theatre, search online and you will find examples of theatres made from cardboard boxes. It is a fun project that you could do with your children.

As a woodworker I have a bin of wood scraps from previous projects. The design and size of my puppet theatre was determined by the wood I had available in my bin. I will explain how I built it, but you can design a theatre with supplies that you have on hand.

I began by making a frame. I used 1/2" thick by 3" wide wood for three sides of the frame and a 1/2" thick by 4" wide wood for the bottom. My thoughts were to try and build the base of the stage as stable as possible so it would not fall over during play. I glued and nailed the frame. Once done I found that the base was not substantial enough to keep the frame from tipping over easily. Using a wider board on the bottom of the frame helped but I still did not feel that it was stable enough. I added feet on each side of the frame that were 11" long. The feet make it difficult to tip the structure over. The frame is 24" wide by 25" tall. Once the frame was done I added a 6" x 24" board across the bottom of the frame. I topped it with a 3" wide board (painted dark blue) to create the stage. I cut notches in the ends of the stage to wrap around the frame.

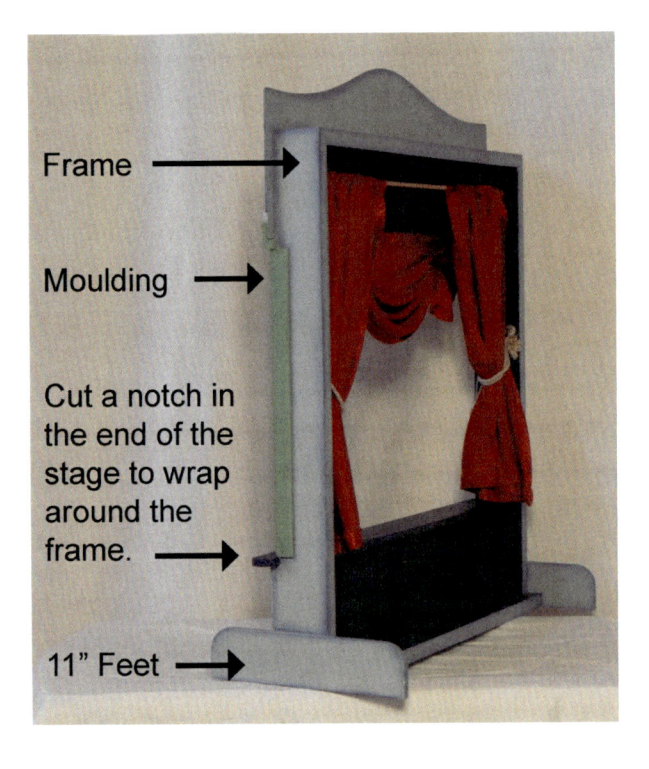

I added a 1/4" thick board across the top of the frame. It was left over from another project and already cut in this shape. The green wood around the stage opening were scraps of moulding. The rope detail that I painted silver were other scraps of wood that were in my bin.

As I stated earlier, I made the theatre from wood that I already had on hand. The size of the wood I had is what determined the size of the theatre. You could make it any size you like.

I think that the paint and embellishments are what really bring this whole project together. I checked for edges that might need to be sanded and then I painted the entire theatre with a base coat of white acrylic paint. I am sure I spent more time deciding what color to paint everything than I did actually painting. I shaded the edges of the wood using a dry brush technique with a darker color of paint.

I purchased wood cutouts from the craft store. The stars, circle for the puppet theatre sign, and the show time clock are all cutouts. They were painted first and then glued to the theatre. If you are not confident painting the lettering on the sign you can trace it. Design the sign on your computer, print it out, and then trace it on the cutout.

The tiny silver stars and the clock face came from my scrapbooking supplies. The hands on the clock were painted blue so they stand out and are movable. The silver swirls on each side of the clock are actually paper clips. All of these elements were simply glued in place. After the glue dried I used a spray polyurethane to seal the entire theatre.

The final detail was adding curtains. I chose a red velour because it resembles velvet. The short valance is a rectangle of fabric that is gathered at each end. The top edge of the valance was glued to the wood. The side curtains were hung from a dowel. I did not realize how easily the curtains would glue to the stage. If I had, I would have also glued the side curtains to the wood. The side curtains were tied up with silver tassels. I had the best time building this project. If I knew it was going to turn out so well, I would have taken more photos of the building process.

143

Templates

You will find **full size templates** on pages 145 to 154. All of the finger puppet templates are on page 154. The remaining pages contain the templates for the masks. Each template states the name of the project and references a page number. After you copy the templates and cut them out, you will be able to match the template to the project using the page number.

Once you have made some of the projects in this book, you may want to create your own masks or puppets. As you are making an animal, think about other animals that have a similar shape. The giraffe mask could easily be changed into a horse, zebra, or cow. The cat mask can also be a cougar, tiger, or leopard. Change the ears on the cat mask and make a fox, bear, panda, or skunk.

The lion mask (*shown below*) is a smaller mask than the ***King Of The Jungle Lion*** (*on page 58*). It is the perfect size for a child. You can follow the directions for the large lion and scale down the size of the features to fit this smaller mask. There are ear and nose templates for this lion on *page 150*. It uses the mask on *page 145* as a base. The eye openings are cut like the cat eyes on the mask on *page 146*. You can change the shape of the eye openings on all of the mask templates to fit any animal you are making. The lion's mane is made from **dreadlocks** that were found at Dream Felt (*see **Resources** page 155*). You could substitute any yarn for the mane. Make similar size loops and felt each loop to the mask. The yarn is attached in one long length.

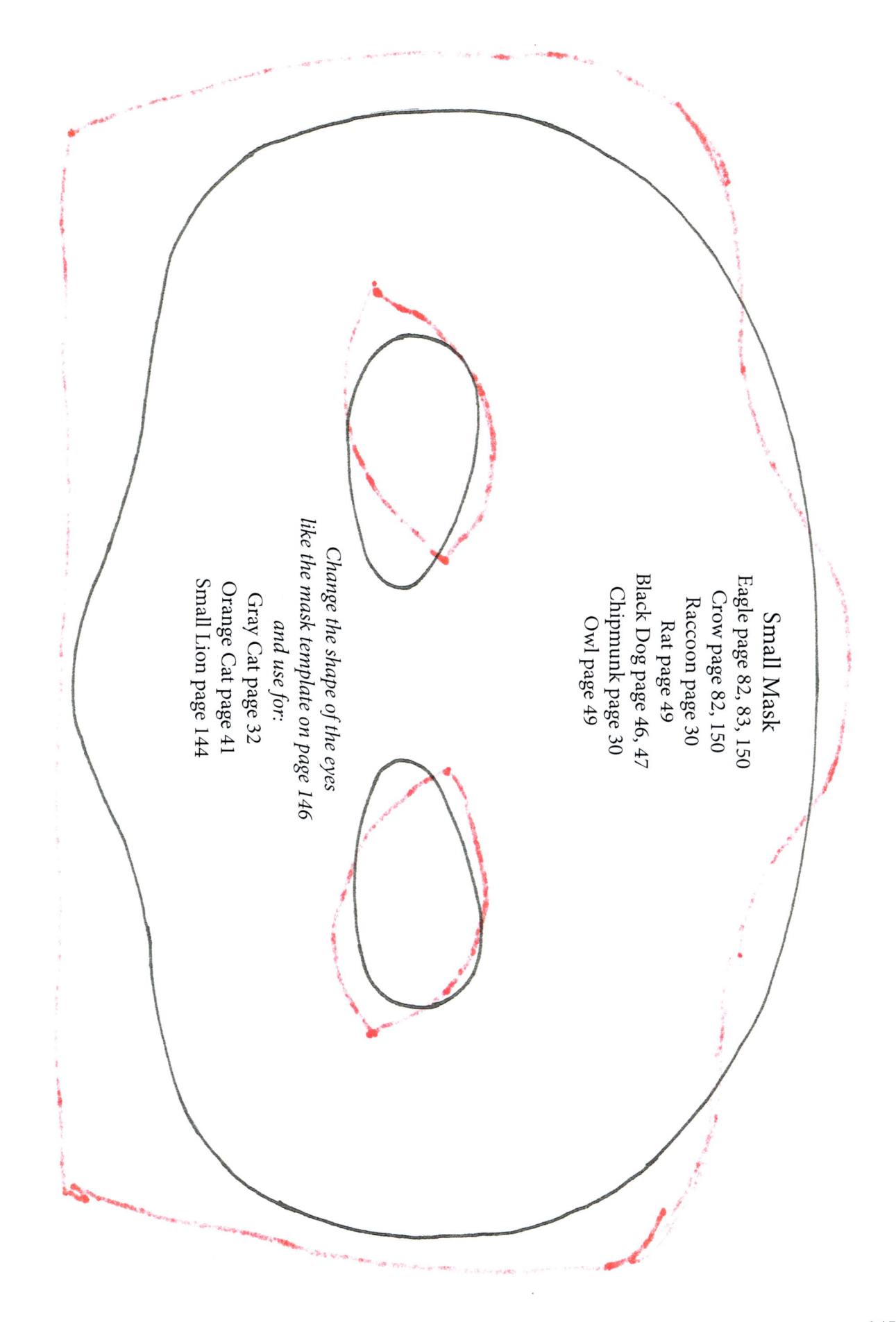

Small Mask
Eagle page 82, 83, 150
Crow page 82, 150
Raccoon page 30
Rat page 49
Black Dog page 46, 47
Chipmunk page 30
Owl page 49

Change the shape of the eyes like the mask template on page 146 and use for:
Gray Cat page 32
Orange Cat page 41
Small Lion page 144

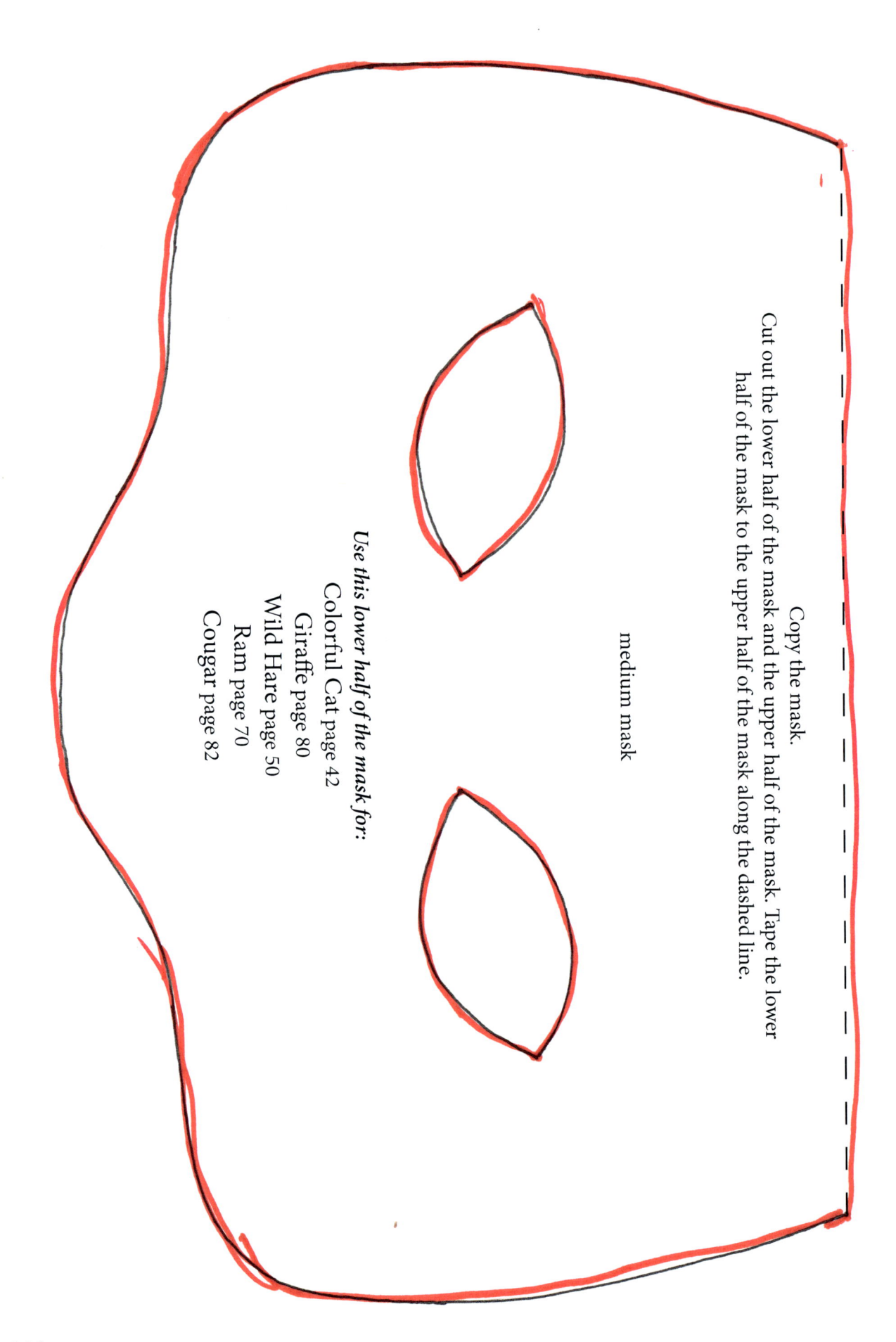

Copy the mask. Cut out the lower half of the mask and the upper half of the mask. Tape the lower half of the mask to the upper half of the mask along the dashed line.

medium mask

Use this lower half of the mask for:
Colorful Cat page 42
Giraffe page 80
Wild Hare page 50
Ram page 70
Cougar page 82

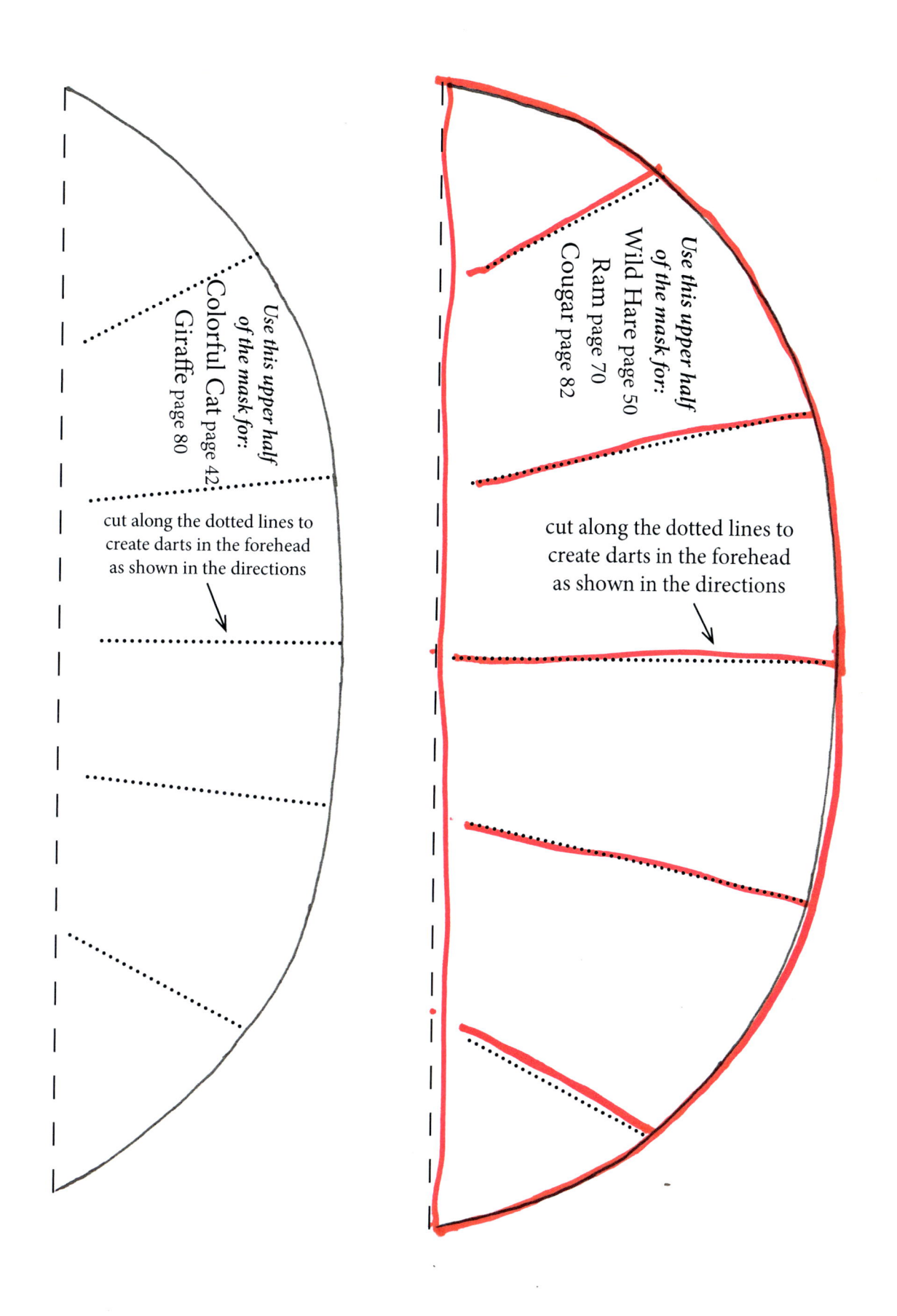

Use this upper half of the mask for:
Colorful Cat page 42
Giraffe page 80

cut along the dotted lines to create darts in the forehead as shown in the directions

Use this upper half of the mask for:
Wild Hare page 50
Ram page 70
Cougar page 82

cut along the dotted lines to create darts in the forehead as shown in the directions

147

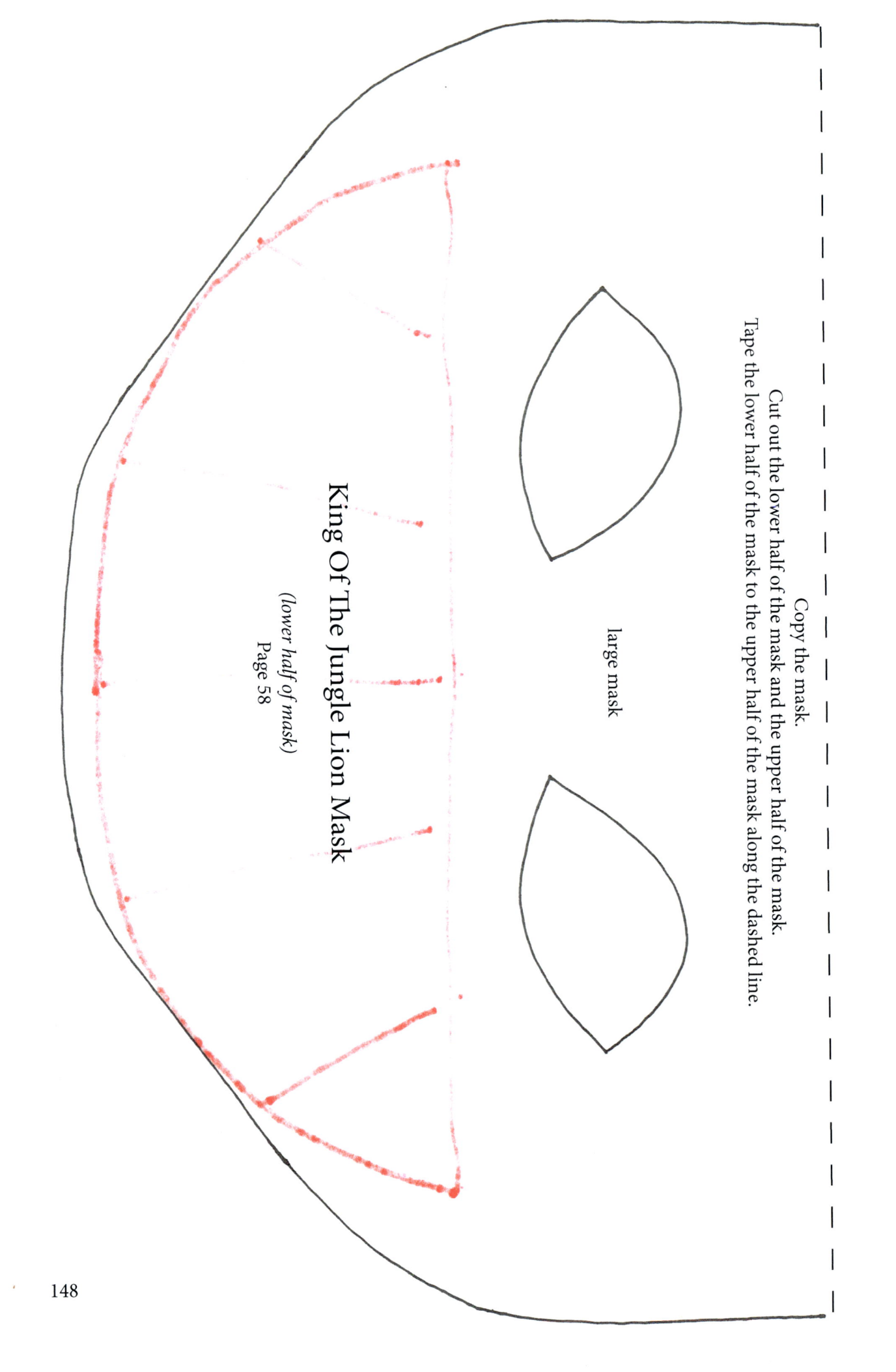

King Of The Jungle Lion Mask

(lower half of mask)
Page 58

large mask

Copy the mask.
Cut out the lower half of the mask and the upper half of the mask.
Tape the lower half of the mask to the upper half of the mask along the dashed line.

148

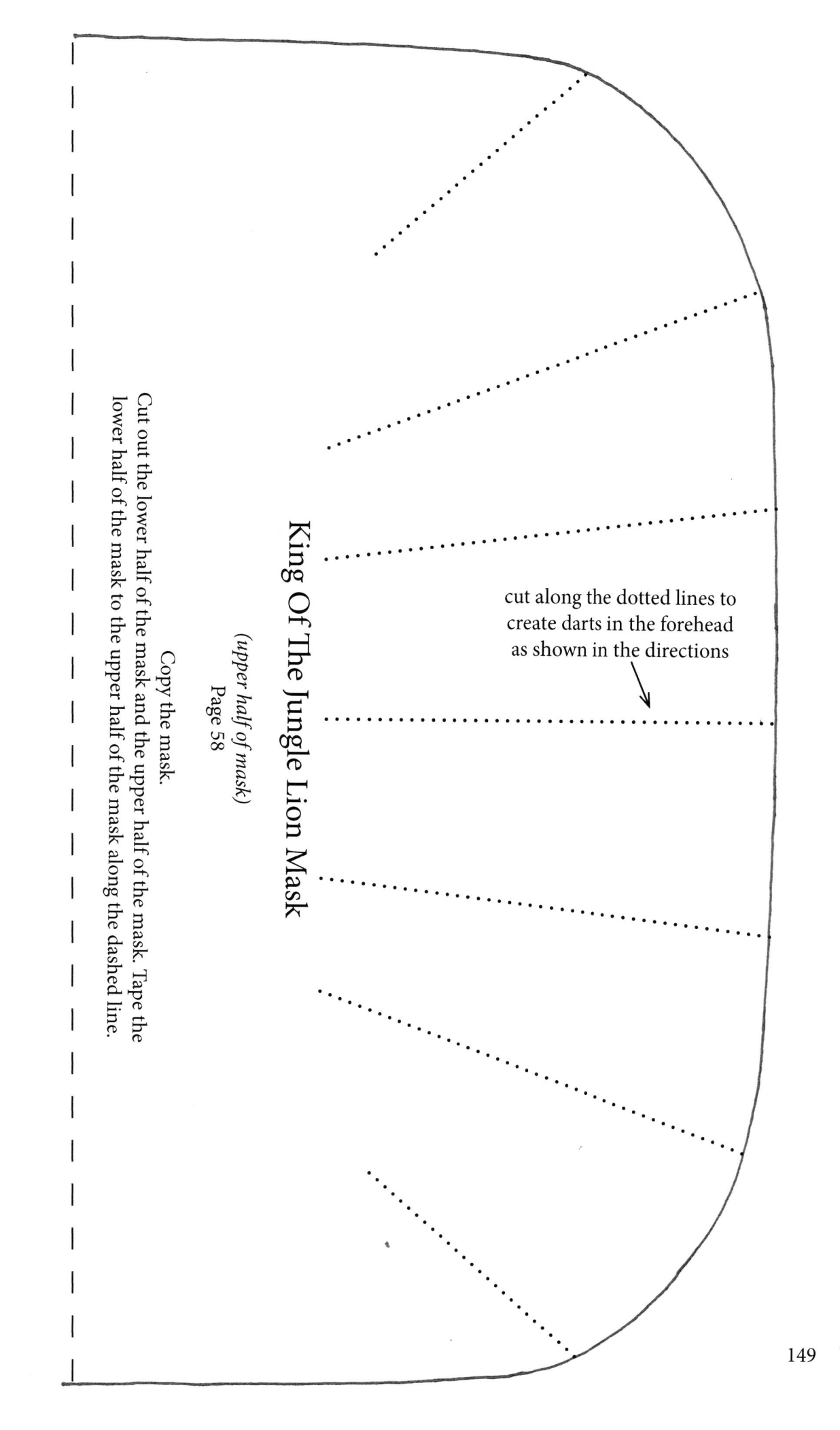

King Of The Jungle Lion Mask

(upper half of mask)
Page 58

cut along the dotted lines to create darts in the forehead as shown in the directions

Copy the mask.
Cut out the lower half of the mask and the upper half of the mask. Tape the lower half of the mask to the upper half of the mask along the dashed line.

Chipmunk's Ear
Page 30

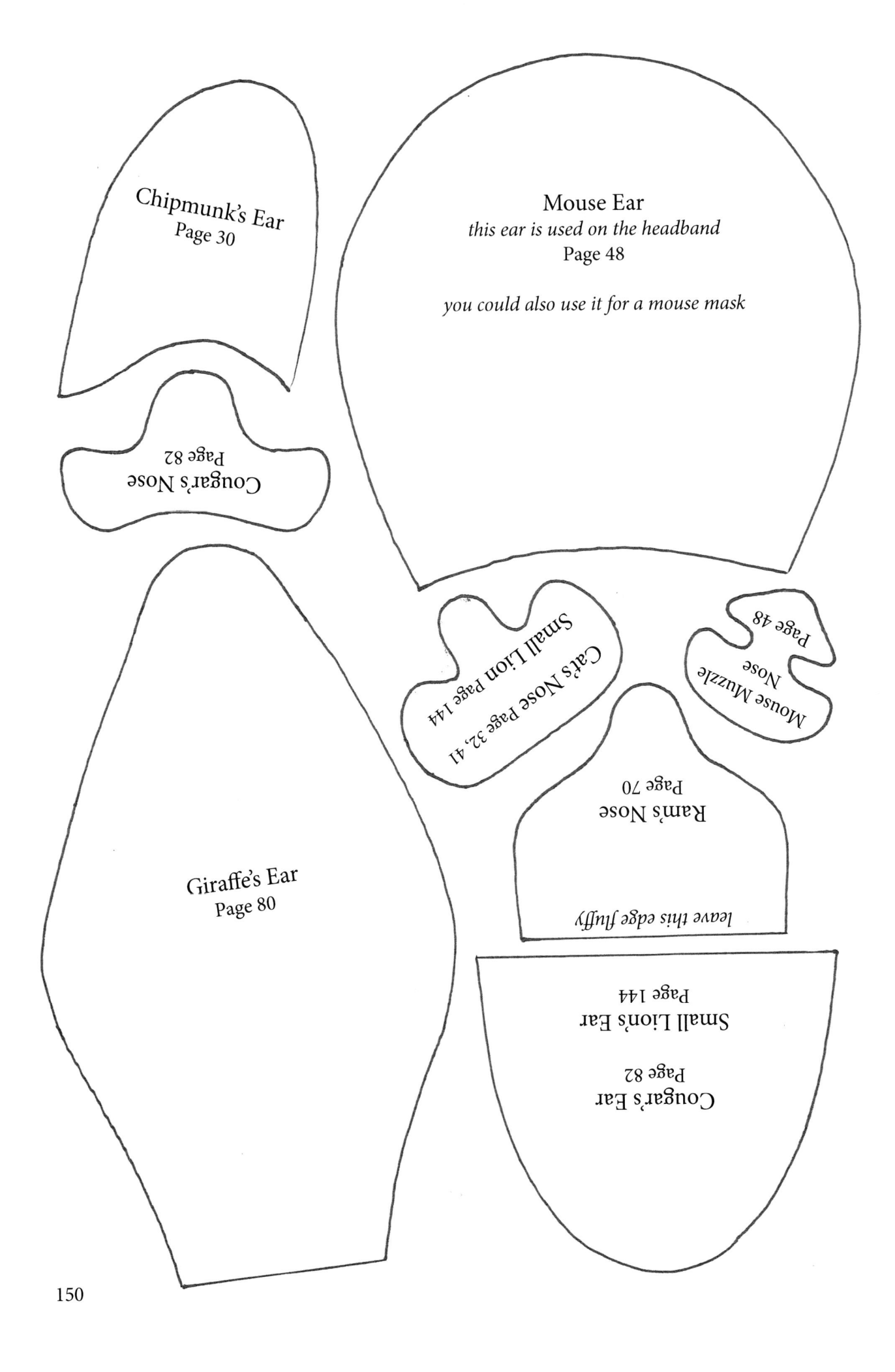

Mouse Ear
this ear is used on the headband
Page 48

you could also use it for a mouse mask

Cougar's Nose
Page 82

Small Lion
Cat's Nose Page 32, 41
Page 144

Mouse Muzzle Nose
Page 48

Ram's Nose
Page 70

leave this edge fluffy

Giraffe's Ear
Page 80

Small Lion's Ear
Page 144

Cougar's Ear
Page 82

150

Rat's Ear
Page 49

Colorful Cat's Ear
Page 42

Teeth
may be used for
rabbit, mouse, or
chipmunk
Page 48

King Of The Jungle
Lion's Nose
Page 58

Cat's Ear
Page 32, 41

King Of The Jungle
Lion's Ear
Page 58

Colorful Cat's Nose
Page 42

Rat's Nose
Page 49

151

Ram's Ear
Page 70

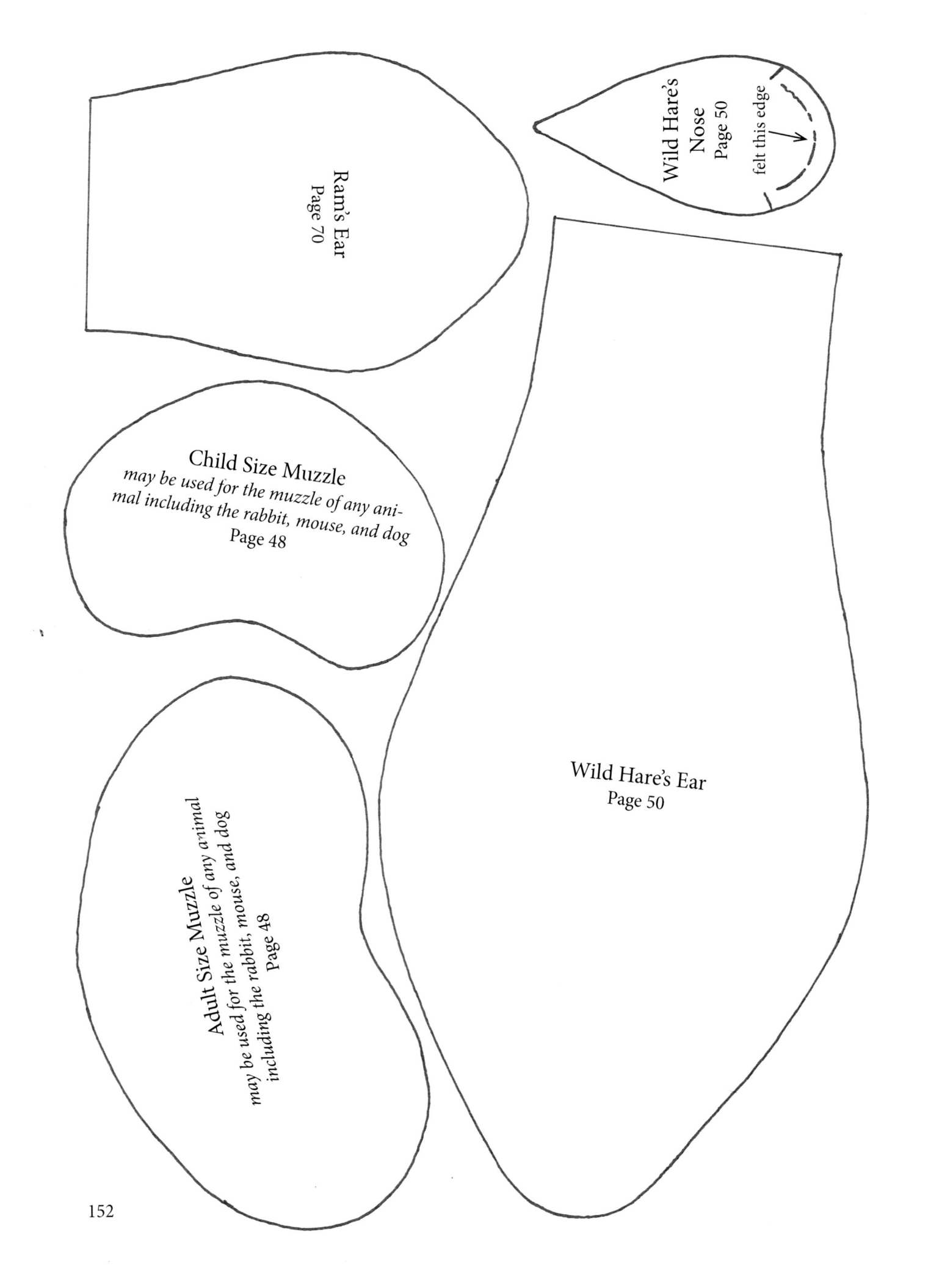

Wild Hare's Nose
Page 50
felt this edge

Child Size Muzzle
may be used for the muzzle of any animal including the rabbit, mouse, and dog
Page 48

Adult Size Muzzle
may be used for the muzzle of any animal including the rabbit, mouse, and dog
Page 48

Wild Hare's Ear
Page 50

152

The Eagle's Beak
page 82, 83, 150

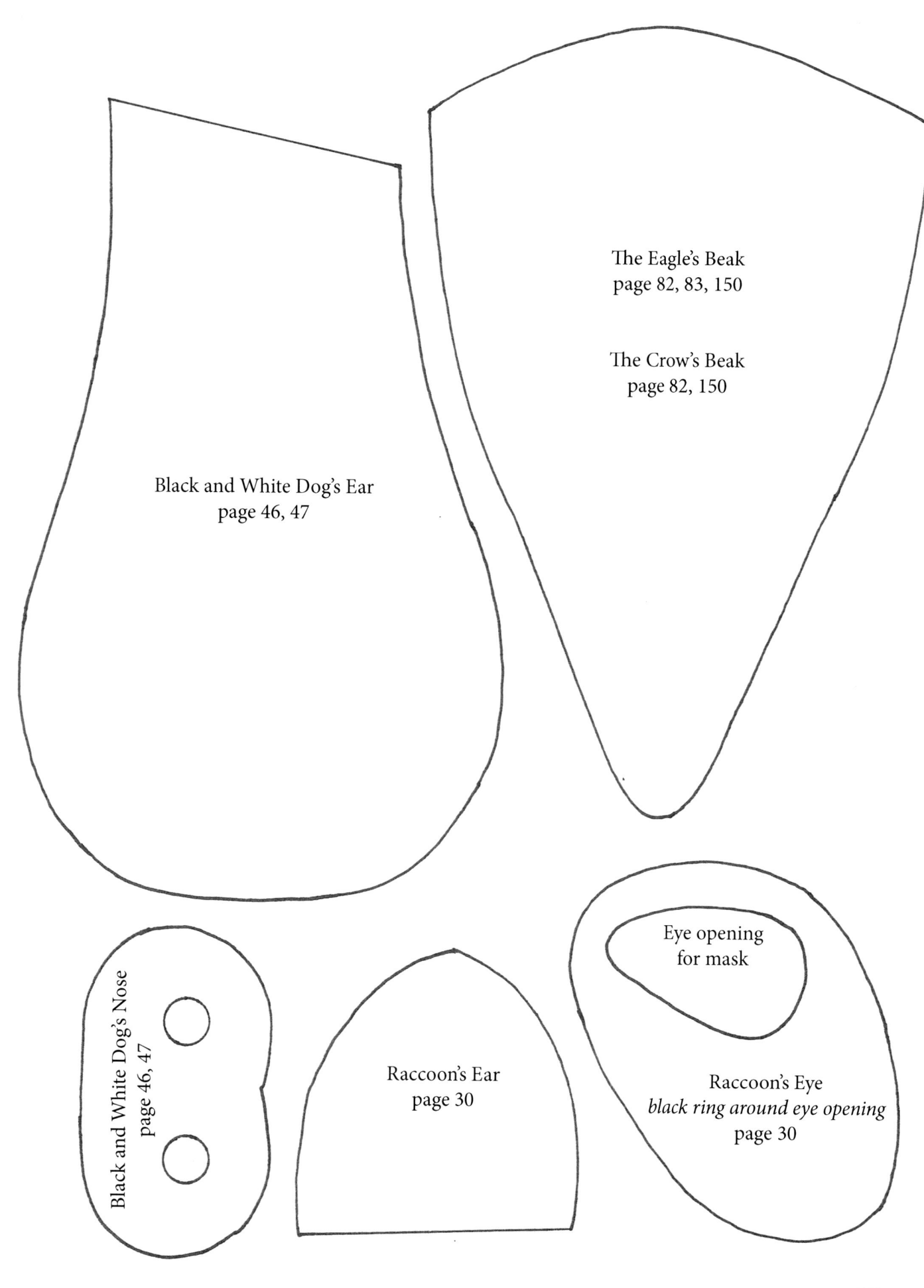

The Crow's Beak
page 82, 150

Black and White Dog's Ear
page 46, 47

Black and White Dog's Nose
page 46, 47

Raccoon's Ear
page 30

Eye opening for mask

Raccoon's Eye
black ring around eye opening
page 30

153

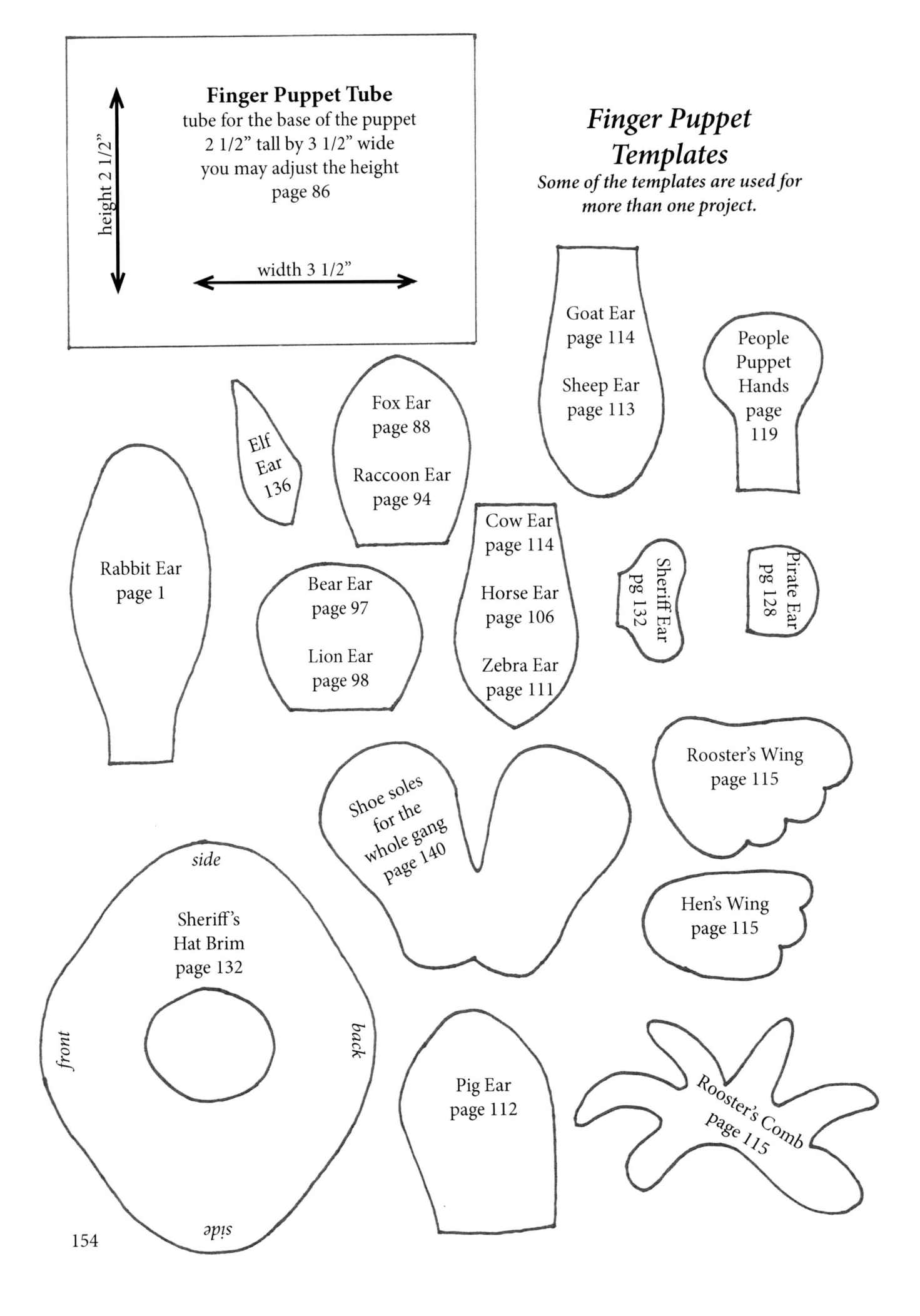

Finger Puppet Tube
tube for the base of the puppet
2 1/2" tall by 3 1/2" wide
you may adjust the height
page 86

height 2 1/2"

width 3 1/2"

Finger Puppet Templates
Some of the templates are used for more than one project.

Goat Ear page 114

Sheep Ear page 113

People Puppet Hands page 119

Elf Ear 136

Fox Ear page 88

Raccoon Ear page 94

Rabbit Ear page 1

Bear Ear page 97

Lion Ear page 98

Cow Ear page 114

Horse Ear page 106

Zebra Ear page 111

Sheriff Ear pg 132

Pirate Ear pg 128

Shoe soles for the whole gang page 140

Rooster's Wing page 115

Hen's Wing page 115

side

Sheriff's Hat Brim page 132

front

back

side

Pig Ear page 112

Rooster's Comb page 115

154

Resources

Dream Felt
www.dreamfelt.com

The Felted Ewe
www.thefeltedewe.com

The Woolery
www.woolery.com

New England Felting Supply
www.feltingsupply.com

Weir Crafts
www.weircrafts.com

Lisa Joyce Yarns
www.lisajoycedesigns.com
(*hand spun wool used for the mane on the **lion's mask** page 58*)

Living Felt
www.livingfelt.com

Felt Alive
www.feltalive.com
www.needlefeltingsupplies.com

Glass Eyes Online
www.etsy.com/shop/GlassEyesOnLine
www.glasseyesonline.com

155

The Old Man

My focus in this book is animal masks, but I could not end without answering a question many of you may have. Can I make people masks? Yes you can. You can make anything that your imagination can dream up. Remember that once you create the base for a mask it is a blank canvas that may be sculpted into any shape, animal, or person.

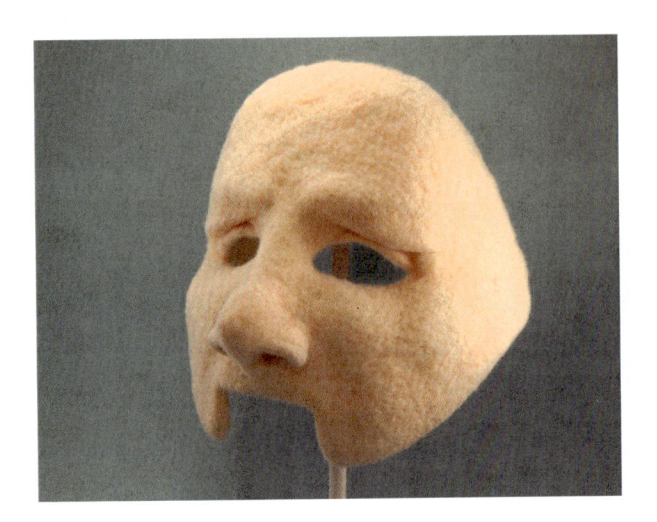

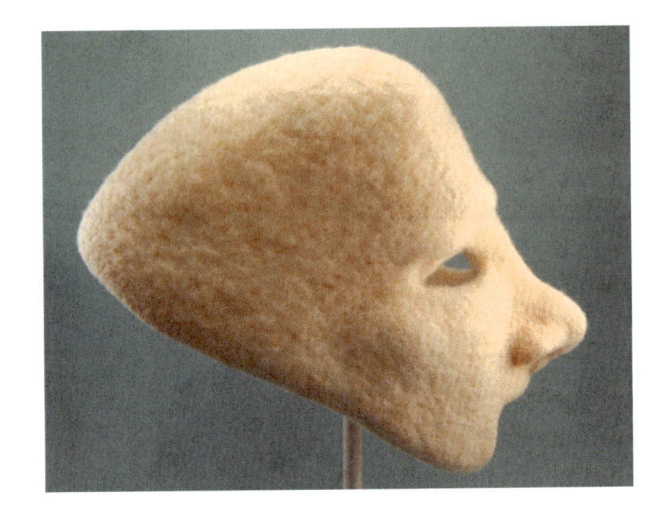

I chose the old man mask to illustrate three components that you may incorporate into any mask. First I chose to extend the mask to the back of the head. I did this because I wanted to give the old man a bald spot on the top of his head. When you put the mask on it will comfortably rest on the top of your head. The second thing I did was to omit the mouth. I wanted the wearer of the mask to be able to use their own exposed mouth. Adding the moustache conceals the edge of the mask around the mouth. The third thing I did was to make the nostril holes open through the base of the mask.

I looked at a photo of a real ear while sculpting. The ears *below* are all on the same piece of foam. The *third photo* is of the finished ears. Notice how much the ears shrink and condense after felting.

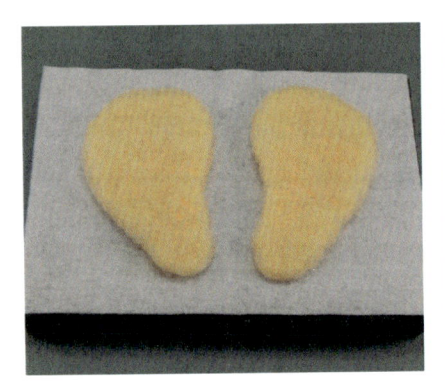

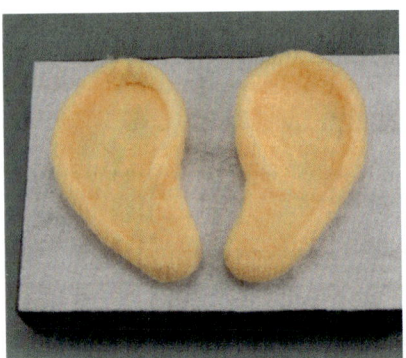

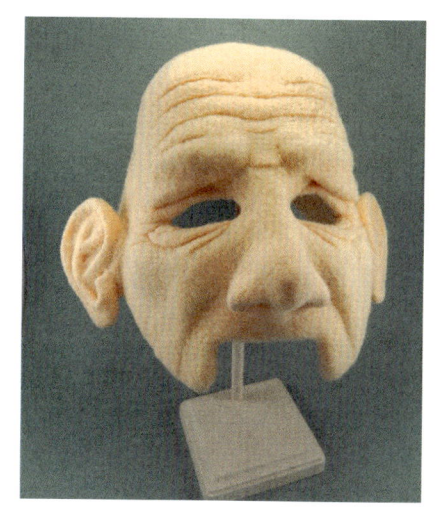

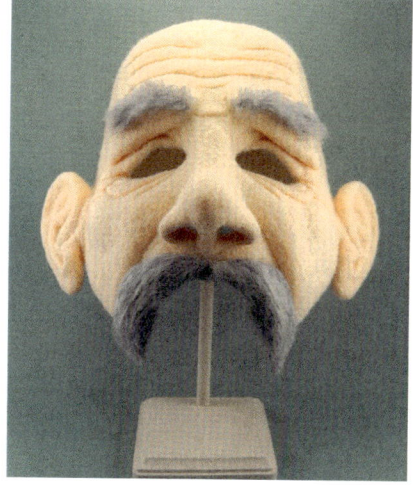

Wrinkles are edges that may be made on the sculpture or on the foam work surface.

The eyebrows, moustache, and hair are varying shades of gray wool roving.

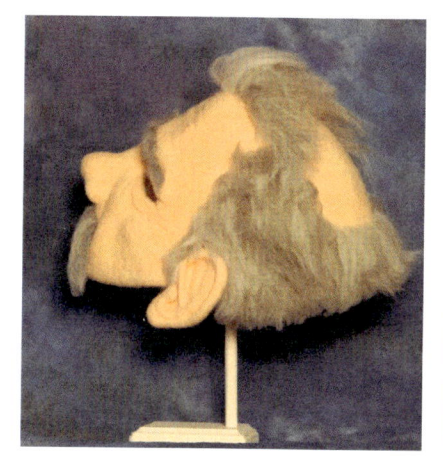

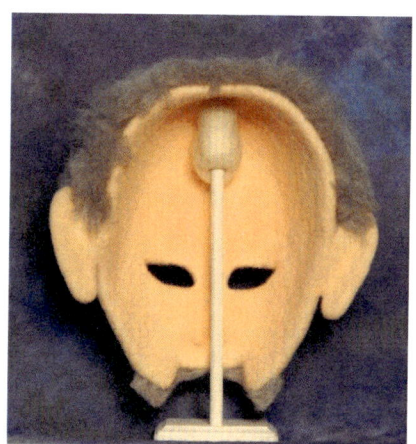

The center photo above shows the back view of the mask. It also shows a **mask display stand** that is explained on *page 83*.

The techniques used to make this old man are the same techniques used on all the projects throughout this book. After you felt a few projects you will gain the confidence to bring to life some of your own ideas and designs. I am continually amazed at how the same techniques can produce a simple sculpture or a detailed work of art. Once you have experienced the magic of needle felting you will begin to refer to it as *needle sculpting*.

157

About The Author

My mother was an artist and I always wanted to be just like her. As a little girl, I was in awe of the way she could pick up a pencil and sketch a portrait that looked so real. She was truly gifted and I worked hard to copy her. My mother gave me the confidence to become a self-taught artist. I have worked hard to develop the skills to paint, weave, sew, and become a woodcarver. I also enjoy writing magazine articles and teaching workshops on various topics.

I praise God for the gifts he has given me and I feel blessed to be able to share the things I have learned with others.

Please visit my website:
www.TereseCato.com

Also by Terese Cato:

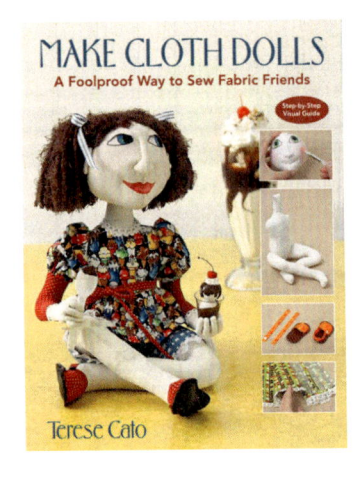

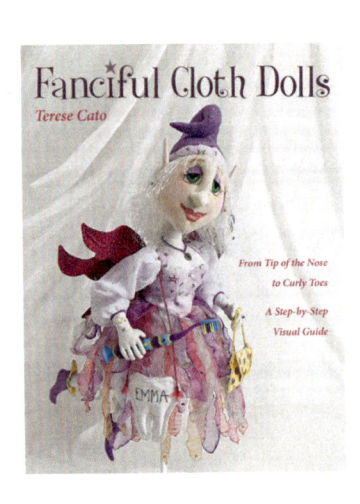

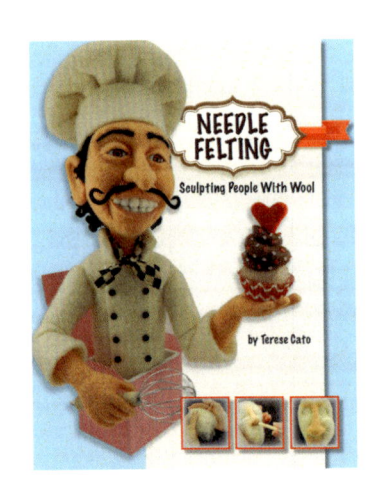

Challenge your creativity!

Made in the USA
San Bernardino, CA
04 January 2017